W9-ACN-473

"Trivial Complaints"

"Trivial Complaints"

The Role of Privacy in Domestic Violence Law
and Activism in the U.S.

Kirsten S. Rambo

www.gutenberg-e.org

COLUMBIA UNIVERSITY PRESS
NEW YORK

Columbia University Press
Publishers Since 1893
New York   Chichester, West Sussex
Copyright © 2009 Columbia University Press
All rights reserved

Library of Congress Cataloging-in-Publication Data

Rambo, Kirsten S.
"Trivial complaints" : the role of privacy in domestic violence law and activism in the U.S. /
Kirsten S. Rambo.
p. cm.
Includes bibliographical references.
ISBN 978-0-231-13557-3 (cloth : alk. paper) — ISBN 978-0-231-50958-9 (e-book)
1. Privacy, Right of.   2. Family violence—Law and legislation.
3. Abused women—Legal status, laws, etc.   I. Title.

K3263.R36 2008
342.08'58—dc22
2008043039

www.gutenberg-e.org

Columbia University Press books are printed on permanent
and durable acid-free paper. This book is printed on paper
with recycled content. Printed in the United States of America.

c 10 9 8 7 6 5 4 3 2 1

References to Internet Web sites (URLs) were accurate at the time
of writing. Neither the author nor Columbia University
Press is responsible for URLs that may have expired
or changed since the manuscript was prepared.

This book is dedicated to all who have faced terror at home—

in honor of those who have survived,

in memory of those who lost their lives,

in support of those who still struggle to be safe

—and to all who work to end it.

CONTENTS

ACKNOWLEDGMENTS

It hardly seems possible to thank all of the many people who helped make this book a reality, but these Acknowledgments represent my best attempt to do so.

First, I am ever grateful to the Gutenberg-e project for their support. I feel exceedingly fortunate to have benefited from the collaboration of the American Historical Association and the Columbia University Press, which together made the Gutenberg-e prize a reality. My sincere thanks go to the impressive staff of the Electronic Publishing Initiative at Columbia (EPIC). Their dedication and talent helped bring this manuscript to life, and I appreciate all the good work and support of Kate Wittenberg, Sean Costigan, Gordon Dahlquist, Karen Sabino Desiderio, Nathaniel Herz, Matthew Nadelhaft, Sharene Azimi, Merran Swartwood, and the marketing team. Robert Townsend and Elizabeth Fairhead at the AHA also helped ensure the success of the Gutenberg-e books and were a true pleasure to work with. My fellow Gutenberg-e authors were a great resource; I have appreciated their friendship and collegiality, and my work always improved as a result of our conversations.

This book began as a dissertation, and I am grateful to Beth Reingold and Mary Odem, wonderful co-chairs whose intellectual and professional guidance proved invaluable throughout the process. Julie Mertus was amazingly helpful despite the many miles between us, and I benefited greatly from her insight and expertise. I would also like to thank the Institute for Women's Studies for its very generous support of my work throughout my time at Emory University. And while their financial support was critical, I also feel tremendously lucky to have found there an atmosphere of true collegiality.

I can't imagine a greater group of colleagues than the friends I found in Women's Studies at Emory. Ginny Bonner and Susan Leisure both provided astute critiques of each draft of the dissertation, and their comments improved it dramatically. I will always be indebted to Jenny Higgins, Paula Jayne, Tiffany Worboy and Donna Troka for the different ways they showed me love and support, all of them providing belly laughs and sanity while also expanding my intellectual horizons. I'm grateful to Maria Bevacqua, Carrie Baker, and Jenny Steadman for their friendship and for paving the way. I am also lucky to have had the benefit of several fantastic mentors in college and graduate school, including Darby Lewes, Barbara McCaskill, and Kim Loudermilk.

All of the people I interviewed were exceedingly generous with their time and support for this project, and I can't thank them enough for sharing their stories with me. I also owe many thanks to Martha Fineman: as a scholar I greatly admire, her thoughtful review of the manuscript and encouragement of the project meant a great deal to me. In addition, the librarians at the Arthur and Elizabeth Schlesinger Library and the National Center on Poverty Law were extraordinarily helpful to me as I sought out and sifted through archival materials, and then navigated getting permission to use images and other items from their impressive collections.

I have been tremendously fortunate to have had the opportunity to join the community of activists and advocates working to end violence against women. I continue to be awed and educated by my colleagues in the movement nationally, internationally, and right here at home, at the Georgia Coalition Against Domestic Violence, Tapestri, the Women's Resource Center to End Domestic Violence, Men Stopping Violence, the Georgia Commission on Family Violence, and many more. Their work is an ongoing source of inspiration.

Anyone who has worked with survivors of domestic violence knows that those who have experienced this violence are the experts in the field. I am honored to continually learn from survivors. It is their knowledge and insights that always move this work forward.

There are many in my personal life who had a hand in this project, too. Providing long-distance love and support were Shannon Skalski, Alexis Radocaj, Maureen Johnson, Peggy Banaszek, and Laurie Sharp—the other sides of the hexagon—as well as Tami Carmichael and Catherine Goodbody. I'm deeply grateful for their friendship over the years and for their continued presence in my life.

Lindsey Siegel—former student and intern, research assistant extraordinaire, current colleague and friend—was instrumental in making this book happen.

Were it not for her heroic efforts, both personally and professionally, who knows what kind of shape this book (or I!) would be in.

Meredith, John, Patrick, Katie, and Anna Murray have helped to ground me, to inspire me, and to encourage and support me in countless ways. I could not have asked for or dreamed of a better sister than Meredith. Her unflagging love and support have made all the difference in my life.

Mildred Rowles and Lois Rambo were two of my earliest sheroes. Smart, funny, and strong, they were the very best role models I could ask for. Richard Rowles provided ongoing encouragement for me to get that "doctor book" written, and his spirit is very much a part of this work.

My parents, Dick and Barbara Rambo, made me believe that this was possible. Their belief in me never wavered, even when mine did. I continue to realize and appreciate in new ways how fortunate I am to have them for parents. They have worked to provide me with opportunities they never had. They've supported me in every way imaginable, almost always with patience and good humor. Long before I undertook this project, they nurtured in me a love of learning, and taught by example the importance of being true to your convictions. I could never adequately express all that they have given to me, or all that they have meant to me. They have always been, and continue to be, my inspiration.

Finally, my deepest gratitude goes to Jeff Al-Mashat. His presence in my life has made this book possible. He has believed in me, and in this project, enough for both of us. He has worked tirelessly and without complaint so that I could have the time and space to follow this path. The depth of his patience and good humor throughout this process has been nothing short of astonishing. He brings out the best in me, and he has somehow managed to make our life together both a comfort and an adventure. For all of this and so much more, I am eternally grateful to him.

PREFACE

A Note about Privacy

As I write, privacy is making headlines. Within the past year we have confirmed two new justices to the United States Supreme Court, and in both cases the potential justices were questioned vigorously at their confirmation hearings about their views on a constitutional right to privacy: whether it exists, what the shape of it might be, and how it might be applied to the issue of abortion. New headlines keep highlighting stories about the mass distribution of personal information as a result of the breach of security systems—at several large corporations and most recently within the military—that were meant to keep personal information private. The passage of the PATRIOT Acts (I and II) in the wake of September 11, 2001, have caused many to question the government's right to scrutinize the lives of private citizens for the sake of national security. These days, many Americans are talking about privacy—as a social concept, a legal concept, and maybe (or maybe not) a constitutional right.

And while the specific issues mentioned above have a distinctly modern flavor, our society's preoccupation with privacy is nothing new. Debates about privacy, its meanings and implications, have been part of our national conversation since this country's earliest days. For those who founded this country, thinking about privacy meant, among other things, grappling with questions such as exactly who could quarter their horses where (and when, and for what purpose). Today, most Americans are more likely to be concerned with privacy as it relates to their medical records or their credit card numbers. Whether the private realm constitutes a physical space (such as home, or private property) or the more encompassing idea of individual bodies or decision-making abilities has been the subject of much debate, and will be explored throughout this book.

Regardless of the particular application, privacy in the United States has always been about balance: safety and security on one hand, and liberty and freedom on the other. Examining this balance raises the question of whether the government has a responsibility to protect its citizens (from violence or terrorism, for example), and if so, to what extent, and how? To what extent can or should the government, in a free society, be allowed to intrude into the home? For example, does the desire to protect the nation from the threat of terrorism justify governmental surveillance of citizens' private phone calls? And where does one draw the line between protection and intrusion?

Privacy as it concerns individuals and their relationship to the state is often inextricably tied to questions of liberty and the substantive due process clause of the Fourteenth Amendment of the Constitution. This amendment declares ". . . nor shall any State deprive any person of life, liberty, or property, without due process of law." Deprivation of life and property are concepts that are readily grasped, but what is liberty? And what would be the "due process" for depriving someone of that liberty? Is liberty simply another way of saying "the right to be let alone"? Or is it something bigger—a right to self-determination, to autonomy, to live the life one chooses to lead? The debate about privacy raises questions about liberty and freedom, key concepts in the construction of "American-ness."

The events of September 11 brought all of these questions into sharp and urgent focus. Subsequent government responses to these events seem to imply that the state (here, the federal government, but more broadly, any governmental actor) does have a duty to protect its citizens, and that some intrusion into the private realm is a necessary means to that end. New questions arise almost daily: if the government can monitor the private mail and library records of its citizens, will it make us all safer? The hope of those who support such actions, of course, is that it will; the fear expressed by those who oppose them is that such intrusions threaten freedom and liberty itself. This discussion about privacy and the state's attempt to protect Americans from acts of terror engages many of the same issues raised in any consideration of the state's responsibility to protect citizens from acts of violence within the home.

The way we understand privacy in this country is vitally important to the way we understand liberty, freedom, and what it means to be an American. The concepts of freedom and liberty, while ever-changing, have always been crucial aspects of the American national identity. And they are also crucial to our understanding of domestic violence and the related issues of reproductive rights and same-sex relationships that I explore in this book. The way that privacy is understood and enacted in each of these cases has implications, not just for the issues themselves, but also for our shared understanding of liberty and freedom.

1. INTRODUCTION

The courts have been loth [sic] to take cognizance of trivial complaints arising out of domestic relations—such as . . . husband and wife. . . . [B]ecause the evil of publicity would be greater than the evil involved in the trifles complained of; and because they ought to be left to family government. . . . For, however great are the evils of ill temper, quarrels, and even personal conflicts inflicting only temporary pain, they are not comparable with the evils which would result from raising the curtain, and exposing to public curiosity and criticism the nursery and the bed chamber.[1]

The problem of domestic violence[2] is one that has persisted in the United States from the country's inception to the present day.[3] And the history of domestic violence in the United States has been inextricably linked with the concept of privacy: legal and cultural understandings of privacy have long influenced the ways in which judges, legislators, activists, victims, perpetrators, and the general public have viewed and responded to this issue. This book examines the history of domestic violence law and activism in the United States from the late nineteenth century to the present day, particularly as they have been affected by various conceptions of privacy. Specifically, it seeks to understand the complex relationship between privacy and domestic violence through a historically situated and contextualized analysis of domestic violence litigation.

While the notion of privacy has acquired a variety of meanings in both legal and nonlegal contexts, it has undoubtedly been a central factor in the development of American political and legal theory. Having been applied to a wide range of issues, from education[4] to pornography[5] to homosexuality[6] to reproduction,[7] privacy has been seen by feminist scholars as both a blessing and a curse for women's rights in the United States. Regardless of the issue being addressed, however, a common factor in the application of privacy has historically been its reinforcing of the traditional, nuclear family. Nowhere has this link been stronger than in the case of domestic violence, in which noninterference by the state into supposedly "private" family matters has, until recently, been the rule rather than the exception—to the great detriment of battered women.

Specifically, privacy has pervaded the issue of domestic violence in the United States in two ways. First, privacy as a legal and constitutional principle with a specific history in Western liberal political thought underlies much of the litigation history. Second, this legal conception of privacy is supported by broader cultural notions about the importance of privacy, a more amorphous, general societal belief that government should not interfere in "private" (i.e., family) matters. While courts and legal advocates have concerned themselves primarily with the first of these conceptualizations of privacy, service providers and victims deal more directly with the second.

In both senses, however, the discourse of privacy as it relates to domestic violence has incorporated specific presumptions about race, class, and sexuality. The concept of privacy has proven to be anything but egalitarian: access to privacy can signify the relative status of individuals in a given society. The Western liberal political tradition that enabled only certain privileged groups of male citizens to move freely between public and private spheres[8] has engendered a legacy in which the privacy of some is valued more highly than that of others.[9] Today, treatment of domestic violence cases and the accompanying emphasis on privacy often presume a white, nuclear (male-headed) family, thereby erasing the experiences of people of color,[10] same-sex couples,[11] and immigrants or nonresidents.[12] As such, the overarching emphasis on privacy that pervades domestic violence litigation contains problematic implications that extend beyond gender lines to encompass a wide range of interlocking issues. This book examines the extent to which concepts of privacy have been imbued with assumptions about race, class, and sexuality and considers their ramifications both for victims of partner violence and for activists within the battered women's movement.

It is important to note that, in addition to service provision and legal advocacy, the battered women's movement has concentrated many of its energies on legislative work. Much of the law governing domestic violence has developed via legislative rather than judicial means (and, in fact, the legislative efforts of the battered women's movement could be the focus of an entirely different study). While this policy-making work has resulted in critical legal protections for women, however,[13] it has not been primarily concerned with issues related to privacy.

Yet conceptions of privacy have proven central to the problem of domestic violence and to the battered women's movement. Notions of privacy have been so influential in shaping this society's ideas about domestic violence—and therefore the movement itself—that an exploration of privacy is essential to a fuller understanding of the subject. Passage of laws has been an important, yet a partial step—as when, for example, courts and service providers have been confronted with non-enforcement of these laws based on conceptions of privacy that keep police from intervening in domestic disputes. This study foregrounds judicial rather than legislative activity, paying particular attention to the role of privacy and the relationship between courts and activists. Legal discourse and judicial narratives, simultaneously reflecting and shaping societal beliefs, provide useful insights into this relationship and various conceptions of privacy.

The late nineteenth century provides a useful context for analysis of more recent anti-domestic-violence efforts for several reasons. First, a review of the case law reveals that it was not until 1871 that state courts began to repudiate the right of chastisement (adopted from English common law, the right of a husband to inflict corporal punishment on his wife for her "misbehavior"). This was a pivotal year in the legal history of domestic violence, for it saw two landmark cases in which the right to chastisement was expressly repudiated.[14] The nineteenth-century cases reveal that when US courts were first confronted with the issue of domestic violence, they grounded their analyses of the problem and their responses in notions of privacy. This early link between privacy and domestic violence in the judicial sphere has continued to influence courts' decisions throughout the history of the battered women's movement, even to the present day.

At the same time that these significant early cases were being decided, the temperance movement was gaining unprecedented momentum. The Woman's Christian Temperance Union (WCTU), which gained prominence as "both the leading temperance organization and the leading women's organization in the United States" in 1873, quickly became a forum for women's activism around a variety of social issues, including domestic violence.[15] From the perspective of the largely middle- and upper-class women able to do activist work at this time, alcohol was very much a woman's problem. Situated so firmly in the domestic domain, women bore the brunt of their husbands' abuse of alcohol.[16] It seemed only natural, therefore, that women would emerge as leaders and workers in the temperance movement, approach the issue from a "woman's perspective," and focus on related issues such as domestic violence. The temperance movement's willingness to address the problem of domestic violence, combined with women's activism on several other fronts—including suffrage and social purity—converged in the early 1870s to form a heightened climate of activism. In this environment, increased public awareness of and discourse about domestic violence engendered the first real public censure of batterers in the United States.[17]

Nonetheless, the first half of the twentieth century saw relatively little activity with regard to combating the problem of domestic violence.[18] The reasons for this decline in activity have been the source of some speculation; what is undeniable, however, is that the early 1970s generated a renewed burst of activism on behalf of battered women that has continued to some degree until the present day.[19] As an outgrowth of the numerous social justice movements of the 1960s, including the civil rights movement and the second wave of the women's movement, the battered women's movement was established in the early 1970s primarily as a means of providing shelter to women in danger.[20] As the movement grew, however, activists expanded the scope of their efforts to include not only the provision of services, but also legal and legislative work to benefit battered women.[21] As a result of this multifaceted approach, activist work increased the visibility of the issue within the public consciousness, therefore ultimately affecting judicial response to the problem of domestic violence.

Case Resources

Roe v. *Wade*

Findlaw (http://laws.findlaw.com/us/410/113.html) (full text)

Oyez (http://www.oyez.org/cases/case/?case=1970-1979/1971/1971_70_18) (oral arguments)

It is significant that this movement emerged on the heels of the hard-fought battle to secure abortio n rights. The progression of reproductive rights cases that led to the landmark *Roe* v. *Wade*[22] decision in 1973 ultimately grounded the right to abortion in legal notions of privacy. Characterizing abortion as a highly personal decision, pro-choice legal advocates urged the state *not* to interfere in this private realm. In *Roe*, the US Supreme Court agreed, and this protection of the private sphere played a central role in securing this important right for women.

The decision by courts and activists to frame reproductive rights in terms of privacy, however, has had serious consequences for battered women's advocates. The concept of state noninterference in the private realm that was so critical to the success of the abortion rights movement has also been used to protect batterers within the same private realm. That these two movements emerged almost contemporaneously highlights an important legal paradox, as courts and activists have had to reconcile these contrasting effects upon women's rights of the use of the concept of privacy. This book explores the extent to which concepts of privacy, as articulated within the reproductive rights movement, have informed the judicial strategies of the battered women's movement and influenced judicial opinions in domestic violence cases.

Overall, the book contextualizes the legal history of domestic violence by exploring the ways in which feminist activism has responded to—and shaped—judicial responses to this problem. Using the notion of privacy as a unifying theoretical concept, this book examines the history of domestic violence in this country, both in the courts and on the streets. In other words, the book traces the legal history of domestic violence as well as the ways in which activists responded to and shaped that history. Having examined the significance of the role of privacy in both judicial and activist responses to domestic violence, the book explores recent alternative visions of privacy as an affirmative right, one that is potentially beneficial to battered women.

A BRIEF HISTORY OF PRIVACY

Privacy, a key theoretical component of this study, is a concept that has received a great deal of attention among feminist legal theorists, in part because the legal right to privacy served as the foundation upon which the right to abortion developed.[23] Generally heralded by these scholars for its pivotal role in securing reproductive freedoms for women, the notion of privacy has also been viewed as a double-edged sword because of its role in perpetuating domestic violence.[24] The same privacy that has allowed women control over their bodies with regard to reproductive rights, feminists suggest, has also left them vulnerable to domestic abuse because of the state's reluctance to interfere in the private realm of the home, even to prevent violence. While these theoretical insights have laid the foundation for an exploration of the relationship between privacy and women's rights in the United States, it is important to take the analysis a step further by unpacking the notion of privacy itself. In order to resist oversimplification, an understanding of a variety of shifting and sometimes competing conceptions of privacy is critical.

The notion of privacy has long played a central role in the development of American political theory. The abstract nature of the concept, however, has made it difficult to define, and the term has acquired a variety of meanings that shift widely according to context. For the purposes of this book, three such meanings are significant. First, the concept of privacy is an essential component of traditional liberal political thought, linked as it is to the individualism that underlies that philosophy. Individualism (with its related ideals of autonomy, self-sufficiency, and self-fulfillment) necessarily posits the individual in relation to the state. From this perspective, privacy essentially means the freedom of an individual from state interference. Individual privacy in this sense is an essential component of personal fulfillment: a citizen cannot define, much less pursue, her or his own goals when hampered or restricted significantly by state intervention. This type of privacy is therefore conceived as a negative right, one that does not guarantee benefits, but instead ensures relief from the burden of intrusion by the state.

In fact, two themes related to privacy predominate in the liberal political theory developed by Western philosophers. First, this philosophical tradition prizes individualism and the development of autonomous, self-sufficient, rational actors operating independently. In *The Citizen*, for example, Thomas Hobbes entreats his readers to "consider men as if but even now sprung out of the earth, and suddenly, like mushrooms, come to full maturity, without all kind of engagement to each other."[25] This emphasis on autonomy and self-sufficiency—and rejection of principles of interdependence—forms the basis for much of Hobbes's political theory. As feminist theorist Christine DiStefano observes, Hobbes's mushroom analogy epitomizes his overall presentation of "a thoroughly atomistic subject . . . whose individual rights . . . clearly precede any obligation to belong to a civil society."[26] Similarly, Jean-Jacques Rousseau, who views humans in a more favorable and less selfish light, nonetheless ascribes to them the principle of self-preservation, first and foremost.[27] Furthermore, while Rousseau concedes that humankind's other basic principle is one of pity, he maintains that sociability is not an inherent value for humans, claiming simply that "Man is weak when dependent."[28]

John Stuart Mill, another theorist of political liberalism, also views the individual as the central unit through which to understand human relationships: "Men, however, in a state of society, are still men; their actions and passions are obedient to the laws of individual human nature. . . . Human beings in society have no properties but those which are derived from and may be resolved into the laws of the individual man."[29] Further, Mill addresses the concept of individualism within the context of liberty and personal freedom. As DiStefano notes, Mill's subject "requires a protected zone of thought, expression, and action for his survival and well-being;" this subject is "a self-sufficient and sovereign entity."[30] In particular, Mill emphasizes that individuals must be left alone in the pursuit of their own interests: "the sole end for which mankind are warranted, individually or collectively, in interfering with the liberty of action of any of their number, is self-protection."[31] For Mill, as for Hobbes and Rousseau, notions of individualism are inextricably linked with principles of autonomy, self-sufficiency, self-preservation, and freedom from interference, all of which suggest the importance of privacy for the success of individual actors.

The second and related theme that pervades much of Western political theory is the establishment of distinct public and private spheres of action. The delineation of these spheres can be traced back at least to Plato and Aristotle. In his *Republic*, for example, Plato describes an ideal society in which the patriarchal family unit is abolished in favor of more communal relations and communally held property—at least, for the highest (Guardian) class. Yet in his subsequent work, the *Laws*, Plato reintroduces the patriarchal family structure as well as the holding of private property. In so doing, he creates discrete zones of activity: the public, which constitutes political and civic interaction and power, and the private, which concerns domesticity, nurturing, and reproductive work. In his reinforcement of patriarchal family forms, Plato relegates women in the *Laws* to the private sphere, while assigning the public sphere to men.[32]

Likewise, Aristotle, who adopts a different philosophical approach from Plato's in many other ways, espouses a very similar (and similarly gendered) divide between public and private spheres. Separating the polis, or political life, from the household, or family life, Aristotle determines that each exists as a separate part of the "natural" order, and each is a central unit of civil society. Furthermore, his functionalist approach determines that women's "natural" reproductive role limits them to the private sphere, while men's "naturally" higher intellectual capacity equips them for both the public and private spheres.[33] Subsequent political philosophers have continued to reiterate and reinforce this division, as in, for example, John Locke's assertion that "these two *Powers, Political* and *Paternal, are so perfectly distinct* and separate; are built upon so different Foundations, and given to so different Ends . . ."[34] As feminist scholar Jean Bethke Elshtain observes, this distinction between public and private—as well as its implications for gender roles—has persisted throughout much of Western political theory.[35]

Case Resources
Griswold v. *Connecticut*
Findlaw (http://laws.findlaw.com/us/381/479.html) (full text)
Oyez (http://www.oyez.org/cases/case/?case=1960-1969/1964/1964_496) (oral arguments)

The second form of privacy, as a significant constitutional and legal principle in the United States, follows readily from its centrality to liberal political thought. While a right of privacy is not explicitly mentioned anywhere in the US Constitution, courts and constitutional scholars have found this right implied throughout the document in several places. The Third Amendment, which prohibits the quartering of soldiers "in any house, without the consent of the Owner," and the Fourth Amendment, which protects citizens from "unreasonable searches and seizures," are just two examples. One of the best known articulations of this position was made by Justice William O. Douglas, who, in writing the Supreme Court's opinion in the 1965 contraception case *Griswold* v. *Connecticut*, found the right of privacy implied in no less than six amendments.[36]

Case Resources
Boyd v. *U.S.*
Findlaw (http://laws.findlaw.com/us/116/616.html) (full text)

This undercurrent of respect for privacy within the US Constitution was likely influenced by judicial reasoning of the colonial period. The 1765 case of *Entick* v. *Carrington*[37] in England considered the issue of search (of a private home) and seizure (of private papers), roundly denouncing both practices and asserting the right to the securing of private property. In the 1886 US Supreme Court case of *Boyd* v. *U.S.*,[38] Justice Bradley characterized the *Entick* opinion as "one of the landmarks of English liberty. It was welcomed and applauded by the lovers of liberty in the colonies as well as in the mother country . . . [I]t may be confidently asserted that its propositions were in the minds of those who framed the Fourth Amendment to the Constitution."[39] Extrapolating from the *Entick* opinion, Bradley outlined an even more emphatic right of privacy in *Boyd*:

> The principles laid down in this opinion affect the very essence of constitutional liberty and security. . . . [T]hey apply to all invasions on the part of the government and its employees of the sanctity of a man's home and the privacies of life. It is not the breaking of his doors, and the rummaging of his drawers, that constitutes the essence of the offence; but it is the invasion of his indefeasible right of personal security, personal liberty and private property . . . [I]t is the invasion of this sacred right which underlies and constitutes the essence of [the *Boyd*] judgment.[40]

In this way, Bradley espoused a right to privacy far more expansive in scope than the Fourth Amendment upon which it drew.

Case Resources
Olmstead v. *U.S.*
Findlaw (http://laws.findlaw.com/us/277/438.html) (full text)

A few decades later, Justice Brandeis cited *Boyd* while articulating a right to privacy in the 1928 US Supreme Court case *Olmstead* v. *U.S.*[41] In his dissenting opinion in *Olmstead*, Brandeis characterized the privacy right with a phrase often cited by both judges and legal scholars since then: "The makers of our

Constitution . . . conferred, as against the government, *the right to be let alone*—the most comprehensive of rights and the right most valued by civilized men."[42] This phrasing and the notion of privacy as, fundamentally, "the right to be let alone" have been crucial to subsequent legal formulations of privacy as a negative right—the freedom from state intervention in the home.[43]

Case Resources

Paris Adult Theatre v. *Slaton*

Findlaw (http://laws.findlaw.com/us/413/49.html) (full text)

Oyez (http://www.oyez.org/cases/case/?case=1970-1979/1972/1972_71_1051) (oral arguments)

Throughout the twentieth century, the Supreme Court continued to develop privacy as a negative right, a right strongly rooted in (and applicable to) domestic and family issues. In a series of early-twentieth-century decisions, the Court interpreted the Fourteenth Amendment to protect various aspects of marital, parental, and domestic rights and relationships,[44] concluding that it has thereby "respected the private realm of family life which the state cannot enter"[45] and that "[t]his privacy right encompasses and protects the personal intimacies of the home, the family, marriage, motherhood, procreation, and child rearing."[46] Furthermore, the Court recognized "the right of a man to retreat into his own home and there be free from unreasonable governmental intrusion,"[47] as well as "the right of each individual 'to a private enclave where he may lead a private life.'"[48] The gendered ramifications of this series of decisions was revealed most tellingly in the 1973 case of *Paris Adult Theatre* v. *Slaton*, in which Chief Justice Burger blithely acknowledged that "the 'privacy of the home'" previously asserted by the Court "was hardly more than a reaffirmation that 'a man's home is his castle.'"[49] As anti-domestic-violence advocates would soon learn, this formulation of privacy—as a negative right protecting "the king of his castle" from state intrusion—could be exceedingly dangerous for women.

Case Resources

Poe v. *Ullman*

Findlaw (http://laws.findlaw.com/us/367/497.html) (full text)

Oyez (http://www.oyez.org/cases/case/?case=1960-1969/1960/1960_60) (oral arguments)

Eisenstadt v. *Baird*

Findlaw (http://laws.findlaw.com/us/405/438.html) (full text)

Oyez (http://www.oyez.org/cases/case/?case=1970-1979/1971/1971_70_17) (oral arguments)

At the same time, however, the right to privacy was proving—rather paradoxically—to be an invaluable tool for securing women's reproductive rights. In fact, the arena in which the right of privacy has perhaps been most fully developed is that of reproductive rights. In 1961, Justice Harlan's powerful dissent in the contraception case *Poe* v. *Ullman* recognized the plaintiffs' "right to enjoy the privacy of their marital relations free of the enquiry of the criminal law."[50] Four years later, in *Griswold*, the Court's majority opinion referred to "the notions of privacy surrounding the marriage relationship" and "a right of privacy older than the Bill of Rights."[51] This right was quickly expanded beyond the confines of the marital bedroom, however; the Court's opinion in the 1971 case of *Eisenstadt* v. *Baird* asserted that "If the right of privacy means anything, it is the right of the individual, married or single, to be free from unwarranted governmental intrusion into matters so fundamentally affecting a person as the decision whether to bear or beget a child."[52] Finally, in the landmark 1973 *Roe* v. *Wade* opinion, the privacy right was construed to include, specifically, the abortion right: "This right of privacy . . . is broad enough to encompass a woman's decision whether or not to terminate her pregnancy."[53] Over several decades of reproductive litigation, therefore, the Court's definition of the privacy right, which began by protecting the sanctity of the marital home, expanded to include the individual freedom to make the most personal decisions.

Finally, it is useful to consider the concept of privacy as it has been engaged by many feminist theorists. Primarily, feminist analyses of the concept of privacy or private life have focused on its dichotomous relationship with the concept of public life. While acknowledging its many centuries as a firmly entrenched facet of Western political theory, feminist scholars in this century have begun to question the utility of this dichotomy as a theoretical paradigm. First, they have asserted that the public/private dichotomy is essentially a false construct, especially when viewed through the lens of gender. The fragility of the paradigm is apparent, they contend, when one considers that actions within the private sphere always have consequences with the public sphere, and vice versa. Feminist legal theorist Catharine MacKinnon raises this issue in her discussion of abortion:

> The private is public for those for whom the personal is political. In this sense, for women there is no private, either normatively or empirically. Feminism confronts the fact that women have no privacy to lose or to guarantee.[54]

Viewed in this light, the line separating the public and private spheres is blurred, if not erased altogether.

Second, feminist scholars have observed that the public/private dichotomy has been instrumental in excluding women from participating in public life, because the dichotomy itself is gendered, with men traditionally being identified with the public sphere of government, paid labor, and so on, and women being relegated to the private sphere of home and family.[55] Furthermore, feminist theorists have argued that the concept of privacy plays a crucial role in perpetuating gender inequality. MacKinnon, for example, has argued that "[w]hen the law of privacy restricts intrusions into intimacy, it bars changes in control over that intimacy through law. The existing distribution of power and resources within the private sphere are [sic] precisely what the law of privacy exists to protect."[56] The legal concept of privacy, she suggests, falsely presumes an equality between the sexes, to women's great danger. In other words, "abstract privacy protects abstract autonomy, without inquiring into whose freedom of action is being sanctioned, at whose expense."[57]

The notion that privacy perpetuates inequality is particularly true in the case of domestic violence, as many feminist scholars have observed. Elizabeth Schneider asserts, "The concept of privacy encourages, reinforces, and supports violence against women. . . . Privacy says that what goes on in the violent relationship should not be the subject of state or community intervention. . . . Privacy operates as a mask for inequality, protecting male violence against women."[58] While Schneider's comment refers specifically to domestic violence in the late twentieth century, her critique hints at a problem rooted in traditional Western political thought. In short, the feminist critique of the concept of privacy calls into question both its falsely dichotomous relationship with the public sphere and its role as a justification for the continued subordination of women.

Each of these concepts of privacy has affected the issue of domestic violence in both legal and social contexts. Entering the US legal system with a strong foundation in political liberalism, the notion of privacy conferred a degree of privilege upon individual, male citizens. Within political liberalism, the citizen is conceptualized as the male head of a household, and therefore as the representative of that household within the public and political arenas.[59] Thus, the protection afforded to individual citizens by virtue of privacy has also been accorded to the male heads of nuclear families. Indeed, two types of privacy have developed this way: individual privacy, granted to individual citizens, and familial privacy, granted to traditional, nuclear families.[60] Both courts and the larger society have emphasized each of these types of privacy at different times, with varying implications for women. As the following chapters will show, the concept of individual privacy, while not without its flaws, has the potential to be useful and empowering for women, as, for example, in the case of the struggle for reproductive rights. Privacy rooted in marital or familial status, on the other hand, has too often had devastating consequences for battered women seeking safety.

The following excerpts of judicial opinions in domestic violence cases of the nineteenth century provide a fairly representative illustration of the extent to which judges' respect for this familial privacy effectively erased the notion of legal recourse for battered women:

> Family broils and dissentions cannot be investigated before the tribunals of the country, without casting a shade over the character of those who are unfortunately engaged in the controversy. To screen from public reproach those who may thus be unhappily situated, let the husband be permitted to exercise the right of moderate chastisement . . . without being subject to vexatious prosecutions, resulting in the mutual discredit and shame of all parties concerned.[61]
>
> In order to preserve the sanctity of the domestic circle, the Courts will not listen to trivial complaints. If no permanent injury has been inflicted, nor malice, cruelty, nor dangerous violence shown by the husband, it is better to draw the curtain, shut out the public gaze, and leave the parties to forget and forgive.[62]

In cases such as these, the duty to protect marital privacy was clearly a much higher priority for judges than protecting women from abusive husbands.

CENTRAL ISSUES

The value of the legal notion of privacy has been highly contested, yet some feminist scholars have suggested that, properly conceived, it has the potential to empower women. Feminist scholars such as Elizabeth Schneider,[63] Patricia Boling,[64] and Dorothy Roberts[65] have called for a new, alternative vision of privacy: one that, in Schneider's words, "encompasses liberty, equality, freedom of bodily integrity, autonomy, and self-determination."[66] This book answers that call in part by exploring alternative models of privacy that are potentially empowering for battered women.

The book illuminates the ways in which concepts of privacy (both in the legal sense and in the broader, social sense) have influenced domestic violence litigation and activism, and, therefore, the lives of battered women themselves. In so doing, it provides insight into the ways that judges have historically viewed the construct of the traditional, nuclear family, as well as the notion of privacy and the problem of domestic violence. Additionally, this study examines how the concept of privacy has been subverted and transformed through feminist activism, and envisions the next step in this process—that is to say, where do we go from here? Given that privacy is undeniably entrenched in our legal system, the book explores how it might be used to provide more, rather than fewer, options for victims of domestic violence. The way that advocates for reproductive rights were able to co-opt the notion of privacy in the service of women's rights is instructive here. Likewise, the arena in which privacy is being contested and negotiated most vigorously in recent years, that of sexual orientation, also provides useful context for this discussion.

The book addresses these questions: What, historically, have been the ramifications of the legal and cultural emphasis on privacy for the lives of battered women? In what ways have notions of privacy reinforced the primacy of the traditional, male-headed household? To what extent has the discourse of privacy presumed a heterosexual victim, and what have been the implications of those assumptions for victims and activists? How have the limitations of domestic violence law influenced the rhetoric and strategies of battered women's advocates? How have the advocacy strategies of the battered women's movement shaped the meaning of domestic violence law in the courts?

Furthermore, the book also considers the ways in which early (nineteenth-century) efforts to combat domestic violence served as a precursor to subsequent (late-twentieth- and early-twenty-first-century) activism. What have been the most pressing issues for these later battered women's advocates, and in what ways have those issues been addressed in the courtroom? To what extent has the reproductive-rights movement's usage of legal concepts of privacy influenced activists and courts with regard to domestic violence? In what ways and to what extent has the battered women's movement been successful in securing safety for women and changing societal notions of privacy and domestic violence through its use of the courts? To what extent have these reconceptualizations challenged or reinforced stereotypical views about race, class, and sexuality? Finally, is the concept of legal privacy inherently detrimental to women's rights, or does it contain the potential for liberation?

In the course of this exploration, the book explores feminist developments of alternative models of privacy that are both innovative and potentially powerful. Drawing upon these feminist contributions as well as more traditional approaches, this analysis seeks a state response to domestic violence that is based on empowerment, rather than paternalism or indifference.

METHODOLOGY

The book relies primarily upon three types of sources and three related methodologies. Sources include significant court cases addressing issues of domestic violence and privacy, literature of the US battered women's movement, and interviews with lawyers and activists. I have employed three methodologies—archival research, content analysis, and semi-structured interviews—to gather and analyze this information.

Archival research is critical to the book in several ways. First, an examination of the literature of the battered women's movement has helped to ascertain the goals of feminist activists at particular junctures, both within the courtroom and in society at large. This literature encompasses a range of materials, including published books and articles (from both mainstream and scholarly presses as well as law reviews), pamphlets and promotional materials, and internal publications such as memoranda, newsletters, and more. For early activist writings on domestic violence, I have undertaken archival research of *The Lily*, *The Revolution*, and the *Woman's Journal*, three national women's journals of the late nineteenth century. For research into the battered women's movement of the late twentieth century, I have mined the archives of numerous organizations within the movement, including the National Organization for Women Legal Defense and Education Fund (NOW-LDEF), the National Coalition Against Domestic Violence (NCADV), the Battered Women's Directory Project, and the National Council on Women and Family Law and its National Battered Women's Law Project (NCOWFL, NBWLP), housed in the Arthur and Elizabeth Schlesinger Library on the History of Women in America. In addition, I have also consulted the personal papers of battered women's movement activists, as well as the full collection of *Aegis* (the former national magazine of the battered women's movement published by the National Communications Network), also housed in the Schlesinger Library. For legal briefs and other case-specific materials, I drew upon the archives of the United States Supreme Court and the National Center on Poverty Law (NCPL; formerly National Clearinghouse for Legal Services).

This archival research also helped to determine the legal cases upon which this study focused. The criteria for choosing cases were twofold: cases were selected based upon their jurisprudential significance and their importance to battered women's activists. In most instances, these criteria overlapped, as activists are generally most concerned with cases that will have the most far-reaching ramifications. While searches of the LEXIS database indicated cases of jurisprudential significance, examination of the movement's literature was helpful in identifying those cases that were of most concern to (and therefore received the most attention from) feminist activists.[67] Feminist participation in these cases is broadly conceived and took a variety of forms, including, but not limited to, legal representation of battered women, organizing and finding plaintiffs for class-action lawsuits, collective financial support of litigants, publicizing cases in local and/or national media, and the submitting of amicus briefs by feminist organizations.

I then undertook content analysis of these cases, focusing specifically on the facts of the case as presented by both parties, the court's decision, and the court's reasoning. Because issues of race, class, or sexuality (of both victims and perpetrators involved in the case), as well as the political orientation of victims' counsel (i.e., whether feminist activist or not) often played a critical role in the presentation and outcome of the case, these factors were examined for relevance as well. Often, the role of amicus briefs was also examined. Within the cases, judicial attitudes toward privacy, families, and gender relations are of particular importance for this study. Judicial opinions, including decision and reasoning, provided fertile ground for this inquiry. Contemporaneous popular media (e.g., newspapers, television, etc.) representations of notable cases were also examined, primarily as a means of determining activists' strategies in bringing particular cases to the attention of the general public.

Finally, I conducted interviews with ten current and former activists and lawyers who have addressed problems of domestic violence and privacy in their work. These semi-structured interviews took place over the course of thirteen months. Most interviews lasted between an hour and an hour and a half, with the shortest lasting thirty minutes and the longest lasting over two and a half hours. When permission was granted, I tape-recorded the interviews and selectively transcribed them afterward.

Additionally, secondary sources in feminist legal theory and women's history such as those mentioned above provided historical and contextual breadth for this analysis. By examining the issue from each of these perspectives concurrently (judicial, activist, and scholarly discourses), the book illuminates the relationship between activists and the courts around the problem of domestic violence and privacy.

CHAPTER OUTLINE

In the second chapter, I examine the judicial paradigm of privacy and domestic violence that developed prior to the emergence of the battered women's movement in the 1970s. Focusing primarily on the late nineteenth century, this chapter explores landmark domestic violence court cases of this era, examining jurisprudential developments and the ways in which judges applied notions of privacy to the problem of domestic violence. Early activist efforts on behalf of battered women are also explored as a means of illuminating the relationship between courts and activists at this time.

The third chapter explores the battered women's movement that developed in the late 1960s and early 1970s, in the midst of the anti-rape and reproductive rights movements. I begin this chapter by examining the influence of these two movements on the battered women's movement. In terms of activism, the anti-rape movement brought experiential wisdom and synergy (as well as some internal conflicts) to the battered women's movement. And, being grounded so

firmly in cultural and judicial notions of privacy, the reproductive rights movement had serious implications for the burgeoning anti-domestic-violence movement, as well. This chapter also discusses those implications, first by tracing the
reproductive rights movement's conceptualization and usage of concepts of privacy, and then by exploring the legal paradox that resulted from the two movements' contrasting uses of privacy. Ultimately, I conduct a critical case study of a
landmark domestic violence case, *People* v. *Liberta*,[68] a case that drew on both
anti-rape- and reproductive rights movement strategies. Most significantly, the
lawyer-activists working on *Liberta* developed an innovative theory of privacy
which, I suggest, could serve as a model for future battered women's litigation,
and I explore the nuances and possible ramifications of that model here.

Case Resources

DeShaney v. *Winnebago County Department of Social Services*

Findlaw (http://laws.findlaw.com/us/489/189.html) (full text)

Oyez (http://www.oyez.org/cases/case/?case=1980-1989/1988/1988_87_154) (oral arguments)

Castle Rock v. *Gonzales*

Findlaw (http://laws.findlaw.com/us/000/04-278.html) (full text)

Oyez (http://www.oyez.org/cases/case?case=2000-2009/2004/2004_04_278) (oral arguments)

Throughout the 1970s and 1980s, the battered women's movement was quickly
expanding its initial focus on service provision, as feminist lawyers and activists
increasingly pursued legal advocacy as a means of achieving justice for battered
women and changing societal notions about partner violence. The fourth chapter
focuses on this legal advocacy of the 1980s. The movement's legal efforts at this
time took creative approaches to the privacy issue, such as mounting class-action
civil lawsuits against police departments for their failure to protect battered
women. This chapter explores this era of litigation, paying particular attention
to the landmark cases of *Bruno* v. *Codd*,[69] *Scott* v. *Hart*,[70] *Thurman* v. *Torrington*,[71]
Sorichetti v. *City of New York*,[72] *DeShaney* v. *Winnebago County Department of
Social Services*,[73] and, most recently, *Castle Rock* v. *Gonzales*,[74] among others.

Case Resources

Lawrence v. *Texas*

Findlaw (http://laws.findlaw.com/us/539/558.html) (full text)

Oyez (http://www.oyez.org/cases/case/?case=2000-2009/2002/2002_02_102) (oral arguments)

In the fifth chapter, I consider how the issue of legal privacy has always proven particularly problematic when applied to intimate same-sex relationships. In direct contrast to the state's ongoing reluctance to intervene in the heterosexual home, gay and lesbian relationships have historically been subject to intense levels of state interference and scrutiny, often via the application of criminal sodomy laws. Here, I explore the historically contentious relationship between the law and homosexuality as a context for examining the often-overlooked problem of same-sex domestic violence. After critical case studies of the homosexual privacy cases *Bowers* v. *Hardwick*[75] and *Lawrence* v. *Texas*,[76] I trace the history of the relatively small number of published cases of same-sex domestic violence. Viewed through the lens of sexuality in this way, the problem of domestic abuse further highlights the necessity for a re-visioning of the legal concept of privacy.

Finally, in the conclusion to the book, I briefly discuss some of the most recent developments in law and activism related to domestic violence and privacy. Drawing on both feminist and more traditional approaches to privacy, I conclude by outlining an alternative model of privacy and some ways in which it might effectively be applied to the problem of domestic violence.

TOWARD A NEW VISION OF PRIVACY

As I trace the historical development of privacy and domestic violence in the following chapters, I critique the ways in which the concept of privacy has been detrimental and dangerous for battered women. At the same time, however, I explore the ways in which it has been conceptualized and used to more promising ends (by theorists, judges, activists, and others), and assess its potential as a tool of liberation. Drawing on this history, I ultimately propose an alternative vision of privacy that could empower rather than constrain. Instead of the traditional conception of privacy as a negative right, this model, which focuses on individual rather than familial privacy, suggests an affirmative right to bodily integrity and autonomy. Available to all individuals equally, it would operate independent of relationship status, and would be grounded in an awareness of equality along lines of sex, race/ethnicity, class, sexuality, and ability. As the complex history of privacy and domestic violence reveals, such a re-visioning of the privacy concept is not only possible, but necessary.

NOTES

1. *State* v. *Rhodes*, 61 N.C. (Phil. Law) 453, 454, 456–57, 459 (1868).

2. In this book, the terms "domestic violence," "domestic abuse," "woman battering," and "intimate partner violence" are all used to refer specifically to abuse against women by their intimate partners. The book does not address issues of elder abuse, child abuse, or sibling abuse, which are sometimes considered within the rubric of domestic abuse. US Department of Justice statistics indicate that women remain the overwhelming majority of victims of this crime (US Department of Justice, Office of Justice Programs, Bureau of Justice Statistics Factbook, *Violence by Intimates*, 1998). This book does not address the issue of male victims of domestic violence. The book refers more often to batterers as men, abusive men, or abusive husbands, because the vast majority of perpetrators are men (*Violence by Intimates*, 1998). However, while much of the historical and legal discourse about domestic violence assumes a heterosexual relationship, this book does not. The problem of homosexual domestic violence, which appears to be as widespread as heterosexual domestic violence, has long been ignored and has only recently begun to receive the serious attention that it deserves in academic, popular, and legal contexts. Domestic violence within homosexual relationships is discussed in greater detail in chapter five.

3. For a more thorough examination of domestic violence in colonial America, see Elizabeth Pleck, *Domestic Tyranny* (New York: Oxford University Press, 1987), and Christine Daniels and Michael V. Kennedy, eds., *Over the Threshold* (New York: Routledge, 1999).

4. See, for example, *Meyer* v. *Nebraska*, 262 U.S. 390 (1923), http://laws.findlaw.com/us/262/390.html (full text); *Pierce* v. *Society of Sisters*, 268 U.S. 510 (1925), http://laws.findlaw.com/us/268/510.html (full text).

5. See, for example, *Stanley* v. *Georgia*, 394 U.S. 557 (1969), http://laws.findlaw.com/us/394/557.html (full text), http://www.oyez.org/cases/case/?case=1960–1969/1968/1968_293 (audio); *Paris Adult Theatre* v. *Slaton*, 413 U.S. 49 (1973).

6. See, for example, *Bowers* v. *Hardwick*, 478 U.S. 186 (1986).

7. See, for example, *Poe* v. *Ullman*, 367 U.S. 497 (1961); *Griswold* v. *Connecticut*, 381 U.S. 479 (1965); *Eisenstadt* v. *Baird*, 405 U.S. 438 (1972); *Roe* v. *Wade*, 410 U.S. 113 (1973).

8. See note 56, below.

9. For one recent example, contrast the US Supreme Court's utter deference to the privacy of "marital bedrooms" in determining the landmark contraception case, *Griswold* v. *Connecticut*, in 1961, with their utter disregard for the bedrooms of same-sex couples in upholding a sodomy law in *Bowers* v. *Hardwick*, in 1986. See also Patricia Boling, *Privacy and the Politics of Intimate Life* (Ithaca: Cornell University Press, 1996): 35 (noting that welfare recipients, for example, are generally granted less privacy than nonrecipients).

10. See, for example, Patricia Hill Collins, *Black Feminist Thought* (London: Routledge, 1990), especially pp. 187–89.

11. See, for example, Ruthann Robson, "Lavender Bruises," *Golden Gate University Law Review* 20 (1990): 567.

12. See, for example, Tien-Li Loke, "Trapped in Domestic Violence," *Boston University Public Interest Law Journal* 6 (1997): 589.

13. See, for example, Susan Schechter, *Women and Male Violence* (Boston: South End Press, 1982): 140–50, 159, 192–202.

14. *Fulgham v. State*, 46 Ala. 143 (1871); *Commonwealth v. McAfee*, 108 Mass. 458 (1871). See also *Knight v. Knight*, 31 Iowa 451 (1871).

15. Ruth Bordin, *Woman and Temperance* (Philadelphia: Temple University Press, 1981): xviii.

16. Ibid., 7.

17. Pleck, *Domestic Tyranny*, 88–97.

18. Ibid., 3–7.

19. Ibid.; Schechter, *Women and Male Violence*.

20. Schechter, *Women and Male Violence*, 29–43.

21. Ibid., 157–84.

22. 410 U.S. 113 (1973).

23. See *Poe* (1961); *Griswold* (1965); *Eisenstadt* (1972); *Roe* (1973).

24. See, for example, Cynthia Daniels, *Feminists Negotiate the State* (Lanham, MD: University Press of America, 1997); Martha Albertson Fineman and Roxanne Mykitiuk, eds., *The Public Nature of Private Violence* (New York: Routledge, 1994); and Catharine A. MacKinnon, *Toward a Feminist Theory of the State* (Cambridge: Harvard University Press, 1989).

25. Thomas Hobbes, *De Cive* (Chapter 8, Section 8.1., in *Selections*, computer version of selected works of Thomas Hobbes, transcribed principally from the Molesworth ed. of 1843, http://chaucer.library.emory.edu/htprop/beck.html.

26. Christine DiStefano, *Configurations of Masculinity* (Ithaca: Cornell University Press, 1991): 84.

27. Jean-Jacques Rousseau, *The Social Contract and the First and Second Discourse*, ed. Susan Dunn (New Haven: Yale University Press, 2002): 84.

28. Ibid., 106.

29. John Stuart Mill, *Logic*, quoted in Martin Hollis, *Models of Man* (Cambridge, England: Cambridge University Press, 1977): 23–24.

30. DiStefano, *Configurations of Masculinity*, 72.

31. John Stuart Mill, *On Liberty*, ed. Edward Alexander (Peterborough, Ontario: Broadview Press, 1999): 223.

32. Elshtain, *Public Man, Private Woman: Women in Social and Political Thought* (Princeton: Princeton University Press, 1981): 20–41; Susan Moller Okin, *Women in Western Political Thought*, revised ed. (Princeton: Princeton University Press, 1992): 43–49.

33. Elshtain, *Public Man, Private Woman*, 41–49; Okin, *Women in Western Political Thought*, 73–80.

34. John Locke, *Two Treatises of Government*, ed. Peter Laslett (Cambridge, England: Cambridge University Press, 1960): 332; original emphasis.

35. Elshtain, *Public Man, Private Woman*.

36. Specifically, Douglas identifies the First, Third, Fourth, Fifth, Ninth, and Fourteenth Amendments as those that create "zones of privacy" (*Griswold*, 484).

37. 19 Howell's State Trials 1029 (1765).

38. 116 U.S. 616 (1886).

39. *Entick*, 626–27.

40. *Boyd*, 630.

41. 277 U.S. 438 (1928).

42. Ibid., 478; original emphasis.

43. See, for example, *U.S. v. Grunewald*, 233 F.2d 556 (1956); *Silverman et al. v. U.S.*,365 U.S. 505 (1961), http://laws.findlaw.com/us/365/505.html (full text); *Tehan v. US*, 382 U.S. 406 (1966), http://laws.findlaw.com/us/382/406.html (full text); *Katz v. U.S.*, 389 U.S. 347 (1967), http://laws.findlaw.com/us/389/347.html (full text), http://www.oyez.org/cases/case/?case=1960–1969/1967/1967_35 (audio); *Stanley* (1969); and *Winston v. Lee*, 470 U.S. 753 (1985), http://laws.findlaw.com/us/470/753 .html (full text), http://www.oyez.org/cases/case/?case=1980–1989/1984/1984_83_133 4 (audio).

44. See, for example, *Meyer*, 399 (in which the Court interpreted the Fourteenth Amendment to include "the right . . . to marry, establish a home and bring up children"); and *Pierce*, 534–35 (in which the Court recognized "the liberty of parents and guardians to direct the upbringing and education of children under their control").

45. *Prince v. Massachusetts*, 321 U.S. 158, 166 (1944), http://laws.findlaw.com/ us/321/158.html (full text).

46. *Paris Adult Theatre*, 49.

47. *Silverman*, 511.

48. *Tehan*, 414, citing *Grunewald*, 581–2.

49. *Paris Adult Theatre*, 66.

50. *Poe*, 536.

51. *Griswold*, 486.

52. *Eisenstadt*, 453.

53. *Roe*, 153.

54. Catharine MacKinnon, *Toward a Feminist Theory of the State*, 191.

55. As Elshtain notes in her discussion of ancient Greek society, "Some categories of human subjects—in Greek society slaves and women were the most important—were confined to private realms of discourse. Truly public, political speech was the exclusive preserve of free, male citizens. Neither women nor slaves were public beings. Their tongues were silent on the public issues of the day" (*Public Man, Private Woman*: 14).

56. Ibid., 193.

57. Ibid., 193.

58. Elizabeth Schneider, "The Violence of Privacy," in *The Public Nature of Private Violence*, ed. Martha Albertson Fineman and Roxanne Mykitiuk, 36–58 (New York: Routledge, 1994): 43.

59. See DiStefano, *Configurations of Masculinity*.

60. Feminist legal theorist Martha Fineman draws the important distinction be-tween familial or marital privacy and individual privacy. She notes that familial pri-vacy, from its earliest incarnations in the United States, was based on family form. In other words, the concept of family was defined by its members (husband, wife, and children), and it was this collection of people living in the same house that earned the right to privacy. A newer form of privacy, she notes, is individual privacy, in which privacy rights accrue to individuals, sometimes regardless of their membership in a family—so that privacy rights are available to single people, for example, as well as married people. This type of privacy is based on the principle of nonintervention, the aforementioned "right to be let alone" by the state. For more on Fineman's formula-tions of privacy, see Fineman, Martha Albertson, *The Autonomy Myth: A Theory of Dependency* (New York: New Press, 2005).

61. *Bradley* v. *State*, 1 Miss. (1 Walker) 158 (1824).

62. *State* v. *Oliver*, 70 N.C. 60, 61–62 (1874).

63. Elizabeth Schneider, "The Violence of Privacy."

64. Patricia Boling, *Privacy and the Politics of Intimate Life*.

65. Dorothy Roberts, "Punishing Drug Addicts Who Have Babies: Women of Color, Equality, and the Right of Privacy," *Harvard Law Review* 104 (1991): 1419.

66. Elizabeth Schneider, "The Violence of Privacy," 37.

67. For a more detailed description of the case selection method for each chapter, see the appendix to the book.

68. 64 N.Y.2d 152 (1984).

69. 419 N.Y.S.2d 901 (1979).

70. *Scott* v. *Hart*, No. C-76-2395 (N.D. Cal., filed Oct. 28, 1976).

71. 595 F.Supp. 1521 (1984).

72. 65 N.Y.2d 461 (1985).

73. 489 U.S. 189 (1989).

74. 545 U.S. 748 (2005).

75. 478 U.S. 186 (1986).

76. 539 U.S. 558 (2003).

2. PRECURSORS TO THE BATTERED WOMEN'S MOVEMENT

Domestic Violence Law and Activism before the 1960s

INTRODUCTION

The concept of privacy that was employed by courts in the late nineteenth century was rooted in the traditions of classical liberal individualism. This notion of privacy was frequently invoked by judges in domestic violence cases. The privacy to which judges referred, however, was rarely acknowledged as part of that specific tradition: these judges did not mention classical liberalism, nor did they try to find a specific "right to privacy" in the US Constitution. Instead, privacy was referred to in vague, amorphous terms. Judges spoke of privacy as if it were a given, an assumed right.

This vagueness meant that the right of privacy could be selectively applied—in certain situations and to certain individuals. Within the context of domestic violence in particular, this right was granted only to men, and to specific men at that. The way in which privacy was invoked in domestic violence cases conveyed a strong affirmation and valuation of the patriarchal, nuclear family form. In these cases, the right of privacy was given to men not just *as men*, but *as the heads of households*. Echoing Locke's formulation of citizen-as-head-of-household, judges' tendency to recognize the right of privacy only for the heads of households made this particular privilege a specifically patriarchal one.

Throughout most of the nineteenth century, states were still debating in their courts and legislatures whether and to what extent wife-beating (or "chastisement")[1] should be legal.[2] The legality of chastisement was indisputably a critical issue for victims of domestic violence. Nonetheless, as some feminist historians have observed, the legal right of chastisement may not have been the most important factor in determining the safety of battered women. Elizabeth Pleck, for example, has observed the significance of social and community sanctions against wife-beating during this era. Noting that several states had passed laws rendering chastisement illegal by the late nineteenth century, she suggests that enforcement of such laws was often ineffectual in comparison with the discipline meted out by community members. A variety of groups and individuals—ranging from victims' family members to church congregations to feminists to vigilante groups, and even the Ku Klux Klan—all took deliberate measures to punish batterers and to protect victims of domestic violence.[3] Of course, the motivation of the group providing the sanctions determined who was protected and in what way. Pleck contends that, given the rarity of divorce and the extremely wide range of possible sentences a convicted batterer might face during this era, "the system of formal regulation against wifebeaters was relatively weak and cumbersome whereas the mechanisms for informal regulation were relatively vigorous and extensive."[4] In Pleck's view, the existence or abolition of a legal right of chastisement played only a partial role in the protection of women abused by their husbands in the nineteenth century.

Likewise, historian Linda Gordon has noted that prosecution was not often a viable option for battered wives who were economically dependent on their abusers. She describes the ambivalence many late-nineteenth- and early-twentieth-century wives exhibited toward having their husbands prosecuted for assaulting them. While they were usually afraid of their abusive husbands, battered wives often petitioned for pardons for these same men, recognizing that their husband's income was essential for supporting their children and themselves.[5] Within the context of economic dependence, the legality of chastisement itself appears to have had only limited significance, for, as many battered women realized, successfully prosecuting an abusive husband often left them with minimal options for survival.

The debate about the existence of a right of chastisement was undeniably a central element in the legal history of domestic violence in this country. Yet, as Pleck's and Gordon's work reveals, other factors (such as community sanctions and economic dependence) have played a considerable role in mitigating chastisement's importance in this history. I would suggest that privacy is another such factor. The story of domestic violence in the courts at this time reveals that the "right to privacy" (or, at least, judges' perception of such a right) often affected the safety of battered women at least as much as the right of chastisement did.

Concepts of privacy held implications and possibilities for activists of this era as well. Because notions of privacy were so strongly ingrained in the issue of domestic violence, questioning those ideas (and/or their relationship to domestic violence) was a potentially powerful gesture. Undermining existing notions of privacy that upheld and supported the acceptance of domestic violence in court and in society at large was a means of attacking the problem of domestic violence itself. The strategies employed by some of the anti-domestic-violence activists of this era indicate that they used this concept to their advantage.

In the late nineteenth century, the link between domestic violence and privacy was a strong and explicit one. An exploration of this relationship reveals that the way in which this link was addressed—by courts and activists—was critical to battered women and to the problem of domestic violence overall. In fact, the choices made by nineteenth-century judges and activists regarding the privacy issue would ultimately set the stage for the same issues to reemerge nearly a century later.

This chapter begins by tracing the historical development of domestic violence cases and activism in the courts throughout the nineteenth century. Here, I undertake a content analysis of the opinions issued during the nineteenth century by state appellate courts in cases of assault and battery of wives by husbands, as well as published opinions from this same era in cases of divorce on grounds of cruelty. I explore the gender, race, and class ideologies informing these judicial opinions and the ways in which those ideologies interacted with judicial and cultural notions of privacy.

Next, I turn to an exploration of anti-domestic-violence efforts undertaken during the latter half of the nineteenth century. These efforts did not constitute a discrete, anti-domestic-violence or battered women's movement; instead, they occurred primarily within the context of the temperance and women's rights movements. This section therefore examines the ways in which the particular strategies and ideologies of these two movements affected the activism undertaken within them to combat domestic violence. I also consider the ways in which these activist efforts confronted the issue of privacy in pursuing their goals.

Having explored the implications of the similarities and differences of the two movements' approaches to the problem of domestic violence, I then trace the history of domestic violence law and activism in the early twentieth century. Generally considered by scholars to be a less active time for law and activism in this arena, this era nonetheless brought several significant developments, both cultural and judicial, to the problem of domestic violence. Finally, the chapter concludes with an analysis of the interaction between courts and activists around the issues of domestic violence and privacy, and a glimpse ahead at the twentieth-century battered women's movement that will be considered in the next chapter.

DOMESTIC VIOLENCE AND PRIVACY IN NINETEENTH-CENTURY COURTS

Initially, the state did not respond to domestic violence as an issue per se. English common law had held that a man had a right to physically punish his wife, an attitude readily adopted in early-American society. Given this prerogative, domestic violence was not an issue from a legal perspective. This prerogative did not face a consistent challenge within the American legal arena until well into the nineteenth century.

A corollary to the doctrine of coverture or marital unity,[6] chastisement was one of a host of "privileges" men acquired upon marriage. According to the marital-unity doctrine, many of a woman's individual rights were effectively negated when she married, as her husband became owner of any property or financial assets she had or might accrue in the future. In turn, a husband was responsible for supporting his wife financially. He also became responsible for her public behavior, as her legal identity became subsumed under his upon marriage. The legal justification for chastisement, therefore, was rooted in the marital-unity doctrine, as William Blackstone explained in his *Commentaries* on English common law in 1765:

> For, as he [a husband] is to answer for her [his wife's] misbehavior, the law thought it reasonable to intrust him with this power of restraining her, by domestic chastisement, in the same moderation that a man is allowed to correct his apprentices or children; for whom the master or parent is also liable in some cases to answer.[7]

Over sixty years later, James Kent's *Commentaries on American Law* echoed Blackstone's treatment of this issue and applied it to the American context:

> As the husband is the guardian of the wife, and bound to protect and maintain her, the law has given him a reasonable superiority and control over her person, and he may even put gentle restraints upon her liberty, if her conduct be such as to require it.[8]

American legal discourse of the early nineteenth century thus unequivocally set the stage for continued state sanctioning of domestic violence.

During that same decade, the first judicial opinion in the United States was written in which domestic violence was overtly condoned. *Bradley v. State* was decided in Mississippi in 1824. In this case, the court explicitly recognized the right of chastisement, and justified it as follows:

> Family broils and dissentions cannot be investigated before the tribunals of the country, without casting a shade over the character of those who are unfortunately engaged in the controversy. To screen from public reproach those who may thus be

unhappily situated, let the husband be permitted to exercise the right of moderate chastisement in cases of great emergency, and use salutary restraints in every case of misbehavior, without being subjected to vexatious prosecutions, resulting in the mutual discredit and shame of all parties concerned.[9]

Several aspects of this opinion are worth noting. First, the importance of privacy is already visible. While the *Bradley* opinion does not refer specifically to a "right of privacy," it invokes a reasoning that clearly prizes domestic privacy. In fact, this opinion suggests that the major reason for allowing husbands the right of "moderate chastisement" is to spare them the shame that would come from having such deeds aired in public. In other words, keeping such matters *private*—and avoiding "public reproach"—is far more important than punishing the violent act. Additionally, the judge suggests that prosecution would publicly embarrass both the abuser and the abused equally, as the husband's violence would somehow render both parties' characters suspect. In this first opinion, not only is privacy used to justify the state's refusal to condemn domestic violence, but this unwillingness to prosecute batterers simultaneously masquerades as a form of protection for battered women. Overall, privacy's function in court as a defense for batterers (and therefore as an impediment to the safety of battered women) has a firm foundation in this opinion.

While *Bradley* is best known to scholars for its recognition of the right of chastisement, its justification for that right—in notions of privacy—may be even more significant. Throughout the nineteenth century, as courts debated the right of chastisement, attitudes about privacy often overshadowed this discussion by ultimately deciding the outcome of the case. For example, *State v. Black*, a North Carolina case from 1864, echoes *Bradley*'s affirmation of the right to chastisement by grounding that right in a respect for the privacy and sanctity of the domestic sphere:

> the law permits [the husband] to use towards his wife such a degree of force, as is necessary to . . . make her behave herself; and unless some permanent injury be inflicted, or there be an excess of violence . . . the law will not invade the domestic forum, or go behind the curtain. It prefers to leave the parties to themselves . . . to make the matter up and live together as man and wife should.[10]

In another opinion, just four years later, the same court refused to recognize the right of chastisement. The outcome of the case, however, ultimately differed very little from that of *Bradley* or *Black*, for the judge refused to convict the abusive husband of assault and battery. In this case, the husband's lack of a right to beat his wife was rendered inconsequential by the privacy issue:

> The courts have been loth to take cognizance of trivial complaints arising out of domestic relations. . . . [B]ecause the evil of publicity would be greater than the evil

involved in the trifles complained of. . . . However great are the evils of ill temper, quarrels, and even personal conflicts inflicting only temporary pain, they are not comparable with the evils which would result from raising the curtain, and exposing to public curiosity and criticism the nursery and the bed chamber.[11]

This opinion also states explicitly that the "violence complained of would without question have constituted a battery if the subject of it had not been the defendant's wife."[12] Because of the relationship of the victim to the perpetrator, therefore, the sanctity and inviolability accorded to the marital "bed chamber" was enough in this case to turn an otherwise-criminal act into an acceptable part of domestic life.

Racial politics, including attitudes that existed both within and outside of minority communities, added further complexity to the issue of privacy. First, some African Americans, concerned about the way in which their status in the larger society would be affected by the publicizing of domestic violence cases, implored victims within their own community to keep such incidents private. In addition, white police imposed their own racial, class, and ethnic prejudices in the arresting and reporting of domestic violence incidents, ultimately paint-ing for judges as well as for the general public a biased, race- and class-specific portrait of batterers and their victims. Various forms of racial and other prejudice were used within the courtroom against perpetrators as well as victims. Thus, by disproportionately punishing African-American, immigrant, and poorer bat-terers, judges and police used instances of domestic violence as a means to control nonwhite masculinity.

During the Reconstruction years of the late nineteenth century, in which the horrors of slavery had barely begun to recede, the self-preservation of the black community remained a high priority.[13] As many black feminist theorists have observed, an essential component of this self-preservation (one that re-mains to this day) consisted of not airing the "dirty laundry" of the community to the larger society. As Beth Richie notes, "Too many blacks still think this [domestic violence] is a divisive issue that should not be aired in public." She continues, "It is a painful, unsettling task to call attention to violence in our community. You may find yourselves feeling caught by the trap called loyalty. There is already so much negative information about our families that a need to protect ourselves keeps us quiet."[14] Such sentiments were even more prominent in the late nineteenth century, a time that many African Americans saw as cru-cial for their integration into American society.[15]

The hesitation to expose negative aspects of black family life was founded on a quite legitimate fear that whites would use them in the service of racial stereo-typing. When this hesitation translated into a request for black women to keep incidents of domestic violence private, however, it left these victims with fewer options than ever. Several African-American newspapers of the time unfortunately did just that. The *Savannah Colored Tribune*, for example, showed little sympathy for battered women of color:

> The habit of these dirty colored women of arresting their husbands every time they
> have a family quarrel is becoming intolerable and should either be stopped or col-
> ored men should stop marrying. White families quarrel and disagree as much as
> colored do but you never hear of white women however low they may be running to
> the magistrate to have their husbands jailed.[16]

Here, racial and class stereotypes served as a means of promulgating the goal of privacy. Presumably responding to white America's stereotypes about the inferior nature of African-American culture, the author seems defensive: if the "dirty colored women" would simply keep such matters in the private realm where they belong, the implication is, they would stop degrading their race below the "lowest" of the whites. Battered black women are left with an unthinkable dilemma: to suffer the abuse in silence as a matter of race loyalty, or to attempt to seek legal recourse and consequently suffer the very real possibility of being ostracized from within the community.

This dilemma was further complicated for women in minority communities by the racial prejudices apparently informing law enforcement at this time. Police of this era made significantly more domestic violence arrests of immigrant men and men of color than of white men, with immigrant men being most commonly arrested in the North (where fears of Irish, Hungarian, and other immigrants echoed the racial prejudice of the South), and African-American men in the South.[17] For instance, Pleck reports that

> Between 1889 and 1894, fifty-eight out of sixty men arrested for wifebeating in
> Charleston, South Carolina were black. . . . [I]t seems likely that some white as well
> as black husbands were beating their wives in Charleston and that the racial differ-
> ential in arrests there reflected the unwillingness of the police to arrest white
> wifebeaters.[18]

Limited historical records make it impossible to know the extent to which these arrest patterns reflect or distort actual patterns of domestic violence incidents or reports. Nonetheless, other contemporaneous evidence suggests that such numbers are undoubtedly influenced by prevailing attitudes of the era that viewed wife-beating as the recourse of the "dangerous classes."[19]

Such race, class, and ethnic biases emerged in the courtroom as well as in the police force. Feminist historians have questioned whether, in some cases, judges' willingness to repudiate the right of chastisement, like police willingness to arrest abusive husbands, was more reflective of a wish to control black and immigrant masculinity than of a desire to protect battered women.[20] In one of the most well-known cases repudiating the right of chastisement, *Fulgham* v. *State*, both the victim and the perpetrator were emancipated slaves. In this 1871 case, the wife had protested her husband's chastisement of one of their children as being too harsh. In response, the husband struck her twice on the back with a board. After the husband was indicted on charges of assault and battery, he appealed the decision. The Alabama Supreme Court allowed the prosecution, declaring that "the wife is not to be considered as the husband's slave."[21] In another decision repudiating the right of chastisement in 1894, the Supreme Court of Mississippi referred to "a belief among the humbler class of our colored population of a fancied right in the husband to chastise the wife."[22]

Siegel asks, with regard to the *Fulgham* opinion, whether the court's apparent sympathy for the abused wife was meant "to ensure that the woman was not treated like a 'slave,' or to prevent her recently emancipated husband from asserting the 'privileges' of a master?"[23] The larger issue raised by this question—the extent to which judges used domestic violence as a means of controlling nonwhite masculinity—resonates far beyond the *Fulgham* case. The words judges chose in domestic violence cases involving racial and ethnic minorities suggest that their intentions were not solely focused on protecting women from abuse. The overt reference to the race and class of the *Harris* couple, together with the implication of a husband who does not know his place ("fancying" a right that does not belong to him), is just one example.

As with racial, ethnic, and class prejudices, judges' stereotypes about gender roles also reinforced their ideas about privacy and domestic violence. In particular, Barbara Welter observes that the "cult of true womanhood" cultivated during the late nineteenth century emphasized piety, chastity, submissiveness, and domesticity.[24] Likewise, the flip side of these same gender ideologies enabled judges to confer an unspoken right of privacy on men as heads of their households and "kings of their castles." In this way, gender roles and notions of privacy were mutually reinforcing. According to this logic, it was only natural that the husband, as head of the household (a unit protected from government interference), deserved control of his wife, particularly if she were to transgress her proper role. The cult of true womanhood, however, did not apply to all women equally: in fact, the attainment of "true womanhood" was largely impossible for women of color and poor women, solely as a result of their race or class status. Thus, in the same way that privacy as the head of the household was less available to African-American, immigrant, or poor men than it was to middle- or upper-class white men, courts' gendered expectations of women differed by race and class as well.[25]

Gender ideologies such as the "cult of true womanhood" formed the basis for a great deal of judicial justification for the refusal to penalize domestic abuse. The same year the *Fulgham* case was being decided in Alabama, the Supreme Court of Iowa expressed a very different opinion in *Knight* v. *Knight*. In this case, the Supreme Court affirmed a lower court's refusal to grant Mrs. Knight a divorce on the grounds of cruel treatment. The opinion suggests that her own "misconduct" had provoked the violence, thereby rendering her ineligible for a divorce on such grounds. After noting with disapproval that the wife possessed "a will which never yields,"[26] the opinion continues:

> The gentle, fragile, submissive woman might be entitled to a divorce which would scarcely furnish the amazon just cause of complaint. . . . We have not a particle of doubt that if she had justly appreciated the responsibilities and duties of her position, had properly regarded the feelings of her husband, had restrained her pride and guarded her temper, she might have remained one among the most honored and the most cherished of wives.[27]

The *Knight* opinion, with its subtle invocation of class distinctions (between the "gentle, fragile" woman [i.e., a true lady] and the [presumably rougher, unrestrained, not submissive, and unladylike] "amazon"), is also a powerful reminder that conforming to prescribed gender norms was essential to the nineteenth-century woman's safety.

Knight, however, was actually a milder echo of an earlier New Hampshire case, *Poor* v. *Poor*. Like *Knight*, *Poor* was a divorce case in which the court rejected the wife's claim of extreme cruelty (based on, among other offenses, her husband's "beat[ing] her cruelly with a horse-whip [and] imprison[ing] her in the cellar").[28] Instead, the opinion notes that the wife was "of a high, bold, masculine spirit; . . . and not always ready to submit, even to the legitimate authority of her husband."[29] Mrs. Poor's unwillingness to submit to her husband's authority as the head of the household was, in the eyes of the court, provocation and justification for the abuse she suffered. The opinion suggests that "she escaped with quite as little injury as she could have had any right to expect, in such an attempt to take his castle by storm."[30] Furthermore, the court contended, "due to the relation in which she stood to her oppressor, if she could not obtain his consent by kindness and condescension, she should have submitted in silence to the wrong he was doing her."[31] In this no-win formulation, wives should submit to their husbands as a prerequisite for their own safety. If, however, this approach fails and they are abused anyway, they should simply acquiesce and endure the abuse. The opinion concludes with this admonition: "the wife has no right to complain . . . she drew upon herself the chastisement she received, by her own improper conduct. . . . Her remedy is to be sought, then, not in this court, but in a reformation of her own manners. Let her return to the path of duty."[32] In essence, Mrs. Poor's failure to conform to gender-role expectations—which the court read as a refusal to submit to her husband's legitimate authority as head of his household—effectively erased any legal recourse whatsoever for the violence she endured.

These gender ideologies were often explicitly rooted in the doctrine of Christianity. Many judicial opinions in domestic violence cases of this era quoted liberally from the Bible. In particular, judges referred to the proper role of a wife, and her transgression of that role, as justification for the abuse itself as well as the court's refusal to intercede on her behalf. Of Mrs. Poor, for example, the court asked, "what course of conduct did duty prescribe to a Christian wife and to a member of the church? . . . [C]harity that suffereth long and is kind . . . not only believeth and hopeth, but *beareth and endureth all things*."[33] Another case cited the book of Genesis in defense of an abusive husband's behavior: "Unto the woman it is said, 'Thy desire shall be to thy husband, and he shall rule over thee,' Genesis, ch. 3, v. 16."[34] Likewise, other elements of Christianity also influenced the outcome of domestic violence cases. In some cases, women were denied divorce despite evidence of cruel treatment because they were alleged to have committed adultery, a sin which presumably justified the violence they experienced.[35]

Within the context of such strict gender roles, the concept of shame—specifically, avoiding bringing shame to men—looms large. Judicial opinions of this time give the impression that adherence to prescribed gender and marriage roles is of such importance that divergence from them would result in a humiliation that should be avoided at all costs. Again, keeping the violence private—especially by refusing to punish it—was a means of avoiding this humiliation. The *Joyner* v. *Joyner* opinion, which pardoned a husband's physical violence in light of his wife's "provocation" of the abuse, declared that "if . . . the wife persistently treats her husband with disrespect, and he submits to it, he . . . loses the respect of the other members of his family, without which he cannot expect to govern them, and forfeits the respect of his neighbors."[36] The author of the opinion in another domestic violence case lamented, "It would be hard if, for the single act [of violence], he must incur the forfeiture of forced separation, the record of which must forever be a source of mortification to himself . . ."[37] Echoing the "mutual discredit and shame" alluded to in the *Bradley* opinion several decades earlier, these opinions referred to the humiliation of publicity. Unlike *Bradley*, however, neither the *Richards* nor the *Joyner* opinion identified the violence itself as the source of embarrassment. Instead, these judges feared the shame a husband might suffer within the community if he were exposed to be anything less than the ruler of the household. A husband's violence toward his wife is seen here as a legitimate mechanism for reinforcing both his dominant position in the household hierarchy as well as the privacy of that sphere.

Similarly, the concept of "family government" that emerged in several domestic violence cases during the late nineteenth century only reinforced these ideals. Several judges of this era interpreted the adage about the husband as the "king of his castle" quite literally. This concept, which combined gender-role ideologies with the utmost respect for marital privacy, led judges in some cases to view the nuclear family as a self-governing unit. This unit was not to be disturbed by the reach of state government except in the most extreme of cases. The author of *State v. Rhodes* relied upon this formulation very explicitly in his refusal to indict a husband for assault and battery:

> Our conclusion is that family government is recognized by law as being as complete in itself as the State government is in itself, and yet subordinate to it; and that we will not interfere with or attempt to control it, in favor of either husband or wife, unless in cases where permanent or malicious injury is inflicted or threatened, or the condition of the party is intolerable. . . . Every household has and must have, a government of its own, modelled to suit the temper, disposition and condition of its inmates.[38]

Given its status of near-immunity from state intervention, this formulation of family government provides husbands, as the heads of that "government," with a staggering amount of power, particularly in relation to domestic abuse. And while the final sentence of the excerpt suggests that such an arrangement might take into account the interests of all family members, there is no indication that any judge of this era was seriously considering the possibility of women or children as equal partners in such government. As another judge observed,

> It has not been denied that he [the abusive husband] is the legal head of the whole family, wife and children inclusive; and I have heard it urged from no quarter that he should be brought under subjection to a household democracy. All will agree, I apprehend, that such a measure would extend the right of suffrage quite too far.[39]

This hierarchy is clearly echoed by other judges in simple statements such as "Every man must govern his household"[40] and references to "the rights and power of the husband as head of the family."[41] Under a system in which physical abuse is often viewed by judges as a legitimate exercise of this power, and courts grant the abuser himself the authority to rule over his wife, the privacy of the home clearly privileges and protects men, thereby often eliminating any legal recourse for a woman experiencing violence at home.

Just as individual judges' approaches to this issue inevitably vary, legal options for battered women likewise varied widely by state throughout the second half of the nineteenth century, as courts continued to ponder the existence of a right to chastisement. As early as 1838, a Delaware court declared that "the wife must be protected. We know of no law that will authorize a husband to strike his pregnant wife a blow with his fist, such as has been inflicted on this woman."[42] Here, the court sees its role quite clearly as that of protector, presumably at least in part because the wife was pregnant. Only four years later, a New York court came to a much different conclusion, arguing that complete repudiation of the chastisement right would lead to moral corruption: "In asserting the principle on which the barbarous practice of correction was abolished, the courts should beware of the opposite extreme. . . . Much as we may congratulate ourselves on the abolition of unreasonable severity, such an achievement would but poorly compensate for the general corruption of domestic morals."[43] An 1857 Pennsylvania opinion expressed a similar sentiment, concluding that "it is a sickly sensibility which holds that a man may not lay hands on his wife, even rudely, if necessary . . ."[44] Throughout the nineteenth century, there was no judicial consensus on the issue of the right to chastisement. Even if such consensus had existed, some courts' decisions about whether to punish abusive husbands depended more upon the court's view of privacy than on the role of chastisement itself. Therefore, any battered woman's chances in a given courtroom were fairly impossible to predict.

As the nineteenth century drew to a close, however, such a consensus was in sight. In fact, the extent to which the legal response to domestic violence was beginning to coalesce seemed quite promising by 1871, for that year saw two landmark cases and one powerful concurrence in which the right to chastisement was expressly repudiated. In the Massachusetts case of *Commonwealth v. McAfee*, a husband had caused his wife's death by striking her on the cheek and temple while she was intoxicated, thus causing her to fall and hit her head. The trial judge refused to endorse the defendant's contention that he "had a legal right to administer due and proper correction and corporeal [sic] chastisement on his wife," and the Massachusetts Supreme Court affirmed: "Beating or striking a wife violently with the open hand is not one of the rights conferred on a husband by the marriage, even if the wife be drunk or insolent."[45]

The *Fulgham* case, discussed earlier for its racial implications, was the other landmark case repudiating chastisement that year. The Alabama Supreme Court, deciding to allow the husband's prosecution, declared that

The husband is . . . not justified or allowed by law to use [any weapon] for [his wife's] moderate correction. . . . And the privilege, ancient though it be, to beat her with a stick, to pull her hair, choke her, spit in her face or kick her about the floor, or to inflict upon her like indignities, is not now acknowledged by our law. . . . [I]n person, the wife is entitled to the same protection of the law that the husband can invoke for himself. . . . Her sex does not degrade her below the rank of the highest in the commonwealth.[46]

Fulgham, like *McAfee*, was an indication that the legal system had begun to recognize domestic violence as unacceptable behavior.

Bolstering these two cases' refutation of the right of chastisement was the concurrence in Iowa's *Knight v. Knight* case that same year. This concurrence, written by Justice Miller, represents a stark contrast to the misogyny and gender stereotyping in the *Knight* majority opinion, condemning the majority's suggestion that the wife deserved the abuse by failing to be a "fragile, submissive woman." Although he concurred in the *Knight* judgment for jurisdictional reasons, Miller flatly rejected the majority's position on domestic violence. Instead, he protested,

> [the plaintiff's] faults are no justification or even palliation of the husband's ill-treatment of her; nor should she be denied all remedy for such ill-treatment because she has not been at all times an *humble* and *submissive* wife. . . . No provocation, in my opinion, will justify a man in cruel and inhuman treatment of his wife, or deprive her of her right to be divorced.[47]

Thus, while *Knight* did not represent a victory, either for the plaintiff in the case or for battered women more generally, Miller's concurrence—especially when viewed alongside the *Fulgham* and *McAfee* opinions—represented a significant development in the legal response to domestic violence.

This trend toward legal refutation of the right of chastisement emerged as a confluence of factors. As legal historian Reva Siegal observes, public discussions of wife abuse became increasingly complex as the nineteenth century progressed.[48] Increased industrialization, urbanization, and immigration were bringing significant changes to the shape and character of American life and allowing many to envision a different future for the nation, one that reflected a variety of social changes. Although many cases since *Bradley* had very specifically recognized a right of chastisement, the various social movements gaining prominence in America by the mid-1800s (including the abolition, suffrage, and temperance movements) had begun challenging previously held beliefs about acceptable behavior. Societal norms regarding such issues as drinking and slaveholding were called into question, and fundamental values became subject to re-examination. As abolitionists chided slaveholders for their "barbaric" physical abuse of slaves, temperance advocates wondered publicly how "civilized" men could, under the influence of alcohol, cruelly beat their wives. Within this climate of social change, attitudes about domestic violence began to shift in both popular and legal discourse.

Likewise, as courts began to condemn domestic violence, the community response to this problem changed as well. Elizabeth Pleck's examination of community response during this era concludes with the observation that as punishment for batterers became more formalized (with courts administering official state sanctions), communities' sense of responsibility for this discipline declined.[49] This analysis suggests that the nature of the legal system itself reinforces the privacy paradigm. Specifically, the legal system's emphasis on individual culpability takes the mechanism for social control away from local communities. Indeed, the presence of formal justice administered at the individual level lessens the perceived need for more informal responses at the community level. In this way, the shifting community response to this problem is another factor strengthening the link between privacy and domestic violence.

At the same time, however, the issue of community response serves as an important reminder of the disjuncture between the role of privacy in domestic violence cases in court, and its role in domestic violence situations at home. The privacy that appeared in judicial opinions as a right that was naturally held by heads of households seemed to suggest that domestic violence was an issue to be dealt with inside the home. Nevertheless, church, neighborhood, and even vigilante groups had for years responded to this ostensibly private violence strongly and often publicly, with acts ranging from expulsion of batterers from church congregations to public flogging of batterers.[50] The nature and prevalence of such actions indicate that the home—and the problem of domestic violence—was never quite as private as those judicial opinions might lead one to believe.

In addition to local and community groups, groups of women activists were responding to the issue of domestic violence at this time as well. These activists working to end spousal abuse addressed this problem from a range of diverse perspectives and from within a variety of organizations and social movements. They also employed a wide array of strategies in their attempts to combat the problem. While some strategies and some movements were more effective than others, one of the most compelling characteristics of this era is the extent to which these activists were able to disrupt the privacy paradigm with regard to domestic violence.

ANTI-DOMESTIC-VIOLENCE ACTIVISM IN THE LATE NINETEENTH CENTURY

For those working to end domestic violence in the late nineteenth century, the privacy issue presented unique ideological problems, for their efforts emerged within the context of numerous other contemporaneous movements, each with different theoretical and strategic approaches. Most notable among these were the temperance reform movement and the women's rights movement. While the influence of other social trends was certainly felt at this time as well, the majority of activism on behalf of battered women was aligned with either or both of these causes. As such, anti-domestic-violence efforts at this time did not constitute a discrete, cohesive, or organized movement. Indeed, only one organization in the nineteenth century, the Protective Agency for Women and Children, located in Chicago, sought specifically to protect abused wives.[51] Instead, activism that addressed the problem of domestic violence at this time usually occurred under the rubric of either the women's rights or the temperance movement. A comparison of these two movements is particularly useful, therefore, for an examination of the ways in which their strategies and ideologies differed with regard to domestic violence.

While individuals within both the women's rights and temperance movements addressed the problem of domestic violence through speeches, writings, and other means, neither of these movements adopted any formal stance on this issue. Nor did the leadership of either movement ever officially proclaim the eradication of domestic violence to be one of its goals. Nonetheless, the late-nineteenth-century activist efforts outlined in this chapter merit scholarly attention, as they represent the first wave of anti-domestic-violence activism occurring within the context of organized social movements.

Before examining these efforts against domestic violence, however, it is important to unpack the concept of the "women's rights movement" through which much of this activism occurred. Historians of the women's rights movement during the nineteenth century agree that this movement was characterized by several sharp ideological divisions, particularly with regard to the issue of suffrage. These divisions led to the formation of numerous different organizations pursuing a variety of strategies, with varying degrees of success. As Steven Buechler observes, women's rights activism in the latter half of the nineteenth century and the opening decades of the twentieth century occurred in three phases.[52] Each of these phases was marked by the creation, prominence, dissolution, or merger of various organizations, as competing priorities and ideologies within the movement shifted over time.

Buechler defines the first phase, the period from 1840 until 1869, as the origin of the women's rights movement. During the early years of this period, activism on behalf of women's rights occurred fairly informally, within the context of the abolitionist movement, as no formal organizations yet existed for the purpose of furthering women's rights. Nonetheless, by the late 1840s, numerous conventions were being held to address the subject of women's rights. The Civil War first disrupted then eventually galvanized the burgeoning women's rights movement. Initially, the war diverted potential activist attention from the cause of women's rights, yet the national debates about equality in voting that followed the war helped to focus the women's movement on the issue of suffrage. In this first phase, therefore, activists in the women's rights movement quickly focused on universal rights and suffrage, aligning their cause with that of African Americans. Thus, by the end of this phase, women's rights activists had created their first formal organization, the American Equal Rights Association, that overtly linked issues of racial and sexual equality.[53]

This willingness to address issues of race and sex simultaneously would prove to be a contentious one for the women's rights movement during its second phase, from 1869 to 1890. During this phase, women's rights activists often found themselves having to choose whether to prioritize suffrage for African Americans or for women. Within both abolitionist and women's suffrage groups, activists often felt that alliance with the other group would weaken their own chances for success. At the same time, some women's rights activists felt that continued allegiance to the abolitionist and Republican interests represented their *only* chance for success. This philosophical and strategic dispute eventually caused a rift between some of the leading figures in the women's rights movement, leading to the formation of rival suffrage organizations.[54]

Susan B. Anthony and Elizabeth Cady Stanton, impatient with the Republicans' seeming reluctance to wholeheartedly embrace the cause of women's suffrage, broke their ties with Republicans and, in 1869, opposed the passage of the Fifteenth Amendment because, in granting suffrage to black men, it reiterated the disenfranchisement of all women. Later that year, Stanton and Anthony formed the National Woman Suffrage Association (NWSA), devoted to supporting all women's issues and to being an organization "controlled and defined by women" first and foremost.[55] Several months later, woman suffragists who were more loyal to their Republican roots, including Lucy Stone and Henry Blackwell, formed the American Woman Suffrage Association (AWSA), which reflected those loyalties.[56] The differences between these two groups, however, consisted not merely in their political allegiances, but also in their ideologies. As Buechler notes, "The ideological posture of [NWSA] was decidedly radical, identifying the connections between women's oppressions and tracing them ultimately to marriage and the sexual division of labor. The ideology of [AWSA] stopped short of such a holistic critique of women's position, restricting its focus to the right to vote."[57] Nonetheless, these ideological differences, so prominent upon the formation of the two groups, did fade over time. Given the proliferation during the 1870s and 1880s of organizations devoted to women's issues apart from the cause of suffrage (including the temperance movement, which had strong female leadership and often focused on the concerns of wives and mothers), NWSA and AWSA focused much of their energies on simply "maintain[ing] the vitality and political focus of these . . . organizations in an increasingly crowded organizational field."[58] As a result, the overt political successes of these organizations during this period were limited; indeed, their main success of this era was simply maintaining the existence of the movement, which would eventually regain momentum after 1890.

As the leadership of NWSA and AWSA changed and the groups' ideological differences grew less apparent, they eventually merged in 1890 to form the National American Woman Suffrage Association (NAWSA), thereby ushering in the third phase of women's rights activism. This third phase, lasting from 1890 until the passage of the Nineteenth Amendment in 1920, witnessed the growth of NAWSA into a large organization with more broad-based appeal (and a greater diversity of perspectives) than either NWSA or AWSA had previously held. NAWSA's inclusive stance, however, also rendered it less focused than either of its parent organizations had been, and it was challenged in 1914 by the emergence of a rival organization, the Congressional Union (CU), which had developed from within its own ranks. The CU shortly merged with the Woman's Party to become the National Woman's Party (NWP), which employed more radical tactics such as pickets and hunger strikes to call attention to the suffrage cause. In the face of such radical tactics, NAWSA came to be perceived as moderate by comparison. Ultimately, this interplay between the two factions within the movement, in concert with the employment of both state-level and federal strategies, led to the passage of the Nineteenth Amendment in 1920.[59]

My discussion of anti-domestic-violence activism within the women's rights movement focuses primarily on the second phase, for several reasons. First, this is the era in which the majority of activism around domestic violence occurred. This time period also corresponds with the proliferation of domestic violence court cases that I have examined earlier in this chapter. The journals that addressed the problem of domestic abuse, such as the *Revolution*, the *Woman's Advocate*, and the *Woman's Journal*, were also published during this time period. Finally, as Buechler observes, this phase was characterized by the proliferation of numerous other women's causes, including the temperance movement, and this context is helpful for my comparison of the two approaches.

I have deliberately contextualized the late-nineteenth-century women's rights movement in this way, emphasizing the ideological and strategic differences within the movement, in order to avoid oversimplifying the nature of the movement itself. It is not my intention to present the women's rights movement at this time as a cohesive, ideologically unified whole that can be easily contrasted with the temperance movement. Nonetheless, I believe that with regard to the issue of domestic violence, several useful distinctions can be made between the efforts undertaken by women's rights activists and those undertaken by temperance activists. For, while it is true that different groups of women's rights activists approached the issue of suffrage in different ways, the movement itself was inherently somewhat more radical than the temperance movement.

The temperance movement did not, for the most part, challenge the assigna-tion of women to the private sphere; instead, it simply sought increased power for women within this domestic arena. This fairly conservative approach did not seek to disrupt the framework of the public/private divide, but rather to work within it. In contrast, the women's rights movement deliberately sought to move women into the public sphere; both the radical and conservative factions within the movement worked, via the drive for the enfranchisement of women, to al-low women access to the traditionally male-identified arena of politics. As a re-sult, despite the ideological divisions that existed within these movements, it can be said that the women's rights movement was, broadly speaking, somewhat more radical in nature than the temperance movement, and this basic differ-ence had interesting implications for the two movements' approaches to the problem of domestic violence.

Furthermore, despite ideological differences within the women's rights movement, women's rights activists shared similar approaches to the problem of domestic violence. As Elizabeth Pleck has noted, "Although Stone and Black-well were regarded as the conservatives of the women's rights movement, their analysis of crimes against women was virtually identical with that of Stanton and Anthony. They, too, believed that abuse of wives grew out of a husband's ownership of his wife as a form of property—'domestic tyranny,' as they some-times called it."[60] Like Pleck, I believe that it is both possible and useful to speak in terms of a "women's rights" approach to domestic violence that, while not entirely unified, can nonetheless be distinguished in many ways from the temperance approach to this problem.

Of course, it is important to recognize that the overall division between the two movements is far from exact. The most obvious factor problematizing this distinction is the fact that some of the same activists participated in both strug-gles at various points in their careers. Elizabeth Cady Stanton, for example, notably aligned with the more radical faction of the women's rights movement during its second phase, had previously worked with temperance reformers dur-ing the mid-1800s.[61] In addition, like all movements, both the women's rights and the temperance movements housed internal divisions and experienced changes over time.[62] Overall, however, they can be said to represent two differ-ent approaches to the issue of domestic violence in the late nineteenth century.

Indeed, several feminist historians have noted the more conservative tenor of the temperance movement in comparison to the overtly political, sometimes radical nature of the women's rights movement.[63] This characterization presents a meaningful framework with which to compare the two axes of nineteenth-century efforts against domestic violence. At the same time, it remains critical to resist the temptation to generalize this description beyond its usefulness.

This discussion acknowledges and explores this division between ostensibly conservative and radical movements, while also observing the inevitable complexities that problematize such a dichotomy, including the often-overlapping agendas of the two movements.

Perhaps the most obvious theoretical difference between the two pertains to the ways in which they addressed the notion of "separate spheres." The prevailing gender ideology of the middle and upper classes of the time, "separate spheres" implied that the public sphere of business, commerce, and political life belonged or should belong to men, while the private sphere of the home and domesticity was the natural domain of women.[64] Conflicting responses to this principle often meant very different strategies for combating domestic violence. On one hand, the temperance movement often reinforced traditional separate spheres ideology by promoting an end to alcohol abuse and physical abuse as a way to restore the peaceful domesticity of the private sphere.[65] Simultaneously, within the more radical branches of the women's rights movement, activists were advocating a complete overhaul of patriarchal families, identifying these homes as sites of risk and oppression rather than safe havens for women. These contrasting approaches to the ideology of separate spheres highlight an issue that had significant implications for the issue of domestic violence.

DOMESTIC VIOLENCE AND THE TEMPERANCE MOVEMENT

Given the somewhat more conservative nature of the temperance movement, it may initially seem surprising that much of the activism on behalf of battered women in the nineteenth century was carried out under the rubric of the temperance movement. There are several reasons for this pairing. The heightened climate of activism of the post–Civil War years saw many former abolitionists turning their attention to other causes, the temperance movement being one of the primary beneficiaries of that energy. From the perspective of the largely middle- and upper-class women able to do activist work at this time, alcohol was very much a woman's problem. Being situated so firmly in the domestic domain, women were seen to bear the brunt of their husbands' abuse of alcohol, particularly when men returned to the home intoxicated and violent. It seemed logical, therefore, that women would emerge as leaders and workers in the temperance movement, approach the issue from a woman's perspective, and focus on related problems such as domestic violence. Most notably, the Woman's Christian Temperance Union (WCTU), which gained prominence as "both the leading temperance organization and the leading women's organization in the United States" in 1873, quickly became a forum for women's activism around a variety of social issues, including domestic violence.[66]

For the most part, the temperance movement dealt with the problem of domestic violence indirectly. Many temperance workers at this time believed alcohol to be the sole cause of domestic abuse, and this belief logically suggested that eradication of alcohol consumption would eliminate the violence. Thus, temperance workers were more likely to raise the issue of domestic violence as another reason for promoting abstinence from liquor than they were to confront the violence per se. It only furthered the temperance cause to raise the subject of domestic violence as one in a long list of evils resulting from alcohol consumption. In this way, the previously taboo subject of domestic violence suddenly began appearing in temperance journals and publications. The *Lily*, which was a "journal devoted to temperance and literature" edited by Amelia Bloomer, proclaimed that "Women are the principal sufferers from intemperance. . . . [T]he insults, the blows, the murders which flow in such awful profusion from the intemperance of husbands, fathers, sons, brothers, fall with heaviest, most crushing force upon woman."[67] Early on, temperance advocates linked the abuse of alcohol with the abuse of women.

The temperance movement did not hesitate to rely upon traditional notions of woman's moral superiority when addressing the issue of domestic violence. Urging women readers to avoid the company of intemperate men, Cora Leslie wrote to the *Lily*,

> Alas, what should we be, if we should follow in the path of these would be "lords of creation!"—Licentiousness, gambling, profanity, and intemperance are among the qualifications which belong to many of them. . . . And if we can withstand all these temptations, which make victims of so many of the sterner sex, are we not in reality, the superiors? Should we not look with *pity* upon such *frail, weak-minded* specimens of humanity?[68]

By invoking and embracing traditional stereotypes of woman's inherent moral superiority, temperance workers made their position a difficult one for even their most conservative opponents to dispute. At the same time, pushing those ideas further to portray men as weak-minded and inferior—and to question their position as "lords of creation"—allowed these activists to claim a power and a legitimacy for their cause that such traditional ideas did not usually foster.

This gender stereotyping, rooted in claims of women's moral superiority, was prominent even when temperance workers supported the cause of woman suffrage. These activists sometimes promoted voting rights for women as a means of winning temperance, and therefore restoring peace to the domestic sphere. As

Buechler observes, "For temperance reformers, the right to vote was conceived as a means of carrying out women's traditional, culturally scripted duty of protecting the home rather than the symbol and substance of an emancipatory movement to gain women's rights and promote sexual equality."[69] This approach assumed that women's stronger sense of morality would naturally lead them to support the temperance cause at the polls—and would thereby help to save women's lives in the process. One temperance worker asked, "[H]ow many wives would have been saved from premature graves, to which they were hurried by misery or murder . . . from the anguish of brutal curses and still more brutal blows had women been endowed with the right of suffrage from this question *alone*, only twenty years ago?"[70] The higher standard of ethics that women would bring to the political process if suffrage were granted was seen as an additional benefit. This same writer contended that woman's right to vote, even if only on the single issue of temperance, "would promote domestic tranquility; for it is much more frequently disturbed by men than by women," and furthermore "[women's] presence [at the polls] would shame or soften the worst [men] into . . . good behavior, and improve the behavior of the rest."[71]

Despite the often conservative rhetoric it employed, the temperance movement was nonetheless quite radical in many ways. In some cases, temperance writers used prevailing notions about morality and women's roles to argue for the dissolution of abusive marriages. A Mrs. Swisshelm, for example, contended in the pages of the *Lily* that "it may be very angelic for a pure-minded, virtuous woman to love and caress a great drunken beast, but . . . we have not the slightest pretensions to being an angel." She continued, "[S]o far from its being a duty for a wife to live with a drunken husband it is a violation of the laws of God, and the dictates of common sense and common decency."[72] While this invocation of traditional stereotypes appears quite conservative on its face, the use of these notions to subvert traditional marriage ideals is actually an unexpectedly radical strategy.

Likewise, temperance advocates' defense of women's rights could be fierce at times:

> What rights have the drunkards [*sic*] wife and children? . . . What right have [men] to make laws which deprive her of every comfort, strips [*sic*] her of every friend, and dooms [*sic*] her to a wretched existence? . . . It is useless for our sex to seek redress at the hands of the law, from the cruel wrongs inflicted upon them, for it will give them none—it does not recognize their right to protection. . . . [I]t is not only the right, but the duty of those trampled upon, to assert their claim to protection.[73]

The discourse of rights found here, while powerful, was rare for temperance activists, and was much more frequently employed by suffragists, whose cause was more obviously linked with rights for women. The notion of women asserting themselves—in fact, being obligated to assert themselves—was equally unconventional within a movement that often used women's supposed meekness to its advantage. Temperance workers' willingness to align themselves with this controversial cause and this heated rhetoric, however occasionally, demonstrates the seriousness, and perhaps even the desperation, with which they approached the issue of women's safety from violent husbands.

Likewise, some temperance activists did not hesitate to express their frustration with the movement's seemingly insurmountable opposition and slow progress. One exasperated temperance worker wrote to the *Lily* that women might be tempted to "warn the dram-sellers . . . not to encroach on our hearth; and if they persisted . . . *burn down* their establishments with [a] clear . . . conscience."[74] Such a comment bears the hallmarks of radical change that are nonetheless couched within some fairly conservative terms. Clearly, this kind of a dramatic call to action certainly helps to underscore the gravity with which temperance activists viewed their cause. At the same time, the female possessiveness of the domestic arena reflected in this statement ("our hearth") reinforces traditional separate spheres ideology—women are incited to take radical measures, but only if their domain, the domestic realm, is perceived to be threatened.

Despite the occasional inflammatory rhetoric offered by temperance activists, neither the movement itself nor its treatment of domestic violence posed a significant threat to the patriarchal family form or to the pervasive ideology of separate spheres. It is certainly true that the movement demonstrated some radical moments, allying itself with controversial causes and employing language designed to shock traditional sensibilities. Overall, however, the more common strategy of the temperance movement was to work within, rather than against, prescribed gender roles and accepted social boundaries—most significantly, the concept of separate spheres. Temperance workers often embraced these notions as a means of increasing the power and legitimacy of their cause (as, for example, when demanding the rights that should naturally accrue to them as the morally superior sex).

While this strategy was an effective means of portraying the movement as a moderate and reasonable one, temperance activists' reluctance to reject the separate-spheres model only reinforced traditional notions of privacy. Accepting their confinement to the domestic domain as implied by separate spheres, temperance workers then asserted their interest in controlling that arena by demanding safe and alcohol-free homes. In so doing, they helped to elevate the nuclear-family home as a sacred space, protected from outside influence—just as early notions of privacy had traditionally construed it.

Unfortunately, with regard to stopping domestic violence, this strategy was a precarious one, for several reasons. First, anchoring the problem of domestic violence so tightly to the problem of alcohol consumption required that temperance activists be correct in their primary assumption; namely, that banning alcohol would automatically eliminate violence in the home. Second, this strategy also meant that the elimination of domestic violence would *only* happen if the campaign for temperance were successful. As a result of these two factors, the temperance movement, while certainly successful in raising some awareness about domestic violence, was ultimately unable to make significant strides against it. Instead, however inadvertently, the rhetoric and strategies of the movement did serve to reinforce cultural notions of privacy and of the home as an impermeable space.

DOMESTIC VIOLENCE AND THE WOMEN'S RIGHTS MOVEMENT

Although their cause was often linked with the temperance movement, suffragists and women's rights advocates confronted the issue of domestic violence much more directly than did their colleagues working for temperance. For suffragists, the link between winning their goal and ending violence was not as clear as it was for temperance workers; no one would argue that winning the vote would automatically eliminate domestic abuse. Instead, many women's rights advocates talked about ending domestic violence in the same way they talked about the vote: as a right. Like temperance workers, these activists raised the issue of domestic violence as a means of furthering their overall goal, but they discussed it as part of the larger slate of women's rights that they were seeking.

And while the temperance movement focused (at least externally) on maintaining safe space for women in their traditional domestic roles, the women's rights movement took a different approach. In fact, the women's rights movement—particularly its more radical factions—publicly acknowledged its more far-reaching agenda of securing rights for women that were previously denied to them. For suffragists, the vote was the most crucial right, for it would help them subsequently to secure other freedoms for women. In an 1892 speech entitled, "The Solitude of Self," Elizabeth Cady Stanton argued passionately along these lines:

> In discussing the rights of woman, we are to consider, first, what belongs to her as an individual, in a world of her own, the arbiter of her own destiny. . . . Her rights under such circumstances are to use all her faculties for her own safety and happiness. . . . [I]f we consider her as a citizen, as a member of a great nation, she must have the same rights as all other members, according to the fundamental principles of our

government. . . . To deny political equality is to rob the ostracized of a self-respect; of credit in the market-place; of recompense in the world of work; of a voice in the choice of those who make and administer the law; a choice in the jury before whom they are tried, and in the judge who decides their punishment.[75]

Whereas the rhetoric of the temperance movement (like some of the more conservative branches of the women's rights movement) often relied on cultural ideas about the moral superiority of women, the rights-focused discourse employed by Stanton and her colleagues emphasized the equality of women and men. And this equality, as Stanton's speech reveals, was not limited to voting rights; instead, these women's rights workers sought a much more far-reaching equality that affected the realms of labor, finance, law, politics, and even physical and mental well-being. In this sense, woman suffrage was not an end in itself, but rather an important means of pursuing this broad-based vision of equality.

Given the movement's focus on equality and the pursuit of equal rights, it is hardly surprising that its writings often called attention to the subjugation of women that activists witnessed in daily life. Often, the most egregious and moving example of this oppression that these writers pointed to was violence against women, particularly in the home. The *Woman's Journal*, published out of Boston in the late nineteenth century, is filled with many of these examples. Edited by Lucy Stone and Henry Blackwell beginning in 1872, the *Woman's Journal* (later renamed *Woman's Journal and Suffrage News*) did not hesitate to publish detailed accounts of domestic violence along with scathing commentaries linking this violence to the overall societal subordination of women. Indeed, even this journal, published by the faction of the women's rights movement considered to be more conservative in its approach to suffrage, employed a radical and systemic critique of domestic violence. In this way, the approach of the *Woman's Journal* to domestic violence mirrored that of another women's rights journal of the same era, the *Revolution*, published by the more radical Stanton and Anthony.

Articles with titles such as "The Subjection of Wives" were not uncommon in the pages of these journals. In her discussion of the horrors of wife-beating, one writer to the *Woman's Journal* asserts, "These horrors result inevitably from the subjection and disfranchisement of women. . . . Equal Rights and Impartial Suffrage are the only radical cure for these barbarities."[76] Lavinia Goodell wrote an article in the same journal entitled "Ownership of Wives," in which she decries "the 'brain starvation' induced by ages of 'subordination' [that] cannot fail to have told on the mental and moral development of women."[77] Another writer, detailing a list of recent incidents of violence against women in the home and denouncing women's lack of legal redress, observes with exasperation, "Yet women are asked to take part in the celebration of their subjugation."[78] Likewise, in an 1860 public speech supporting divorce laws, Stanton described a marriage "where innocent children, trembling with fear . . . hide themselves from the wrath of drunken, brutal fathers . . . as they see the only being on earth they love, dragged about the room by the hair . . . , kicked and pounded, and left half dead and bleeding on the floor?"[79] She continues, "Our law-makers have dug a pit, and the innocent have fallen into it. . . . The mass of the women of this nation know nothing about the laws, yet all their specially barbarous legislation is for woman."[80] Stanton concludes by advocating a new model of marriage based on the concept of equal rights: "[T]here is one kind of marriage that has not been tried, and that is, a contract made by equal parties to live an equal life, with equal restraints and privileges on either side."[81] While this approach was in some ways much more direct than that taken by temperance workers, it had a similar effect. By citing the most heinous and provocative examples of the subordination of women—namely, domestic violence—these writers were able to bolster the case for women's rights overall.

These activists were also willing to use (and to exhort others to use) political means as the tools of social change. British feminist Frances Power Cobbe, author of the influential article, "Wife-Torture in England," printed in the *Woman's Journal*, made specific recommendations to Parliament regarding legal recourse for poor women. In this article, she cogently argues that while wealthy women may obtain divorces for their safety, poor women are unable to afford them. In response to this inequity, Cobbe outlines for Parliament a bill that seeks to resolve a number of issues affecting the safety of poor battered women, including orders of protection, child custody, and financial support. The full text of the bill, entitled the Wives' Protection Bill, was reprinted in the *Woman's Journal*.[82] Having gathered the support of "many eminent legal authorities," Cobbe urges readers to support this and similar bills.

A different kind of political activism took place in the United States, where American feminists petitioned the governor of Pennsylvania to review the conviction of Hester Vaughn. Vaughn, a domestic servant and victim of domestic violence, had been impregnated by her employer and subsequently fired by him. After giving birth alone, she was found lying with her dead infant next to her. Convicted of infanticide, Vaughn had been sentenced to death. Upon hearing of her case, these activists wrote and spoke frequently about it in an attempt to generate publicity on Vaughn's behalf. They also visited her in prison, raised money for her, staged a public protest of her sentence, and petitioned the governor for her pardon, which they eventually secured.[83] In the process, they demanded, among many other things, that "in all civil and criminal cases, woman shall be tried by a jury of her peers; shall have a voice in making the law, [and] in electing the judge who pronounces her sentence . . ."[84] Not content merely to correspond with Governor Geary, a delegation of these activists also visited him in person, demanding an audience with him in order to plead their case.[85] One of these activists, a Mrs. Kirk, also paid a visit to the judge in the case, urging him to consider domestic violence from the woman's perspective.[86] The Vaughn case was an unusually extreme and high-profile example of women's rights activism at this time. Nevertheless, the strategy of direct intervention in political and judicial realms that the Vaughn case represented was in keeping with the women's rights movement's agenda of securing equal rights of participation in these arenas for women.

In addition to the myriad of important practical uses presented by access to law and politics, these activists also demonstrated a sophisticated awareness of the symbolic importance of law. Promoting the Wives' Protection Bill, for example, Cobbe suggests that no matter how small the number of women who might take advantage of such a bill, its presence as a possible recourse for battered women would be extremely significant nonetheless. In fact, she suggests, the mere existence of such a law "would act very effectually on the husband as a deterrent to violence."[87]

Suffragists and women's rights activists also brought a radical economic analysis to the issue of domestic violence. Cobbe's bill, designed to help battered women secure freedom both financially and physically, is just one example. Likewise, Rhoda Munger, writing for the *Woman's Journal*, characterizes abandonment and forced poverty as a form of violence. Munger recounts the story of a woman in Little Rock who was impregnated and then abandoned to live in poverty by a man who lived in luxurious conditions in the same town. Describing the conditions in which the woman lived (without food, wood for warmth, or medicine), and ultimately died of consumption, Munger describes her abandonment as "cruel and brutal," referring to the father of her child as "her murderer."[88] Drawing these theoretical links between physical and economic violence, women's rights workers pursued a holistic approach to the issue of domestic violence, seeking solutions that were deeply rooted and systemic.

Perhaps most significantly, advocates for women's rights engaged in publicity of the issue of domestic violence as a means of combating it. Their writings reveal that they pursued this course both explicitly and implicitly. Calling into question the prevailing "public sentiment," which "sympathizes with the man who has killed his wife 'because he loves her,'"[89] they sought to change public perception by raising awareness about the realities of domestic violence. In so doing, they challenged existing norms that suggested that domestic matters should remain private at all costs. While these efforts proved to be rather small in scale, they nonetheless reveal an awareness among these activists of the importance of bringing this problem into the public sphere. An activist in Boston, for example, wrote in the *Woman's Journal* that "there seems no better way than to show up these dreadful things in their true colors, and keep them before the people continually and persistently, until they are led to trace out the causes that lead to such terrible results and apply the remedy."[90] Likewise, Cobbe recognized the importance of this strategy when she wrote, "it is indispensable that some specimens of the torture to which I refer should be brought before the reader's eye."[91] While judicial opinions repeatedly expressed a reluctance to "invade the domestic forum" or "raise the curtain" on the abuse—thereby denying legal redress to battered women—women's rights activists recognized that bringing this problem out of the private realm would be a critical first step in addressing it.

To that end, the *Woman's Journal* promised, in 1876, to publish on a regular basis a list of crimes recently committed against women. This effort was thwarted, however, once the editors realized that the number of such incidents was so great that "to do so would convert the *Woman's Journal* into a mere 'Police Gazette.'"[92] They did, however, publish selective lists of such incidents, culled from a variety of local newspapers and focusing mainly on domestic violence. Often, these lists did read almost as a police blotter, providing names, dates, and details of the incidents, with little or no accompanying comment, as in the following entry: "Decatur, Ill., January 3.—John McEvers, a saloon-keeper at this place, shot his wife through the back of the head with a rifle to-day, the ball coming out in front and tearing away her lower jaw. She is still living but will probably die. McEvers is in jail." The effect of these lists, provided under such headings as "Crimes of a Single Day," was to demonstrate the frequency and the severity of these attacks, in a seemingly objective fashion. In this way, activists attempted to shed light on the sheer magnitude of the problem by destroying the veil of silence and secrecy surrounding it, while leaving little room for argument. While the impact of this strategy was necessarily limited by the small size of the *Woman's Journal*'s audience, this tactic nonetheless reveals a desire on the part of these activists to challenge domestic violence by exposing it to public scrutiny and stripping it of the protection of privacy.

Despite its strong rhetoric and often radical strategies, this movement's approach to domestic violence had some conservative elements, as well. Women's rights activists often relied on the same gender stereotypes used by temperance advocates, referring to women as "defenseless"[93] or invoking condescending images of social class differences between victims and activists. In her description of battered wives (by which she is, incredibly, attempting to solicit sympathy for them), Cobbe paints the following picture: "Poor, stupid, ignorant women as most of them are, worn out with life-long drudgery, burdened with all the pangs and cares of many children, poorly fed and poorly clothed . . ."[94] The disdainful-yet-pitying tone of this description seems almost incongruous in the face of the tireless work Cobbe was doing on behalf of economically disadvantaged battered women.[95] Yet contradictions such as these only serve to underscore the complexity of the movement, which resists characterization as solely and simply radical. Like the temperance movement, the women's rights movement was a multidimensional effort that encompassed the opinions and perspectives of a broad range of activists.

COMMON PERSPECTIVES

In fact, the two movements shared several common elements. The most prominent and probably most significant of these for the issue of domestic violence was their shared critique of the justice system. Throughout the writings of both movements, harsh and pointed criticisms of American law and the American justice system are pervasive. Writing in the *Woman's Journal* about wife-beaters, one activist declared, "Not one in ten of this class of criminals receive their just deserts; nor will they, so long as money, the plea of emotional insanity, and perjury, defeat the ends of justice."[96] A writer in the *Lily* lamented, "The dispensers of justice will condemn the wronged and ruined, while they suffer the oppressor and destroyer to go free."[97] Although adopting a more charitable approach to the law, Cobbe also admits its failings: "the existing law, even worked with the extremest care and kindness, cannot and does not prevent the repetition, year after year, of all the frightful cruelties, beatings, burnings, cloggings, and tramplings . . ."[98] The weaknesses of the existing legal system as a means of protection for battered women, whether due to corruption or just inadequacy, were a source of tremendous dissatisfaction for activists of all kinds working to end domestic violence.

Even more frustrating for these workers was the sense that the legal system failed women because it either deliberately ignored or refused to take seriously the problem of violence in the home. Articles in the *Woman's Journal* and the *Revolution* with such titles as, "Christian England Gives Two Pounds for Whipping Your Wife," expressed outrage over the virtually nonexistent punishments meted out to men who attacked and beat their wives. Judicial wrist-slapping in the form of minimal fines sent a clear message regarding the degree of gravity with which courts approached this problem.[99] Judges', politicians', and society's apparent lack of concern for battered wives in the face of staggering, concrete evidence of the problem's magnitude was equally disheartening to activists. Writing from England, Cobbe quotes judicial statistics of the vast numbers of women "brutally assaulted" in the home, only to lament that "the newspapers go on boasting of elementary education, and Parliament busies itself [with other matters]; but this evil remains untouched!"[100]

Both temperance reformers and women's rights advocates were quick to point out the roots of this apathy toward the problem of domestic violence: the gender bias that was so easily observed in legal and political arenas. A writer to the *Revolution* described the plight of a woman imprisoned for "riotous conduct" for asking her husband for child support after finding him living with another woman. If the situation had been reversed, this writer asserted, "not a court of justice in the land but would have acquitted the outraged husband should he have shot and killed both wife and paramour. Are we to dignify such legal partiality as this by the name of justice?"[101] A temperance worker cynically echoed this complaint: "Such is the consistency of the law in this land of boasted liberty and equality!"[102] The fact that women were being denied justice solely by virtue of being female outraged activists across ideological lines. When addressing the problem of domestic violence, it was not difficult to see the connection between disregard for women in the courtroom and in the home.

The reason for the gender bias in law and government that was most frequently cited by activists was the complete male domination of—and lack of female representation in—these areas. In fact, of all the critiques activists leveled at the political and judicial systems, this issue generally revealed the most cynicism and hostility. "Woman has all the rights she wants, has she? Not while we have men empowered to make such laws as these," one woman wrote in the *Revolution*.[103] Temperance reformers also recognized the perils of this lack of representation: "[Woman] tamely submits to be governed by such laws as man sees fit to make, and in making which she has no voice."[104] While such critiques might suggest a belief in a liberal "add-women-and-stir" solution to this problem, other writers formulated even more radical critiques. One such writer first advises, "Let it be remembered that Man has always legislated for Woman, and does so still. That he is not only her lawgiver, but her judge and juror."[105] She then ultimately links this problem to the prevalence of domestic violence, viewing them together as different manifestations of the root problem, the overall subordination of women.

These critiques of the flawed political and judicial systems, shared by both temperance and women's rights workers, represent a significant component of nineteenth century efforts to combat domestic violence. That this range of activists responded so critically and so vehemently to problems within the judicial system suggests both their awareness of its power and their belief in its potential as a source of liberation to battered women.

COMPARISON AND EVALUATION OF THE TWO MOVEMENTS

This point of common ground between these two ideologically diverse movements is quite significant, not least because this unified critique laid the groundwork for future battered women's advocates to seek judicial reform. At the same time, the contrasting ways in which the two movements approached a variety of related issues is instructive here. For example, the two groups reacted very differently to the prevailing contemporaneous ideology of separate spheres. Temperance reformers worked within that paradigm very deliberately, relying on traditional notions of women's moral superiority and supposed reign over the domestic sphere as a source of authority and power in the service of achieving their goal. Advocates for women's rights, on the other hand, publicly renounced this division very early in their movement, denouncing men for "assigning [women] a sphere of action," and declaring that "it is time she should move in the enlarged sphere which her great Creator has assigned her"[106]—thereby suggesting that the realm in which women should live encompassed the whole world, given to them by God, and not the tiny sphere assigned to them by men.

In the larger sense, temperance activists were careful, at least outwardly, to avoid any appearance of upsetting the male power structure even as they worked to combat domestic violence. Women's rights advocates' approach to the problem, by contrast, seemed as radical as their other demands—for the vote, for divorce reform, for education and employment rights for women—as each one was a direct assault upon existing male power. Although the public personae of the two movements differed in this way, their goals were often overlapping, as was their membership. With regard to domestic violence, then, it can be said that the two movements ultimately complemented each other. By breaking the taboo around domestic abuse in a "respectable" way, temperance advocates set the stage for their colleagues' more radical-seeming approach to the issues. Likewise, the suffragists' strident demands for women's rights and equality made the temperance advocates' plea for peace in the home seem almost reasonable by comparison.

In very different ways, the two movements began the critical work of loosening the privacy paradigm. Working under the rubric of the anti-drinking crusades, temperance reformers were able to break the silence around the issue of domestic violence and begin to raise public awareness of the problem. Chipping away at this social taboo was a crucial first step in enabling the more overt publicity campaigns that would come later. Women's rights advocates, by publishing detailed lists of atrocities committed against women in their homes, demonstrated an understanding that as long as this problem was perceived as a strictly "private" matter, reform would be impossible. Because of the significant role that privacy played in the issue of domestic violence both judicially and culturally, these activists' work to lift the shroud of privacy that hid these acts of violence was a meaningful endeavor, however limited its effects were in practice.

Additionally, because privacy was so strongly linked to the patriarchal family, undermining this privacy could be construed as attacking the family unit itself. To varying degrees, nineteenth-century activists were in fact doing just that, whether through the women's rights advocates' campaigns for divorce or through temperance reformers' insistence that women had a moral obligation to abandon drunken, violent husbands. These three elements—privacy, domestic violence, and the patriarchal family unit—were intertwined and mutually reinforcing. As a result, attempts to combat domestic violence that failed to disrupt either of the other two elements would thus have a lesser impact upon the problem.

Overall, through its rejection of separate-spheres ideology and its emphasis on helping women to secure independence, the women's rights movement pursued a more aggressive critique of privacy and the patriarchal family. With its overarching focus on procuring safety for women within the traditional domestic domain, the temperance movement presented a much less substantial challenge to either the privacy paradigm or the nuclear family. Interestingly, when courts did begin to repudiate the right of chastisement, they applied the rhetoric of rights and equality, speaking, as the women's rights activists had, of a woman's right not to be beaten.[107] Nonetheless, both the temperance and the women's rights movements served as crucial mobilizing forces for women in the late nineteenth century and laid the groundwork for women's activism, around domestic violence and a host of other issues, for the coming century.

DOMESTIC VIOLENCE LAW AND ACTIVISM IN THE EARLY TWENTIETH CENTURY

For a variety of reasons, activism on behalf of battered women did not reach this level again until well into the next century. As several scholars have noted, this decline in activity around domestic violence dovetails with an overall reduction in the more visible types of feminist activism during this era.[108] Having been focused intensely on the fight for suffrage and the battles over fair labor practices during the first two decades of the twentieth century, feminist activism was much less visible in the ensuing years. Of course, several compelling social issues did receive a great deal of attention from feminist activists at this time— most notably, the anti-lynching and birth control movements[109]—to a much greater extent than any efforts on behalf of battered women.

Historians have suggested several possible reasons for the decline in battered women's activism at this time. Most obvious is the range of successes that feminists had already begun to achieve, both in courts and in legislatures. During the late nineteenth and early twentieth centuries, numerous laws expanding the scope of women's rights were passed in various states throughout the country. Legislatures began to chip away at the doctrine of marital unity, granting women rights to their own property, wages, and representation before the law.[110] Divorce laws were also liberalized during this time, allowing women to seek divorce on grounds of cruelty. Likewise, by 1910, 35 of the 46 states had passed laws classifying wife beating as assault.[111]

Despite these initial advances on both legislative and judicial fronts, however, the early decades of the twentieth century saw very little progressive change in the government's response to domestic violence. As awareness of the problem increased, so did the number of cases brought to court. In response to this growing category of cases, a new development emerged at this time: domestic relations courts. Established because, in the words of one New York City judge, "domestic trouble cases are not criminal in a legal sense," these courts were staffed primarily by social workers.[112] Rather than prosecution, the courts provided services such as counseling for batterers and their wives. The effect of such courts, established in most major cities by the 1920s (and still operating in a modified format in many places today), was "to decriminalize marital violence" and to encourage the preservation of the marriage despite the abuse.[113]

At the same time, two related elements were converging: the rise of social work as a profession, and the growing popularity of the psychological and psychiatric fields.[114] As Linda Gordon observes, the professionalization of the social work field in the early twentieth century led to an increasingly individualized approach to family violence. Seeking legitimacy as a "scientific" field, the social work of this era also deliberately sought to avoid any appearance of the perceived sentimentality about family life that was associated with the nineteenth century.[115]

The increasing respect and prominence accorded to Freudian and other psychological models during the 1940s and 1950s reinforced this focus on individual problems, as opposed to systemic change. In particular, such models often promoted ideals of selflessness and sacrifice as the hallmarks of successful female development, for the attainment of these goals presumably fitted women best for the roles of wife and mother.[116] Freudian notions of women as inherently masochistic were also devastating to battered women of this era, as these ideas affected the ways in which service providers, among others, viewed cases of domestic violence, often leading them to trivialize or dismiss the problem.[117]

The combination of these factors led to an increase in victim-blaming throughout the middle decades of the twentieth century. Because it was the battered wives who generally sought the aid of social workers and therefore became the "clients," these workers in turn focused their efforts on changing the woman herself. After all, just by virtue of seeking social services, the battered wife was, as Gordon observes, "present and influenceable" in a way that the battering husband was not.[118] While social workers focused on "fixing" battered women, emerging psychological models of their inherent masochism reinforced the notion that the fault for the violence might well lie with the victim.

Ironically, the societal gains won by feminists may have contributed to the decrease in public sympathy for battered women.[119] Having secured greater independence via an increasing presence in the paid labor market and increased access to divorce, women were no longer viewed as helpless victims. But at the same time, these changes were still not widely accepted. Paid labor was still seen as a predominantly male domain, and the presence of women (in particular, white and middle-class women) in this arena made many people uncomfortable. Likewise, divorce and remarriage, while more readily available through the courts, were not generally looked upon favorably. Thus, the increased options available to battered women also carried several negative consequences: societal disapproval on the one hand, and decreased sympathy for their plight on the other.[120]

During the middle of the twentieth century, the ways in which victims of domestic violence conceptualized their abuse also seems to have shifted. Gordon has observed the changes in the nature of women's complaints to social workers at this time, and has developed an economic hypothesis. During times of economic stability, she observes, in which women could (and did) depend more upon their husbands for economic support, women complained primarily about nonsupport by their husbands, even in cases in which physical abuse was also clearly present. At these times, women were more likely to blame themselves for the violence, because "economic dependence prevented women's formulation of a sense of entitlement to protection against marital violence, but it also gave them a sense of entitlement to support."[121] Less secure financial times, beginning with the Great Depression, brought more claims of physical violence, even when lack of support was also an issue. This shift, according to Gordon, suggests that economic uncertainty reduced women's expectation of financial support, while their resulting independence actually heightened their sense of entitlement to bodily integrity.[122]

Case Resources

Meyer v. *Nebraska*

Findlaw (http://laws.findlaw.com/us/262/390.html) (full text)

At the same time that activism and social concern for the issue of domestic violence were waning, a strong foundation was being laid for the development of privacy rights, in a series of US Supreme Court cases decided throughout the first part of the twentieth century. One of the most significant of these was *Meyer* v. *Nebraska*, a 1923 case that invalidated a Nebraska statute forbidding the teaching of any language other than English to young children. The Court determined that this statute unreasonably restricted the liberty protected by the Fourteenth Amendment. Specifically, the Court interpreted this Fourteenth Amendment liberty to include, among other things, "the right . . . to marry, establish a home and bring up children."[123]

Case Resources

Pierce v. Society of Sisters

Findlaw (http://laws.findlaw.com/us/268/510.html) (full text)

Just two years later, *Pierce* v. *Society of Sisters* was decided, and became another landmark case in the development of privacy rights. Like *Meyer*, *Pierce* concerned an educational issue. Here, the Oregon Compulsory Education Act, which compelled parents and guardians to send their children to public school, was also challenged as a violation of the Fourteenth Amendment. The Court agreed with this analysis, concluding that the statute interfered unduly with "the liberty of parents and guardians to direct the upbringing and education of children under their control."[124] Building specifically on the *Meyer* opinion, this interpretation of Fourteenth Amendment liberty focused on the freedom of parents to determine the nature of their children's education.

Case Resources

Prince v. Massachusetts

Findlaw (http://laws.findlaw.com/us/321/158.html) (full text)

Finally, in 1944, *Prince* v. *Massachusetts*, involving child labor and religious freedom, solidified this trend. In *Prince*, the Court considered the case of a guardian who allowed her ward to sell religious magazines, in accordance with her religious beliefs but in violation of a Massachusetts statute that restricted children from selling periodicals on public streets. Within the opinion, the Court referred specifically to *Meyer* and *Pierce*, characterizing them boldly and broadly: "[T]hese decisions have respected the private realm of family life which the state cannot enter."[125]

Case Resources

Paris Adult Theatre I v. *Slaton*

Findlaw (http://laws.findlaw.com/us/413/49.html) (full text)

Oyez (http://www.oyez.org/cases/case/?case=1970-1979/1972/1972_71_1051) (oral arguments)

Interestingly, the *Prince* opinion went on to uphold the statute, finding it to be no violation of the Fourteenth Amendment and concluding that "the family itself is not beyond regulation in the public interest."[126] Yet when subsequent cases sought to further establish privacy rights, such as *Paris Adult Theatre I v. Slaton*—which described a "privacy right [that] encompasses and protects the personal intimacies of the home, the family, marriage, motherhood, procreation, and child rearing"[127]—they found the roots of this privacy right in *Prince, Pierce,* and *Meyer.*

For a wide variety of reasons, public sympathy for the issue of domestic violence and activism on behalf of battered women were at much lower levels in the first half of the twentieth century than they had been in the latter part of the previous century. During this same period of time, the basis for the right to privacy was slowly but steadily being developed in the courts. By the time the battered women's movement began to coalesce in the early 1970s, therefore, the judicial stage was set for some difficult legal confrontations based on the issue of privacy in the home. Bolstered further by the recent developments in reproductive rights jurisprudence, the privacy that had developed quietly over the past few decades would be a significant challenge for battered women's advocates to face.

CONCLUSION

The privacy that has historically shaped the issue of domestic violence has often been more of a vague, cultural term than a specifically political or legal one. Yet in the nineteenth century, social and judicial ideas about the importance of privacy held tremendous sway over the fates of battered women, both at home and in court. The right of chastisement that was debated in courts throughout the nineteenth century obviously played a significant role in these cases. Yet the centrality given to this question in many judicial opinions of this era was often negated by considerations of privacy, which frequently determined what the real outcome of the case would be. The race, class, and immigrant status of victims and offenders often proved to be mitigating factors in these cases as well, as the willingness of police and judges to punish batterers often appeared to depend as much on their own biases about African Americans, immigrants, or the poor as on the actual facts of the case. Community response to domestic violence was also affected by judicial treatment of the issue. Often, local groups' sense of responsibility to protect victims and punish batterers reflected their perceptions about the extent to which the state was performing these functions.

On the national scale, activism on behalf of battered women (and against their abusers) happened largely within the context of other social movements. The most prominent of these were the temperance reform effort and the women's rights movement. As some feminist historians have observed, some general ideological differences between these movements existed. Nonetheless, with regard to domestic violence, both movements exhibit a complex mixture of rhetoric and strategies that often resists generalization. In fact, at several points, the agendas of the two movements seem to overlap. Two of the most significant points of overlap involve their pervasive critique of the American justice system, particularly in its treatment of battered women, and the use of publicity as a strategy for combating domestic violence. Publicizing the problem of domestic violence, an explicit strategy of women's rights advocates (and, less explicitly, of temperance workers), was a first step in weakening the privacy paradigm that had kept battered women from finding justice in the legal system.

Despite these initial efforts of the late-nineteenth-century activists, the first half of the twentieth century was a quiet time for anti-domestic-violence activism. The feminist energy that had been focused on suffrage and other battles for equal rights subsided greatly in the ensuing decades. Several factors, including the professionalization of social work and the increasing popularity of particular psychological theories, contributed to a culture of victim-blaming in the arena of domestic violence. Recent gains in gender equality (such as winning suffrage and an increased presence in the paid labor force) may have actually contributed to this problem, causing a decrease in public sympathy for battered women. At the same time, while activism and public understanding of the problem languished, a constitutional right to privacy was being developed in the courts in a variety of cases unrelated to domestic abuse. While these cases initially spoke only vaguely of parental rights as part of the liberty implied in the Fourteenth Amendment, the opinions were gradually used to establish a right of privacy protecting the home from state interference.

The right of privacy that began to take legal shape in these cases would eventually be a jurisprudential lifeline for activists working to secure reproductive rights. After decades of frustration with courts and legislatures, birth control and abortion advocates were finally able to succeed in securing these rights for women by convincing courts that these decisions fell under the rubric of privacy rights and therefore should not be disturbed by the state. Just as reproductive rights workers were winning these victories in court, the battered women's movement was gaining momentum. For these activists, the consequences of privacy rights would be much less felicitous. The paradox that this issue presented for feminist activists—several of whom were working in both movements at the same time—will be explored in the next chapter.

NOTES

1. In fact, nineteenth-century courts used the term "chastisement" to refer to wife-beating. This terminology reflected William Blackstone's description of a man's means of disciplining a wife, child, or servant for whose actions he was legally responsible. William Blackstone, *Commentaries on the Laws of England* v.1 (Oxford: Clarendon Press, 1765): 430.

2. For a more detailed discussion of various state laws passed against chastisement, see Elizabeth Hafkin Pleck, "Wife Beating in Nineteenth-Century America," *Victimology* 4, v. 1 (1979): 60–61.

3. Elizabeth Hafkin Pleck, "Wife Beating in Nineteenth-Century America," *Victimology* 4, v. 1 (1979): 67–71.

4. Ibid., 71.

5. Linda Gordon, *Heroes of Their Own Lives: The Politics and History of Family Violence* (New York: Viking, 1988): 271–74.

6. For more information on coverture and the marital unity doctrine, see William Blackstone *Commentaries on the Laws of England* vol. 1 (Oxford: Clarendon Press, 1765): 430–33 and James Kent, *Commentaries on American Law* vol. 2 (New York: O. Halstead, 1827): 109.

7. William Blackstone, *Commentaries on the Laws of England* v.1 (Oxford: Clarendon Press, 1765): 430.

8. James Kent, *Commentaries on American Law* vol. 2 (New York: O. Halstead, 1827): 180.

9. *Bradley* v. *State*, 1 Miss. (1 Walker) 158 (1824). While phrases such as "moderate," "great emergency," and "salutary" suggest that the court is not necessarily willing to disregard *all* acts of chastisement, the opinion nonetheless condones quite clearly the corporal punishment of wives by their husbands.

10. *State* v. *Black*, 60 N.C. (Win.) 268 (1864).

11. *State* v. *Rhodes*, 61 N.C. (Phil. Law) 453 (1868). For another, similar example, see also *State* v. *Oliver*, 70 N.C. 60 (1874).

12. Ibid., 454.

13. For further discussion of this era, see Angela Davis, *Women, Race, and Class* (New York: Vintage Press, 1983): Ch. 5.

14. Beth Richie, "Battered Black Women: A Challenge for the Black Community," in *Words of Fire*, ed. Beverly Guy-Sheftall (New York: New Press, 1995): 398–99. For more on this issue, see Patricia Hill Collins, *Black Feminist Thought: Knowledge, Consciousness, and the Politics of Empowerment* (London: Routledge, 1990): 187; Barbara Omolade, *The Rising Song of African-American Women* (New York: Routledge, 1994): 89.

15. See Angela Davis, *Women, Race, and Class* (New York: Vintage Press, 1983): Chapters 1, 5, and 6.

16. *Savannah Colored Tribune*, April 22, 1876, quoted in Elizabeth Hafkin Pleck, "Wife Beating in Nineteenth-Century America," *Victimology* 4, v. 1 (1979): 65–66. In a

similar vein, Pleck also cites the *Richmond Planet*, which implored black women to "Stay out of the Police court with your petty quarrels," (April 9, 1890, quoted ibid., 65).

17. Elizabeth Hafkin Pleck, "Wife Beating in Nineteenth-Century America," *Victimology* 4, v. 1 (1979): 65.

18. Ibid.

19. Elizabeth Hafkin Pleck, "Criminal Approaches to Family Violence, 1640–1980," in *Family Violence*, ed. Lloyd Ohlin and Michael Tonry, 16–39 (Chicago: University of Chicago, 1989). For further examples of this sentiment, see Reva B. Siegel, "The Rule of Love: Wife Beating as Prerogative and Privacy," *Yale Law Journal* 105 (1996): 2138–39.

20. Reva B. Siegel, "The Rule of Love: Wife Beating as Prerogative and Privacy," *Yale Law Journal* 105 (1996): 2135–36; Sandra F. VanBurkleo, *"Belonging to the World:" Women's Rights and American Constitutional Culture* (New York: Oxford University Press, 2001): 77–78.

21. *Fulgham v. State*, 46 Ala. 143 (1871), 146.

22. *Harris v. State*, 14 So. 266 (Miss. 1894), 266.

23. Reva B. Siegel, "The Rule of Love: Wife Beating as Prerogative and Privacy," *Yale Law Journal* 105 (1996): 2135.

24. See Barbara Welter, "The Cult of True Womanhood," *American Quarterly* 18 (1966): 151.

25. See Laurie Keiser, "The Black Madonna: Notions of True Womanhood from Jacobs to Hurston," *South Atlantic Review* 60 (January 1995): 97–109.

26. *Knight v. Knight*, 31 Iowa 451 (1871), 455.

27. Ibid., 458.

28. *Poor v. Poor*, 8 N.H. 307 (1836), 313.

29. Ibid., 308.

30. Ibid., 311.

31. Ibid., 312. It is interesting to note that while the court acknowledged the husbands behavior as a "wrong," it apparently saw the behavior as justified in light of the wife's actions.

32. Ibid., 319.

33. Ibid., 312; emphasis in orginal.

34. *Joyner v. Joyner*, 59 N.C. 322 (1862): 325.

35. See, for example, *Shackett v. Shackett*, 49 Vt. 195 (1876).

36. Ibid., 325.

37. *Richards v. Richards*, 1 Grant (PA) 389 (1857), 393.

38. *State v. Rhodes*, 61 N.C. (Phil. Law) 453 (1868), 457.

39. *People v. Mercein*, 3 Hill (N.Y.) 399 (1842), 420.

40. *Joyner*, 325.

41. *Commonwealth v. Wood*, 97 Mass. 225 (1867), 229.

42. *State v. Buckley*, 2 Del. 552 (1838), 552.

43. *Mercein*, 3 Hill (N.Y.) 399 (1842), 410.

44. *Richards*, 392–93.

45. *Commonwealth v. McAfee*, 108 Mass. 458 (1871), 461.

46. *Fulgham*, 147.

47. *Knight v. Knight*, 31 Iowa 451 (1871), 459, 460; original emphasis.

48. Reva B. Siegel, "The Rule of Love: Wife Beating as Prerogative and Privacy," *Yale Law Journal* 105 (1996): 2125.

49. Elizabeth Hafkin Pleck, "Wife Beating in Nineteenth-Century America," *Victimology* 4, v. 1 (1979): 71.

50. Ibid., 67–71.

51. Elizabeth Hafkin Pleck, "Feminist Responses to 'Crimes Against Women,' 1868–1896," *Signs* 8 (1983): 465. This society also protected rape victims, and was utterly unique in its time for its provision of services to abused adult women in addition to children.

52. Steven Buechler, *Women's Movements in the United States* (New Brunswick: Rutgers University Press, 1990).

53. Ibid., 46–48.

54. Ibid., 48–51.

55. Ellen Carol DuBois, *Feminism and Suffrage: The Emergence of an Independent Women's Movement in America, 1848–1869* (Cornell: Ithaca University Press, 1978): 190.

56. Ibid., 162–200; Steven Buechler, *Women's Movements in the United States* (New Brunswick: Rutgers University Press, 1990): 48–51.

57. Steven Buechler, *Women's Movements in the United States* (New Brunswick: Rutgers University Press, 1990): 50.

58. Ibid., 51.

59. Ibid., 53–61; Aileen S. Kraditor, *The Ideas of the Woman Suffrage Movement, 1890–1920* (New York: Columbia University Press, 1965).

60. Elizabeth Hafkin Pleck, "Feminist Responses to 'Crimes Against Women,' 1868–1896," *Signs* 8 (1983): 459.

61. Ellen Carol DuBois, *Feminism and Suffrage: The Emergence of an Independent Women's Movement in America, 1848–1869* (Cornell: Ithaca University Press, 1978): 104.

62. Jed Dannenbaum, in "The Origins of Temperance Activism and Militancy Among American Women," *Journal of Social History* 15 v.2 (1981): 235–52, presents an interesting discussion of the more militant aspects of the temperance movement.

63. See, for example, Elizabeth Pleck, *Domestic Tyranny: The Making of Social Policy Against Family Violence from Colonial Times to the Present* (New York: Oxford UP, 1987):49–66, and Linda Gordon, *Heroes of Their Own Lives: The Politics and History of Family Violence* (New York: Viking, 1988): 250–57.

64. For more details on separate spheres, see Ellen Carol DuBois, *Feminism and Suffrage: The Emergence of an Independent Women's Movement in America, 1848–1869* (Cornell: Ithaca University Press, 1978): 16.

65. Steven Buechler, *Women's Movements in the United States* (New Brunswick: Rutgers University Press, 1990): 52.

66. Ruth Bordin, *Woman and Temperance: The Quest for Power and Liberty, 1873–1900* (Philadelphia: Temple University Press, 1981): xviii.

67. Unknown author, "Feminine Suffrage," *Lily* (December 1, 1851): 90–91.

68. Cora Leslie, "A Chapter on Young Men," *Lily* (April 1849): n. pg.; original emphasis.

69. Steven Buechler, *Women's Movements in the United States* (New Brunswick: Rutgers University Press, 1990): 52.

70. Unknown author, "Feminine Suffrage," *Lily* (December 1, 1851): 90–91. This article, written in support of woman suffrage, provides an example of the way in which the goals of the temperance and suffrage movements often converged, despite some of the differences between them.

71. Ibid., 90.

72. Mrs. Swisshelm, "Plain Talk," *Lily* (June 1, 1849): n. pg.

73. Unknown author, "Woman's Rights," *Lily* (October 1, 1849): n. pg.

74. Mrs. Swisshelm, "Plain Talk," *Lily* (June 1, 1849): n. pg.; original emphasis.

75. Elizabeth Cady Stanton, "The Solitude of Self," *Woman's Journal* (January 23, 1892): n. pg.

76. Unknown author, "Crimes Against Women," *Woman's Journal* (January 15, 1876): n. pg.

77. Lavinia Goodell, "Ownership of Wives," *Woman's Journal* (October 28, 1876): 349.

78. Unknown author, "Centennial Crimes Against Women," *Woman's Journal* (June 17, 1876): 199.

79. Elizabeth Cady Stanton, Susan B. Anthony, and Matilda Joslyn Gage, eds., *History of Woman Suffrage: 1848–1868*, vol. 1 (Salem, NH: Ayer Company, 1881): 719.

80. Ibid., 720–21.

81. Ibid., 722.

82. Frances Power Cobbe, "Wife-Torture in England," *Woman's Journal* (June 1, 1878): 174–77.

83. Unknown author, "The Case of Hester Vaughan," *Revolution* (December 10, 1868): 357; Elizabeth Cady Stanton, "Governor Geary and Hester Vaughan," *Revolution* (December 10, 1868): 353–55.

84. Unknown author, "The Case of Hester Vaughan," *Revolution* (December 10, 1868): 357.

85. Elizabeth Cady Stanton, "Governor Geary and Hester Vaughan," *Revolution* (December 10, 1868a): 353–55.

86. Unknown author, "The Case of Hester Vaughan," *Revolution* (December 10, 1868): 357.

87. Frances Power Cobbe, "Wife-Torture in England," *Woman's Journal* (June 1, 1878): 175. Indeed, this awareness of law as a tool to influence cultural values and social mores has been observed by twentieth-century legal scholars, as well. See, for example, Sean E. Brotherson and Jeffrey B. Teichert, who assert that "The symbolic power of the law in transmitting meaning about such key social concerns as 'family life and ethics' thus lends it great influence in shaping fundamental values. We therefore ought to consider carefully what the law symbolically communicates about who we are, what we value, and how we ought to conduct ourselves in our relationships

and within society." "Value of the Law in Shaping Social Perspectives on Marriage," *Journal of Law and Family Studies* 3 (2001): 29.

88. Rhoda Munger, "A Woman's Wrongs in Arkansas," *Woman's Journal* (August 31, 1878): 280.

89. Unknown author, "Wife-Killing From Affection," *Woman's Journal* (April 20, 1878): 126.

90. Unknown author, "Crimes Against Women," *Woman's Journal* (January 15, 1876): n. pg.

91. Frances Power Cobbe, "Wife-Torture in England," *Woman's Journal* (June 1, 1878): 174.

92. Unknown author, "Crimes of a Single Day," *Woman's Journal* (January 29, 1876): 34.

93. Ibid., 34.

94. Frances Power Cobbe, "Wife-Torture in England," *Woman's Journal* (June 1, 1878): 176.

95. Nonetheless, it is possible that even the derogatory terms employed here are simply meant to underscore the extent of victimhood experienced by battered women who were also poor, thus representing a deliberate strategy on Cobbe's part. I suspect, however, that these terms instead reflect the perceived class discrepancy between the women working publicly to end domestic violence and the women suffering privately from it.

96. Unknown author, "Crimes Against Women," *Woman's Journal* (January 15, 1876): n. pg.

97. Unknown author, "The Rathbun Tragedy," *Lily* (September 1, 1849): n. pg.

98. Frances Power Cobbe, "Wife-Torture in England," *Woman's Journal* (June 1, 1878): 176.

99. Unknown author, "Christian England Gives Two Pounds for Whipping Your Wife," *Revolution* (August 6, 1868): 71. See also "Crimes Against Women," *Woman's Journal* (August 1878: 280), detailing a similar case in the U.S.

100. Frances Power Cobbe, "Wife-Torture in England," *Woman's Journal* (June 1, 1878): 176.

101. Unknown author, "The Case of Hester Vaughan," *Revolution* (December 10, 1868): 358.

102. Mrs. Swisshelm, "Plain Talk," *Lily* (June 1, 1849): n. pg.

103. Unknown author, "The Case of Hester Vaughan," *Revolution* (December 10, 1868): 358.

104. Unknown author, "Woman's Rights," *Lily* (October 1, 1849): n. pg.

105. Lavinia Goodell, "Ownership of Wives," *Woman's Journal* (October 28, 1876): 348–49.

106. "Declaration of Rights and Sentiments," Seneca Falls, 1848.

107. See, for example, *Fulgham*, acknowledging that women are "entitled to the same protection of the law" (1871: 147).

108. Elizabeth Hafkin Pleck, "Wife Beating in Nineteenth-Century America," *Victimology* 4, no. 1 (1979); Elizabeth Hafkin Pleck, *Domestic Tyranny: The Making*

of Social Policy Against Family Violence from Colonial Times to the Present (New York: Oxford University Press, 1987); Linda Gordon, *Heroes of Their Own Lives: The Politics and History of Family Violence* (New York: Viking, 1988).

109. See, for example, Angela Davis, *Women, Race and Class* (New York: Vintage, 1983) and Leslie Reagan, *When Abortion Was a Crime: Women, Medicine, and Law in the United States, 1867–1973* (Berkeley: University of California Press, 1997).

110. See, for example, Norma Basch, *In the Eyes of the Law: Women, Marriage, and Property in Nineteenth-Century New York* (Ithaca: Cornell University Press, 1982) and Joan Hoff, *Law, Gender, and Injustice: A Legal History of U.S. Women* (New York: New York University Press, 1991).

111. Robert T. Sigler, *Domestic Violence in Context* (Lexington, MA: Lexington Books, 1989): 9.

112. Reva B. Siegel, "The Rule of Love: Wife Beating as Prerogative and Privacy," *Yale Law Journal* 105 (1996): 2168.

113. Ibid., 2168.

114. Linda Gordon, *Heroes of Their Own Lives: The Politics and History of Family Violence* (New York: Viking, 1988): 61; Elizabeth Hafkin Pleck, *Domestic Tyranny: The Making of Social Policy Against Family Violence from Colonial Times to the Present* (New York: Oxford University Press, 1987).

115. Linda Gordon, *Heroes of Their Own Lives: The Politics and History of Family Violence* (New York: Viking, 1988): 61–62.

116. Ibid., 281–85.

117. Ibid., 284.

118. Ibid., 281.

119. Ibid., 283.

120. Ibid., 282–83.

121. Ibid., 260.

122. Ibid., 260.

123. *Meyer v. Nebraska*, 262 U.S. 390 (1923), 399. The implication here is that parents have the right to bring up children as they choose.

124. *Pierce v. Society of Sisters*, 268 U.S. 510 (1925), 534–35.

125. *Prince v. Massachusetts*, 321 U.S. 158 (1944), 166.

126. Ibid., 167.

127. *Paris Adult Theatre I v. Slaton*, 413 U.S. 49 (1973), 65.

3. THE PARADOX OF PRIVACY FOR THE BATTERED WOMEN'S MOVEMENT

Rape, Reproductive Rights, and the Case of *People* v. *Liberta*

INTRODUCTION

After several decades of little visible activism against domestic violence in the first half of the twentieth century, the US battered women's movement reemerged in the late 1960s. The movement developed in the midst of the broader struggle for women's liberation, and concurrently with several related social movements, such as the anti-rape,[1] anti-sexual-harassment,[2] and reproductive rights efforts. The influence of (and sometimes coalitions with) these other movements during these formative years helped to determine the nature and goals of the various activist groups that formed to work on this issue. These goals also changed over time. At first, the battered women's movement sought primarily to provide women with physical protection from violence (via shelters). Their agenda quickly progressed, however, to include the more proactive goal of securing legal protections, as well. As it expanded its focus from physical to legal protection, the movement increasingly had to contend with issues of privacy. The anti-rape and reproductive rights movements strongly influenced this trajectory and the ways in which the battered women's movement conceptualized, confronted, and co-opted existing notions of privacy. In many ways, the activism of feminist attorneys in the case of *The People of the State of New York* v. *Mario Liberta*[3] represents a synthesis of these influences. A landmark case overturning the marital rape exemption in New York State, *Liberta* ultimately offered an alternative, empowering model of privacy for battered women.

Feminist scholars and activists working on domestic violence have long recognized that privacy is an essential aspect of the problem. Since *Roe v. Wade*[4] was decided, several feminist legal scholars have considered the ramifications of its particular conception of privacy for the issue of domestic violence.[5] Such analyses generally focus on the paradox created by the contrasting potential uses of privacy: in short, the right of privacy that helped to secure the abortion right for women is also used as a justification for the perpetuation of domestic violence. That is, the same right to privacy that ostensibly prevents the state from interfering with a woman's right to choose abortion simultaneously prevents the state from intervening in a violent home. And in both cases, this conception of privacy is rooted in a judicial respect, almost reverence, for "the sanctum of the home"—in particular, the heterosexual, marital home.[6]

Given this paradox, feminist critiques of privacy ask, what is the appropriate response of a feminist scholar to the privacy issue? The answer is significant, for it has not only ideological but also practical implications. Particularly for legal theorists who are involved in feminist litigation, this question is more than simply an academic one. Some scholars resolve this issue by criticizing *Roe* for employing the privacy analysis at all, suggesting that legal privacy is simply too dangerous a concept for feminists to endorse.[7] Others have suggested that feminists should challenge existing models of privacy, and/or develop alternative models of privacy. Patricia Boling, for example, argues for

> the need for a vantage point that can help us gain some conceptual clarity about (1) what is valuable and worth protecting about privacy and private life; (2) what is dangerous and oppressive about hiding persons or problems in private, depriving them of public significance, and (3) . . . how issues rooted in private life can be made politically recognizable and actionable. . . . Another step might be to think of privacy as a particular kind of political tool used to protect (or suppress) certain interests or aspects of human life. On this view, treating intimate, especially familial, life and personal decision making as private—that is, as off-limits to public scrutiny and government interference—is a political decision, visible in our social values, legal norms, and the fundamental law of our Constitution. Of course, we need to question who decides to value and protect privacy, and whose interests are served by doing so.[8]

In this way, Boling suggests that feminist scholars not reject concepts of privacy altogether, but that they instead consider interrogating, co-opting, and transforming existing models.

Likewise, Dorothy Roberts makes a similar argument, but she goes further by suggesting that such a model is crucial for the empowerment of African-American and poor women.[9] Specifically, she notes, "The definition of privacy

as a purely negative right serves to exempt the state from any obligation to ensure the social conditions and resources necessary for self-determination and
autonomous decisionmaking."[10] Instead, Roberts champions the notion of an
affirmative view of privacy, declaring that

> this approach shifts the focus of privacy theory from state nonintervention to an
> affirmative guarantee of personhood and autonomy. . . . This affirmative view of pri-
> vacy is enhanced by recognizing the connection between privacy and racial equal-
> ity. The government's duty to guarantee personhood and autonomy stems not only
> from the needs of the individual, but from the needs of the entire community. . . . It
> may be possible . . . to reconstruct a privacy jurisprudence that retains the focus on
> autonomy and personhood while making privacy doctrine effective. Before dismiss-
> ing the right of privacy altogether, we should explore ways to give the concepts of
> choice and personhood more substance. In this way, the continuing process of chal-
> lenge and subversion—the feminist critique of liberal privacy doctrine, followed by
> the racial critique of the feminist analysis—will forge a finer legal tool for disman-
> tling institutions of domination.[11]

While Roberts's analysis is undertaken specifically to address issues of reproductive rights, her vision of a new model of privacy is equally applicable to the
problem of domestic violence.

Like Boling and Roberts, Elizabeth Schneider suggests a feminist revisioning, rather than rejection, of the privacy paradigm, and she discusses this
idea specifically in the context of domestic violence. Schneider maintains that
the right of privacy, differently construed, actually contains "radical potential."[12] In order to realize this potential, Schneider suggests, "The challenge is
to develop a right to privacy which is not synonymous with the right to state
noninterference with actions within the family, but which recognizes the affirmative role that privacy can play for battered women. Feminist reconstruction
of privacy should seek to break down the dichotomy of public and private that
has disabled legal discourse and public policy in this arena."[13] By advocating a
feminist appropriation and subversion of the existing right to privacy, these
scholars imply that this right need not be detrimental to the interests of battered
women. Indeed, their work suggests that such an alternative model would have
the potential to advance significantly a variety of women's legal issues. Unfortunately, they often conclude, no such model has yet been articulated.

In reality, however, the case of *People* v. *Liberta* represents just such a model.
Responding directly to the recent reproductive rights privacy litigation, and
demonstrating the influence of the anti-rape movement, *Liberta* serves as a
critical case study of one alternative to the privacy paradox. This chapter, therefore, explores the strategies and influences that led to the *Liberta* opinion, as

well as its implications for battered women and its potential as a model for a new, affirmative right to privacy.

Indeed, this chapter focuses on both the legal and cultural forms of privacy as they have affected the lives of battered women. As discussed in chapter one, both of these approaches to privacy—its formal development as a legal, constitutional right, and its more amorphous existence as a shared cultural value—affect this society's responses to domestic violence. Furthermore, these two forms of privacy are often complementary and mutually reinforcing. In general, while lawyers and judges deal primarily with the legal aspects of privacy, grassroots activists and service providers within the movement confront the more informal, cultural attitudes about privacy. This chapter thus addresses both of these arenas.

The chapter begins with an analysis of the early years of the US battered women's movement, during which it primarily focused on providing shelter and other basic services. In this section, I explore some of the major strategies of those early years, noting in particular the ways in which those strategies reflected an awareness of and a challenge to traditional, cultural notions of privacy. In addition, I examine the significant developments and dynamics within the movement, especially its links to and relationship with the anti-rape movement. I also trace the establishment during this era of the major organizations committed to combating domestic violence, including the formation of the first organization devoted solely to promoting the legal rights of battered women, the National Battered Women's Law Project (NBWLP).

The chapter next turns to an exploration of the other type of privacy with which the battered women's movement has had to contend: privacy as a legal, constitutional right. For, while the battered women's movement was beginning to take shape, advocates for reproductive rights were increasingly winning significant victories in court and further developing the constitutional right to privacy. This section explores this trajectory, examining the contours of the legal right to privacy that resulted from this line of cases. This discussion also traces the ways in which the development of this right explicitly privileged marital relationships, often to the exclusion of all others. My analysis considers the implications of this privileging of marriage and the nuclear family home, both for battered women and for the future of the privacy right.

Within the anti-domestic-violence movement, neither lawyers nor activists responded immediately to the model of privacy articulated in the line of reproductive rights cases that culminated in the *Roe* v. *Wade* decision. Throughout most of the 1970s, they remained focused primarily on providing physical shelter for battered women, on raising public awareness of the problem, and on urging police and other state actors to take the problem seriously and respond appropriately. It was not until the 1984 case of *People* v. *Liberta* that the movement directly confronted—and appropriated for its own benefit—the reproductive rights model of privacy. Therefore, the chapter next provides a critical case study of *Liberta*, paying particular attention to the role of feminist lawyer-activists in formulating this alternative model of privacy. Finally, the chapter concludes with a brief analysis of the ways in which the type of privacy advanced by *Liberta* could be successfully applied to benefit the battered women's movement more broadly.

THE EARLY YEARS OF THE BATTERED WOMEN'S MOVEMENT

The beginning of the battered women's movement is not easily identified by a single event or a specific date. As explained in chapter two, the first half of the twentieth century was relatively quiet with regard to the issue of domestic violence. During the late 1960s and early 1970s, however, activism on behalf of battered women gained momentum, and quickly led to greater social awareness of the problem of domestic violence. This increased public awareness, as well as the advocacy work that generated it, are generally considered to signal the beginning of the US battered women's movement.

EARLY ACTIVISM: PROVIDING PHYSICAL PROTECTION

Indications of the burgeoning movement abounded during these formative years. The late 1960s and early 1970s brought a variety of "firsts" for the issue of domestic violence: the first time wife abuse was reported in major newspapers (1974); the first task force on battered women organized by the National Organization for Women (NOW) (1973); the first time an article on domestic violence appeared in a major scholarly journal devoted to the sociology of the family (1969).[14] The first "speakout" on rape, organized by the New York Radical Feminists, took place in 1971 and paved the way for public and private consciousness-raising about all types of violence against women.[15] The first battered women's shelters were also established during the 1970s;[16] the rapid proliferation of such refuges also suggested the beginning of a movement.

The emphasis on service provision predominated in the movement's early years. As Barbara Hart, longtime activist and lawyer within the movement, observed,

Where we started was not with law, but with shelters, safe houses, support groups, etc. I was, at that point, a social worker, and I don't know that there were any of us that were lawyers, we were all social activists. . . . We just didn't go to law as a solution. . . . So that's the place that we started. . . . My view was not that the law was a particularly useful tool . . . What I saw as much more useful was women's organizing together, women's discourse, women's community.[17]

While the battered women's movement eventually broadened to incorporate legal and legislative initiatives as well, its earliest efforts focused on providing physical protection and basic services to women in crisis, often via the establishment of shelters and safe houses.

Shelters for other disadvantaged groups of people, such as those facing poverty, joblessness, or alcoholism, had existed in the United States for years. Yet refuges created with battered women in mind did not begin to emerge steadily until the mid-1970s. Instead, early shelters for battered women were initially formed on a more ad hoc basis, either operating informally from within a private residence, or co-opting an existing shelter to aid women seeking refuge from abusive partners. Pasadena, California's Haven House, for example, opened in 1964 by the wives of alcoholic husbands, is sometimes considered the first battered women's shelter in the country.[18] While it was created for victims of alcohol-related violence, Haven House quickly became a refuge for many battered women.[19]

Many women began to provide shelter very informally and even by chance. Joan Zorza, who would eventually become a feminist attorney litigating on behalf of battered women, recalls some of her earliest contact with victims of domestic violence. She began working with battered women "completely unintentionally and unexpectedly . . . even before much of this had a name. . . . [I] was totally shocked to discover domestic violence."[20] In her job providing military counseling through the American Friends Service Committee, Zorza often worked from her home. Several of the men she counseled would bring their wives or girlfriends to counseling sessions with them,

because they didn't trust them out of their sight. And then, at ten at night when they were beaten up . . . a number of [the women] found their way—as one of the only places they knew where they could go—onto my doorstep. Being a good soul . . . when someone knocks on your door . . . needing a place to stay . . . I let them in . . . with absolutely no awareness of what it was or what this was about . . . Some of the women stayed for months.[21]

Zorza, who admittedly "kind of backed into" the issue of domestic violence, eventually assisted in the formation of Transition House in Boston, one of the first shelters created explicitly for battered women.[22]

This trajectory, from ad hoc sheltering to more deliberate service provision, mirrors the growth of the movement overall. As women like Zorza—who had been providing refuge in their homes on an individual basis—came together, they created group shelters specifically for battered women:[23] Rainbow Retreat (founded in Phoenix, Arizona in 1973), Women's Center South (Pittsburgh, Pennsylvania, 1973), and Women's House (St. Paul, Minnesota, 1974), were among the first of these.[24] Conceived at the individual, community, and grass-roots levels, these early shelters frequently proved richer in ideology than in financial resources. Often founded by women of color and lesbians,[25] several of these shelters, such as Casa Myrna Vazquez (Boston, 1974) and La Casa de Las Madres (San Francisco, 1976) reflected a progressive politics that sought to eliminate hierarchy between staff and residents and to empower residents within their own communities.[26] In most cases, the lack of formal ties to governmental or other funding sources proved beneficial, allowing founders to determine the goals and ideology of the shelter.

Such idyllic visions of shelter life did not always translate into practice, however. As Zorza notes, conflicts among lesbians and heterosexual women, or among staff and residents, inevitably arose when residents felt that they were being pressured to leave their abusive partner, or all men, for good.[27] Likewise, anti-Semitism was a pervasive problem, according to Zorza, who observes that many shelters in New York City originally refused to accept battered Jewish women, referring them instead to the one shelter in the city created specifically for Jewish women.[28] Many shelters in New York also refused to accept battered immigrant women or anyone else without a social-security card.[29] Given the often admirable goals guiding many shelters, but also the very real problems of racism and homophobia, the degree of success shelters achieved in serving diverse populations seem to have varied widely. Notwithstanding this limitation, these early shelters did more than physically protect women from abusive partners. They also served a symbolic purpose that furthered activists' broader goal of taking domestic violence out of the private realm. As the founders of the National Coalition Against Domestic Violence (NCADV) observed, "those shelters symbolize the right of every woman to be physically protected by the society in which she lives."[30]

FOUNDATIONS IN THE ANTI-RAPE MOVEMENT

The twentieth-century anti-domestic-violence movement in the United States was rooted in and strongly linked to the national anti-rape movement. This connection occurred for several reasons. First, both movements developed within the context of the women's rights and women's liberation movements that began in the 1960s. Both grew out of the increased gender consciousness that women's liberation fostered, including that movement's assertion of a woman's right to control her own body. Additionally, both movements addressed forms of violence against women that were often similar and even overlapping; one could not work to combat rape without gaining increased awareness of domestic violence, and vice versa. Likewise, the anti-rape movement's explicit analysis of rape as a crime of violence, rather than sex, created an inevitable link between the two.[31] As a result, many anti-rape activists ultimately became advocates for battered women. At various points, the two movements joined coalitions or worked together against violence against women in general.

The consciousness-raising that characterized the radical feminism of the late 1960s was a critical component in the founding of the anti-rape movement. Within consciousness-raising groups, women discovered that their experiences of physical and sexual assault were far more common than they had suspected. The prevalence of these revelations led to the first public "speakout" on the subject of rape, held by the New York Radical Feminists in 1971. In her chronology of the anti-domestic-violence movement, longtime activist Yolanda Bako traces its origins to consciousness-raising groups and to this first speakout, which "launched the beginning of a continuous movement to change antiquated laws and public attitudes about rape and other assaults against women."[32] In this way, even these early activist efforts to combat violence against women confronted cultural issues of privacy, and deliberately sought to bring this problem out of the private realm. Publicizing the violence offered several benefits: removing the shame associated with rape and domestic violence, decreasing the feeling of isolation often experienced by victims, and increasing public awareness of the problem.

As the anti-rape movement progressed, many of its initial strategies lent themselves directly to the creation of a battered women's movement. The rape crisis hotlines that were established in the early 1970s,[33] for example, allowed women an opportunity to seek support and to talk openly and anonymously about the violence they suffered.[34] Furthermore, as Hart explains, the rape crisis hotlines inadvertently engendered, among anti-rape advocates, an increased awareness of the problem of domestic violence:

> In those [reading and consciousness-raising] groups [in which she and others participated during the late 1960s and early 1970s], we discovered that many of the . . . women had been sexually abused by their intimate partners—and some by strangers— but mostly it was the coercion and the violence of their partners. So we began talking about it, and then we decided to open up a hotline, a sexual assault hotline, and that hotline generated more calls about physical violence—as contrasted with sexual

violence—than anything else. So the women's center began to talk about, well, so what are we gonna do about this?[35]

As such, the creation of hotlines intended to deal with sexual assault actually initiated some of the earliest anti-domestic-violence activism.

In addition, public awareness and media campaigns launched by anti-rape activists took violence against women out of the private sphere and placed it on the national agenda. Likewise, the movement's critique of existing procedures to deal with rape victims in hospitals, police stations, and courtrooms applied equally to the domestic violence context. As Bako observes,

> Each reform of the anti-rape movement . . . set the stage for considering what was to be done with victims of family violence. . . . As the early 70's were spent confronting the problems of women who were assaulted by strangers, the mid seventies tried to address the flip side of the problem: women and children who were assaulted by men they could easily identify and the state could readily apprehend.[36]

The anti-rape movement continued to affirm that rape was *always* violence, regardless of who committed it. In this way, the movement's increasingly sophisticated analysis of and emphasis on rape as a crime of intimates as well as strangers also assisted in the inevitable progression toward a closer examination of domestic violence.

The many connections between the issues of rape and domestic violence eventually led many activists working on one issue to also work in the other. Yolanda Bako, herself an anti-rape advocate who later helped to found the NCADV, observed that "Many [NCADV] coalition members are long time activists in the areas of rape prevention . . . and . . . other issues that involve self-help and working against the feeling of powerlessness."[37] Likewise, the original Steering Committee members concluded that any group considered for membership in the NCADV "must have an expressed commitment to eliminating violence against women in all its forms."[38] This cross-pollination between movements led to the sharing of ideas and resources among various groups working to end violence against women.

The alliance between anti-rape and anti-domestic-violence activists was also one of necessity. Workers in both movements often found that joining forces and forming coalitions afforded them a stronger voice, greater public presence, and increased financial stability. The attempt to found a women's shelter in Brooklyn, New York was a case in point. This process revealed obstacles in the existing state legislation that would effectively prevent such a shelter from ever being established. Specifically, as Bako explains, "In 1977 there was no provision in the not-for-profit incorporation law of [New York State] to allow women and children to be cared for in a public facility together."[39] Only after assembling a coalition of women from "all the major women's groups in Brooklyn," and spending two years planning, lobbying, and waging media campaigns did the coalition succeed in establishing a center dedicated to reforming this legislation.[40]

Such coalition strategies had numerous benefits for both movements. Activists quickly learned that by seeking reforms related to violence against women broadly conceived, they could achieve several goals at once (for example, training hospital personnel to respond to all violence against women, rather than just sexual assault). This strategy could effect change on various levels, from local community issues such as hospital intake, to police response, to legislative reform. The compilation of statistics for this purpose also benefited from a coalition perspective: defining rape more broadly to include marital and date rape, rather than solely stranger rape, conveyed a much more accurate picture of the reality of sexual assault and served the goals of both the anti-rape and the battered women's movement, both of which confronted marital rape frequently. In fact, as *People* v. *Liberta* would later demonstrate, marital rape served as a point of common ground and significant struggle for the two movements.

Anti-domestic-violence activism also learned several lessons from the anti-rape movement. Battered women's advocates were eager to avoid repeating the mistakes made in anti-rape work, especially with regard to organizational and financial strategies. In particular, the tension between obtaining funding while maintaining ideological purity loomed especially large for these activists. Several of the earliest founders of the NCADV, already active in anti-rape work, critiqued the anti-rape movement from the inside. They condemned "the failure of the anti-rape movement to maintain its feminist philosophy once we created the pressure for government dollars."[41] The position taken by these battered women's advocates toward the anti-rape movement is telling; here, they maintain a critical distance from that movement ("the failure of the anti-rape movement . . .") while simultaneously claiming it ("*we* created the pressure . . ."). This dual stance suggests just how closely the two movements were aligned. Despite the occasional internal tensions, the bonds that existed between the two movements would later prove crucial to their success in the courtroom. Pooling resources and sharing strategies would eventually benefit both movements, most immediately in their efforts to combat marital rape.[42]

ORGANIZATIONAL DEVELOPMENT

The NCADV was one of the most significant and ultimately influential battered women's advocacy groups formed during these years and it continues to provide meaningful support for anti-domestic-violence efforts nationwide. The idea for the NCADV originated at the Houston International Women's Meeting in 1977, where a variety of battered women's advocates agreed to establish a national coalition of groups "to act as a strong political and collective force in working towards ending wife abuse."[43] Resolutions adopted by delegates to the Houston meeting included the following:

> The President and Congress should declare the elimination of violence in the home to be a national goal. . . .

> State legislatures should enact laws to expand legal protection and provide funds for shelters for battered women and their children. . . .

> Programs for battered women should be sensitive to the bilingual and multicultural needs of ethnic and minority women.[44]

Furthermore, the "Proposed National Plan of Action," that resulted from the conference noted that "Nobody knows how many American wives have been beaten. Most State laws don't give the victims adequate protection or even the right to sue their assailants. Police don't like to intervene in what appears to them to be a private family matter. . . ."[45] Even in its infancy, clearly, the battered women's movement had the problem of privacy on its mind.

The original Steering Committee of NCADV included women from across the country, "from diverse backgrounds and experience," who were addressing domestic violence at the grass-roots level.[46] Initial meetings of this group reflected its commitment to empowerment and equality for battered women and to resisting co-optation by more conservative interests or structures. Committee members established twelve specific objectives for the national coalition, prioritizing such goals as securing resources for member organizations, creating and tracking legislation, and working to reform attitudes about violence both among the general public and within the criminal justice system.[47] The establishment of these goals represented some of the battered women's movement's earliest efforts to expand service provision beyond physical shelter. Moving into legislatures and courtrooms, the movement began to seek legal remedies and protections for battered women.

NCADV was by no means the only national organization to develop during the movement's early years, however. Other groups such as the Battered Women's Directory Project and the National Communications Network had earlier paved the way. Led by Betsy Warrior, the Battered Women's Directory Project was a carefully compiled and continuously updated list of programs and projects working on the problem of domestic violence from around the nation. Warrior's compilation proved to be an invaluable resource for activists seeking to build coalitions across regions. It was also quite accessible: interested battered women's advocates could obtain a copy of this directory by mailing one dollar to the Battered Women's Directory Project. In 1976, Warrior had the first edition of the directory published, entitled *Working on Wife Abuse*.[48]

In early 1978, in the course of its duty to investigate sex discrimination, the US Commission on Civil Rights held a Consultation on Battered Women.[49] The consultation took place in Washington, D.C., and drew over six hundred attendees. Some of these attendees were attorneys, academics, and shelter workers, who were invited to the consultation in order to present their perspectives on the problem of domestic violence. Yet many of the six hundred in attendance were activists who had not been invited, but came nonetheless—from across the country—to observe the proceedings. The objectives of the consultation included identifying reliable data as well as existing research gaps and strategies; identifying necessary state-level legal reforms; identifying the short- and long-term support services needed by battered women; assessing the role of the federal government in each of these issues; facilitating communication among activists, researchers, and policymakers; and generating public awareness.[50]

For commission staffers, Warrior's directory served as a research tool: with it, they identified existing organizations and individuals to participate in and testify at the consultation. Having come together for the consultation, many of these women met the evening before the official proceedings and began to flesh out plans for the formation of the National Coalition. Over the course of the next few days, these approximately sixty women elected steering-committee members, developed regional caucuses, and adopted a statement of purpose.[51] As Hart recalls,

> We knew about a number of us (battered women's advocates) around the country, because we had done some networking, so we said, "OK, let's have a meeting—since we're all coming to these hearings, let's meet the night before." And so we met at [George Washington University]. And then we went to the hearings [the next day], and then we met in the bathrooms of the [building where the hearings were held] and decided that we needed to have a national coalition. So that's when we gave birth to the national coalition. And we developed an organizing committee, and we spent some time looking at trying to . . . build the organization, but also to try to get some money . . . So we did some meeting with folks in Congress. . . . So we started at the Civil Rights hearings and then we moved forward.[52]

At the same time that the NCADV was forming and Warrior was coordinating the Battered Women's Directory Project, another effort to foster communication among anti-domestic-violence activists nationwide was also afoot. The National Communication Network for the Elimination of Violence Against Women (NCN) published its first newsletter in April 1977. Formed in response to the frustration and isolation expressed by many anti-domestic-violence activists, NCN sought "to generate a national network and to facilitate a dialogue among women working to eliminate male violence against women, particularly domestic violence."[53] In addition to their stated focus on domestic violence, the activists who worked to create NCN also considered the possibility of issuing a joint publication with the Feminist Alliance Against Rape (FAAR), which was already publishing its own newsletter. After much consideration and negotiation, the two groups agreed to produce a publication that, while mailed singly, would consist of two discrete sections, one by FAAR and one by NCN. The newsletter, which often contained information from the recently formed anti-sexual-harassment group, the Alliance Against Sexual Coercion, as well, addressed a wide range of issues related to violence against women.

After an arduous struggle to find the proper moniker for this publication, the expanded newsletter became known by November 1978 as *Aegis, the Magazine on Ending Violence Against Women*. Articles in the NCN portion of the magazine covered a wide range of topics, such as "Learning from the Anti-Rape Movement" and "Race and the Shelter Movement," as well as regular features such as "National Coalition Against Domestic Violence News" and "Legal Projects and State Legislation." Hart, a member of the *Aegis* collective, describes it as "a very, very radical, progressive place, in which it was very committed to confronting and eradicating race and class barriers—'smashing racism' is probably what we may have said back then. . . . [these were] folks that were very highly committed to addressing issues of race and class."[54] *Aegis* was published bimonthly and then quarterly until it ceased publication in 1987 due to lack of funding.[55] For shelter workers, lobbyists, and lawyers, *Aegis* served as a national resource through which to communicate and strategize.

LEGAL ACTIVISM

Although not created solely as an anti-domestic-violence organization, the National Center on Women and Family Law (NCOWFL), also formed at this time, devoted much of its energy to the legal needs of battered women, via its National Battered Women's Law Project (NBWLP). The NBWLP operated from the premise that "the law . . . can play an integral role in helping battered women and their children to put an end to the violence and rebuild their lives."[56] Unlike NCADV and the Battered Women's Directory Project, which focused primarily on supporting battered women's shelters and refuges, NCOWFL concentrated its efforts in the legal (and occasionally legislative) arenas. Furthermore, according to NBWLP, "Battered women's advocates need help with their law reform efforts. They need technical assistance on their litigation challenges to improper judicial and police response. They need resources for educating the judiciary and court personnel about battery and why certain policies are harmful to battered women and their children."[57] Providing support and information to lawyer-activists litigating on behalf of battered women, NCOWFL and NBWLP served as the most significant national resource for domestic violence litigation for over twenty years. Before it closed its doors in 1996 due to a lack of funding, NBWLP effected change in countless lawsuits of all sizes across the country, including the most influential domestic violence cases of the late twentieth century. These cases included everything from criminal prosecutions of individual batterers to large-scale, class-action lawsuits aimed at making police departments more responsive to domestic violence calls.[58]

The support for individual cases provided by NBWLP ranged from simple provision of information to attorneys to actual participation in the cases through the writing of amicus briefs. At the same time, NBWLP served as a clearinghouse of information about domestic violence litigation to shelters and other grassroots programs, as well as to Legal Aid Societies, legislators, and the media. In addition to producing resource packets and other educational materials on the legal issues related to domestic violence, NBWLP also contributed legal and legislative updates to *The Women's Advocate,* a bimonthly newsletter published by NCOWFL. While a host of other legal advocacy groups, including NOW's Legal Defense and Education Fund (NOW-LDEF), often assisted or participated in domestic violence litigation, NBWLP was the only national organization devoted solely to advancing the legal rights of battered women.

During the early years of the anti-domestic-violence movement, therefore, activism by and for battered women took a variety of forms. The earliest efforts quickly progressed from ad hoc protection of abused women within private residences to the establishment of group shelters. Many activists soon recognized the value of coalition building, and a national network of shelters began to take shape. At the same time, activists hosted conferences and other meetings at which they shared ideas and sought solutions to the problems of domestic violence. They quickly recognized that shelter work was "a Band-Aid approach" and often characterized it as such.[59] The increased communication among battered women's advocates across the country, aided by the publication of *NCN* and then *Aegis,* led to a shift in focus from service provision and physical protection to proactivity and legal protection.

These two arenas—service provision and legal advocacy—mirror the two ways in which the battered women's movement confronted issues of privacy during the 1970s. First, through media and other publicity campaigns, activists challenged cultural ideas about privacy and domestic violence by seeking to demystify the problem and to encourage public dialogue about it. These campaigns specifically encouraged neighbors and other community members to get involved by speaking up and supporting victims of domestic violence, rather than continuing to shroud battered women in shame. Similarly, while legislative reforms often focused on obtaining government funding for shelters and other programs, they also pursued tougher sentences for offenders as a means of sending a public message that battering would not be tolerated.

Second, the movement's lawyer-activists quickly began confronting privacy within the legal arena. Led on the national level by NCOWFL and NOW-LDEF, these judicial reform efforts initially had two priorities: 1) educating judges that domestic abuse could no longer be viewed as merely a private, family matter, and 2) holding police forces accountable for refusing to intervene in such cases. Both of these efforts represented the movement's first challenges to privacy within the legal sphere. The movement's activist and judicial strategies, therefore, complemented each other: while activists attempted to disrupt societal conceptions of privacy by refuting the notion that domestic violence was merely an individual problem, lawyers focused on changing judicial interpretations of privacy that prevented the state from intervening in abusive homes.

LEGAL PRIVACY AND THE MOVEMENT
FOR REPRODUCTIVE RIGHTS

Case Resources

Meyer v. Nebraska

Findlaw (http://laws.findlaw.com/us/262/390.html) (full text)

Pierce v. Society of Sisters

Findlaw (http://laws.findlaw.com/us/268/510.html) (full text)

Prince v. Massachusetts

Findlaw (http://laws.findlaw.com/us/321/158.html) (full text)

This surge of awareness and activity on behalf of battered women occurred just as years of activism and litigation around reproductive rights were coming to fruition. This timing was not coincidental, and its implications were significant. The marital and familial privacy cases of the first half of the twentieth century (including *Meyer*,[60] *Pierce*,[61] and *Prince*)[62] had set the stage for the establishment of a reproductive rights jurisprudence grounded in privacy. Drawing upon these earlier cases, the Supreme Court fashioned a right to privacy that was immediately beneficial to the cause of reproductive rights. The concepts of privacy employed by lawyers and justices in the contraception and abortion cases, however, would inevitably affect domestic violence litigation. An analysis of privacy as developed in the reproductive rights cases is therefore crucial to an understanding of the legal history of domestic violence.

At the root of the cases that eventually led to *Roe v. Wade* was a Connecticut statute that had been enacted in 1879. The bill was introduced in the Connecticut legislature at the same time that a very similar one was brought to the Massachusetts legislature under the influence of noted moralist Anthony Comstock. After several revisions, the Connecticut bill became law in 1879. In its final form, this criminal statute prohibited trafficking in "obscene" materials related to sex or reproduction, and forbade the "use of any drug, medicine, article, or instrument for the purpose of preventing conception."[63] As such, the law implicated both women and doctors, for it made the usage as well as the prescription of contraceptives illegal. The statute, which had been alternately observed and ignored in Connecticut since its inception, ultimately served as the basis for a national debate on the legality of contraception and abortion.[64]

Activists in the Connecticut Birth Control League (CBCL) unsuccessfully sought repeal of the law at every biennial legislative session from 1923 through 1935. Frustrated at their lack of progress, they opened a contraceptive clinic in Hartford in spite of the statute in 1935, which operated successfully and with little public attention for the next five years. The CBCL continued to open such clinics throughout the state without any public censure, until the 1938 opening of a clinic in Waterbury. The Waterbury clinic drew the attention of the local media, prompting a critical response from the local Catholic clergy and engendering public debate about its legality. The furor eventually made its way to the courtroom, and the case *State of Connecticut v. Roger B. Nelson et al.*,[65] decided in 1940 by the state Supreme Court, effectively closed all Connecticut birth control clinics for the next 25 years.[66] While the criminal statute had not yet been enforced, the threat of prosecution it carried served as an effective deterrent to the provision of contraceptive services.

Case Resources

Tileston v. Ullman

Findlaw (http://laws.findlaw.com/us/318/44.html) (full text)

Once the issue had entered the judicial arena—and because legislative remedies seemed next to impossible—birth control activists began to pursue their goal through the courts. (Primarily, their goal consisted of making contraception available to all women; throughout this era, contraceptive measures had been and continued to be available to wealthy women from their private doctors.) The first of these cases to reach the US Supreme Court was *Tileston v. Ullman*.[67] Fritz Wiggin, a lawyer recruited by the CBCL, located the plaintiff,

New Haven doctor Wilder Tileston. Tileston easily documented the cases of three local married women for whom, due to various medical conditions, pregnancy could be fatal. New Haven County State's Attorney Abraham Ullman was named as the defendant in the case. Wiggin argued the case on both state and federal constitutional grounds, claiming primarily that the birth control statute violated the Fourteenth Amendment in two ways: first, by potentially depriving the female patients named by Tileston of "life without due process of law"; second, by depriving Tileston of property—namely, his ability to practice his profession—without due process.[68]

After the Connecticut Supreme Court affirmed the statute, Wiggin and the CBCL appealed to the US Supreme Court. Once the Court accepted the appeal, Ullman responded with an argument that implicitly presaged the debates about privacy that were just about to surface, claiming that "a state has the right to control the marital relations of its citizens."[69] The Court, however, managed to avoid addressing that issue, for it dismissed the case on superficial grounds. The case of *Tileston v. Ullman* did not present a significant case or controversy, the unanimous Court decided, because the arguments about deprivation of life pertained only to the patients (who were not named as plaintiffs), and not to the doctor himself. Additionally, Wiggin's failure to demonstrate any actual threat of prosecution under the statute rendered Tileston's claim of deprivation of property insubstantial.[70]

Case Resources

Poe v. Ullman

Findlaw (http://laws.findlaw.com/us/367/497.html) (full text)

Oyez (http://www.oyez.org/cases/case/?case=1960-1969/1960/1960_60) (oral arguments)

Connecticut birth control activists and lawyers learned several lessons from the failure of *Tileston*. Primarily, they needed to bring a case that was technically flawless, thereby allowing the Court to reach the merits of the case. Second, as their new attorney, Yale Law School professor Fowler Harper, suggested, the public debates and controversy that continued to surround the issue of birth control in Connecticut would make it virtually impossible to get the statute repealed in the Connecticut courts. Instead, Harper recommended a strategy that involved planning to lose in Connecticut, so that they could concentrate their energy on getting a case to the US Supreme Court quickly. Lee Buxton, a physician who had previously testified at legislative hearings about the dangers of the 1879 statute, eagerly agreed to participate in the case. Buxton had seen numerous patients who had suffered severe physical and emotional damage as a result of unintended pregnancies, and one of these, a woman who had lost three infants in three years as a result of congenital defects, ultimately became the plaintiff in the case that Harper brought to the US Supreme Court,[71] *Poe* v. *Ullman*.[72]

Unlike his predecessor Wiggin, Harper argued his case explicitly on privacy grounds. He criticized the Connecticut statute for "purport[ing] to regulate the behavior of married persons in the privacy of their homes in an arbitrary manner which restricts their liberty and seriously jeopardizes the lives and health of spouses." Referring to "the right to marry [and] establish a home" that the Court had affirmed in *Meyer*, Harper asserted that this right "necessarily implies the right to engage in normal marital relations." He further insisted that "The normal and voluntary relations of spouses in the privacy of their homes is regarded as beyond the prying eyes of peeping Toms, be they police officers or legislators."[73] By claiming the constitutional right to "marital relations" and couching such a right in privacy terms, Harper formulated the origins of a right to marital privacy.

Despite their presentation of what they believed to be a technically sound case, the efforts of the birth control advocates were frustrated once again. The justices determined, again, that the lack of a sufficient case or controversy prevented them from reaching the merits of the case. This time, the problem lay not with having the wrong plaintiffs. Instead, the utter lack of enforcement of the 1879 statute led the Court to conclude that this case, like *Tileston*, did not present a sufficient case or controversy for adjudication. While the statute and the ensuing litigation had forced the closure of all of the contraceptive clinics in the state for years, no person had yet been prosecuted under the statute. Justice Frankfurter authored the plurality opinion in *Poe*, noting "[t]he lack of immediacy of the threat" of prosecution, and asserting that "This Court cannot be umpire to debates concerning harmless, empty shadows."[74]

This time, however, the Court was far from unanimous. Three other justices joined Frankfurter's opinion, and one concurred. Two of the four dissenting justices filed lengthy and significant opinions. Justice Douglas's dissent argues strenuously that the Court should have reached the merits of the case and recognized the statute as an invasion of the right to privacy, which he locates in the Fourteenth Amendment. Relying upon *Meyer*, he concludes that the familial rights affirmed therein were "said to come within the 'liberty' of the person protected by the Due Process Clause of the Fourteenth Amendment." This liberty, Douglas claims, "includes the right of 'privacy.'"[75] With the 1879 statute, Douglas contends, "the State has entered the innermost sanctum of the home. . . . That is an invasion of the privacy that is implicit in a free society."[76] Justice Harlan's dissent is even more substantial and more powerful; he articulates "these married persons['] . . . right to enjoy *the privacy of their marital relations* free of the enquiry of the criminal law."[77] After a lengthy analysis of substantive due process doctrine,[78] Harlan locates the privacy right in the Fourth and Fourteenth Amendments, contending that "the Constitution protects the privacy of the home against all unreasonable intrusion of whatever character."[79]

With regard to future privacy cases, two aspects of Harlan's dissent were particularly significant: first, his reliance on substantive due process, which, by allowing a much broader interpretation of the Fourteenth Amendment, made the right to privacy much easier to locate and justify. Second, Harlan was careful to confine this reading of privacy to the *marital* bedroom. He notes that "a statute making it a criminal offense for *married couples* to use contraceptives is an intolerable and unjustifiable invasion of privacy."[80] His repeated emphasis on "marital relations," "married persons," "married couples," "lawful marriage," and "marital intimacy" as deserving of privacy implies that people and relationships outside of those parameters might not be so worthy.[81] In fact, Harlan subsequently makes this distinction clear: "I would not suggest that adultery, homosexuality, fornication and incest are immune from criminal enquiry, however privately practiced."[82] Ultimately, in addition to his privacy argument, much of Harlan's dissent rests on the privileges that should be afforded to people who are legally married:

> Adultery, homosexuality and the like are sexual intimacies which the State law forbids altogether, but the intimacy of husband and wife is necessarily an essential and accepted feature of the institution of marriage, an institution which the State not only must allow, but which always and in every age it has fostered and protected.[83]

By tying privacy rights so strongly to the marital relationship, Harlan imbues the right to privacy with meanings that do not necessarily accrue to it, meanings that would have significance both for reproductive rights activists in the short term and for domestic violence activists in the long term.[84]

Not altogether surprised by the Court's ruling in *Poe*, the leadership of what had become the Planned Parenthood League of Connecticut (PPLC) had already planned their next course of action. Less than five months after *Poe* was decided, PPLC President Estelle Griswold and Dr. Buxton opened a contraceptive clinic—coupled with a press conference—in New Haven. The media attention had the desired effect: Griswold and Buxton were arrested almost immediately, thereby forcing enforcement of the 1879 statute.[85] The case that resulted from the arrest slowly made its way, as Harper intended, to the US Supreme Court.

Case Resources

Griswold v. Connecticut

Findlaw (http://laws.findlaw.com/us/381/479.html) (full text)

Oyez (http://www.oyez.org/cases/case/?case=1960-1969/1964/1964_496) (oral arguments)

The Court in *Griswold v. Connecticut*[86] was not nearly as divided as it had been for *Poe*; only two justices dissented. Justice Douglas authored the fairly brief majority opinion. Unlike Harlan's dissent in *Poe*, Douglas's majority opinion in *Griswold* makes the privacy right seem much less tangible. Referring to the *Pierce* and *Meyer* precedents, Douglas argues in terms of "peripheral rights"—those rights that, like the right to choose how to educate one's children (as in *Pierce*), are not explicitly stated in the Constitution, but can be construed therein nonetheless.[87] Such cases, Douglas contends, indicate that "specific guarantees in the Bill of Rights have penumbras, formed by emanations from those guarantees that help give them life and substance. . . . Various guarantees create zones of privacy."[88] He located these "zones of privacy" in no less than five amendments, including the First, Third, Fourth, Fifth, and Ninth, ultimately concluding that "the right of privacy which presses for recognition here is a legitimate one."[89] Despite his reluctance to pin down a single source for the privacy right itself, Douglas's invocation of it is nonetheless strident; he concludes by asserting "a right of privacy older than the Bill of Rights—older than our political parties, older than our school system."[90]

Having paid careful attention to the *Poe* dissents, the PPLC lawyers stressed the importance of marriage to the privacy right in the materials and arguments they presented for *Griswold*. Douglas's majority opinion echoes this sentiment, citing the importance of the "intimate relation of husband and wife"[91] and concluding with a rousing tribute to the institution of marriage itself:

> Would we allow the police to search the sacred precincts of marital bedrooms for telltale signs of the use of contraceptives? The very idea is repulsive to the notions of privacy surrounding the marriage relationship. . . . Marriage is a coming together for better or for worse, hopefully enduring, intimate to the degree of being sacred. It is an association that promotes a way of life, not causes; a harmony in living, not political faiths; a bilateral loyalty, not commercial or social projects. Yet it is an association for as noble a purpose as any involved in our prior decisions.[92]

With this exaltation of marriage, the Court reversed Connecticut's controversial contraception statute.

The three written concurrences, while debating the exact constitutional location of the right to privacy, nonetheless acknowledge it, and base their arguments on the concept of marital privacy. Relying heavily on the Ninth Amendment, Goldberg's concurrence (in which two other justices join) asserts the right of privacy as "a fundamental personal right."[93] Goldberg's argument, which draws specifically on Harlan's *Poe* dissent, claims constitutional protection for "a particularly important and sensitive area of privacy—that of the marital relation and the marital home," as well as "the traditional relation of the family—a relation as old and as fundamental as our entire civilization."[94] Thus, as the Court debated the Connecticut statute—from *Tileston* to *Poe* and finally to *Griswold*—the judicial conception of privacy continued to take shape. By the time the Court finally invalidated the 1879 statute in 1965, its members generally agreed that there was, in fact, a constitutional right to privacy. Although the specific source of this right was still being debated, the nature of it was not: the right to privacy pertained to the activities of the home—more specifically, the bedroom, and even more specifically, the marital bedroom. This characterization of privacy as a right enjoyed by married people in their homes would not easily fade.

Just two years later, however, a contraceptive case that had nothing to do with married couples began taking shape in Massachusetts. Unlike the Connecticut statutes, which had prohibited contraceptive use by married people, the laws in Massachusetts at this time forbade only the distribution of contraceptives to unmarried individuals. At the urging of Boston University students, contraception activist William Baird gave a public lecture on BU's campus. Baird did not hide his intention to test the Massachusetts statutes by forcing a court case. During his lecture, he denounced the law for "dictat[ing] . . . the privacy of your bodies" and distributed information on vaginal foam contraceptives. Due to the press coverage Baird and BU had successfully attained prior to his visit, police officers were present at the lecture, and Baird was arrested on the spot as he had hoped.[95]

Case Resources

Eisenstadt v. Baird

Findlaw (http://laws.findlaw.com/us/405/438.html) (full text)

Oyez (http://www.oyez.org/cases/case/?case=1970-1979/1971/1971_70_17) (oral arguments)

This case, too, eventually made its way to the US Supreme Court. Writing for the majority in *Eisenstadt v. Baird*,[96] Justice Brennan describes the statutes as violative of the Equal Protection Clause of the Fourteenth Amendment. He contends that the distinction that the statutes made between married and unmarried persons was entirely invidious and could not be supported by any rational relationship to a valid state interest. The Massachusetts statutes simply failed the rational basis test required for equal protection analysis and were therefore unconstitutional. The court invalidated the statutes, allowing contraceptives to be distributed in Massachusetts to people regardless of marital status.

Brennan's opinion, however, also relies heavily on *Griswold*, paying particular attention to the uses of privacy and its relationship to marriage in that case. Toward the end of the opinion, Brennan writes,

> It is true that in *Griswold* the right of privacy in question inhered in the marital relationship. Yet the marital couple is not an independent entity with a mind and heart of its own, but an association of two individuals each with a separate intellectual and emotional makeup. If the right of privacy means anything, it is the right of the individual, married or single, to be free from unwarranted governmental intrusion into matters so fundamentally affecting a person as the decision whether to bear or beget a child.[97]

In addition to simply invalidating the statutes on equal protection grounds, the *Eisenstadt* opinion thus offered a deliberate revision of the right to privacy. The marital relationship that had been such an essential component of the privacy right only seven years earlier in *Griswold* was now deemed superfluous: while the privacy right remained intact, its scope was significantly broadened to include both married and single people. At the same time, privacy seemed to be losing its association with a tangible physical location. No longer confined to the bedroom, whether marital or otherwise, privacy was beginning to encompass the far more abstract realm of individual decision-making.

Another defining feature of the *Eisenstadt* opinion was its noticeable lack of concern with the question of where the privacy right was located in the Constitution. Whereas the *Griswold* opinion upon which this case relied had repeatedly struggled to locate and justify this right, *Eisenstadt* simply assumed it to be a given. By the time *Eisenstadt* was decided, *Griswold's* internal debates about where, how, and to what extent the privacy right existed seemed obsolete. In addition, Brennan's wording—specifically, "the decision whether to *bear* or beget a child"—hinted strongly that the privacy right might be applied to the question of abortion as well. Although *Roe v. Wade* was already well underway by the time *Eisenstadt* was decided, this case confirmed that the Court was already beginning to consider the possibility of viewing abortion in terms of the right to privacy.

In 1969, a women's liberation group at the University of Texas sought to provide information on birth control to single women—information that was not readily available to such women under existing Texas law. In the course of providing this information, they received a great number of requests for information on abortion as well. Having learned of fairly reliable abortion providers both in Mexico and in Texas, they began a referral service. Concerned that their efforts might be punishable under Texas's antiabortion statute, they consulted a young lawyer they knew named Sarah Weddington regarding the legality of providing abortion information and referrals. After researching Texas abortion law, Weddington remained unsure, and the group suggested filing a federal lawsuit to test the constitutionality of the statute.[98] As Weddington further explains,

> When the group here in Austin originally asked me to get involved, it was because they had collected information about the safe places for women to go for abortion—both safe in the sense of going to other states, like California, where it was already legal, . . . or safe as in here in Texas, where it was illegal, . . . but . . . there were better places than the bad ones, and to try to keep [the women] out of the bad ones. So they wanted to know if they could, you know, put [the information] in the campus newspaper, or could they respond to an interview request from the campus newspaper or local press members about the information. Or, whether they could be prosecuted if it became known they had been collecting the information and were happy to make it available to people—could they be prosecuted as accomplices to the crime of abortion? So that was the question I originally started working on, and then [I] found the *Griswold* case, and a lot of other cases that were pending relating to the issue of abortion and abortion regulation.[99]

Weddington quickly found several plaintiffs for the test case, including Norma McCorvey, a pregnant, single woman whose search for an abortion was ultimately unsuccessful, and who was therefore forced to carry her unwanted pregnancy to term.[100] For the purposes of the test case, McCorvey would be referred to as Jane Roe. Dallas County District Attorney Henry Wade was named as the defendant in the suit. One of the central arguments of Weddington's initial complaint was that the Texas statute infringed upon Roe's *"right to privacy in the physician-patient relationship."*[101] By implying that the privacy right might exist not only between married couples, but also between a woman and her doctor, this particular emphasis suggested that the privacy right was indeed moving out of the bedroom and away from the marital relationship.

Initially, Weddington and her colleagues had no indication that their case would turn out to be so central: "When we decided to file a case, it was really with the thought that we would help get some *other* case to the Supreme Court—because we would be helping to build this mountain of litigation going on around the country, and therefore increase the chances that the Supreme Court would accept some case on the issue. We didn't think it would be ours!"[102] Yet, by the time the Court did agree to hear *Roe*, the momentum that the series of privacy and contraception cases had been gathering, coupled with growing national debates about the legality of abortion, ensured that *Roe* would be a pivotal case.[103]

Case Resources
Roe v. *Wade*
Findlaw (http://laws.findlaw.com/us/410/113.html) (full text)
Oyez (http://www.oyez.org/cases/case/?case=1970-1979/1971/1971_70_18) (oral arguments)

The majority opinion in *Roe*, authored by Justice Blackmun and joined by six other justices, is notorious for its length, complexity, and tripartite analysis, in which a woman's right to choose abortion is balanced with the state's interest in protecting potential life. After a lengthy analysis of the legal and medical "history of abortion" in England and the United States,[104] Blackmun asserts that these competing rights vary depending upon the trimester of pregnancy, according the state increasing regulatory power over abortion with each successive trimester.

Before establishing this balancing act, however, Blackmun turns to the privacy issue, noting immediately that "the Constitution does not explicitly mention any right of privacy."[105] Nonetheless, he asserts, "The Court has recognized that a right of personal privacy . . . does exist under the Constitution," and determines that its precise location is not entirely relevant. Ultimately, he concludes, "[t]his right of privacy . . . is broad enough to encompass a woman's decision whether or not to terminate her pregnancy."[106] Blackmun is also careful, however, to outline the limitations of the privacy right. The opinion notes, "The Court's decisions recognizing a right of privacy also acknowledge that some state regulation in areas protected by that right is appropriate. . . . The privacy right involved, therefore, cannot be said to be absolute."[107] By extending the privacy right to include abortion, while simultaneously and deliberately acknowledging its limitations, the *Roe* opinion represents both a culmination of privacy jurisprudence as well as a guidepost for future litigation.

Over the course of several decades of reproductive rights litigation, therefore, the Court's definition of the privacy right, which had originated in the recognition of the sanctity of marriage, had expanded to include the individual freedom to make the most personal decisions. The right had broadened significantly, from protecting only married persons to including single persons, and from a tangible, location-specific right (i.e., freedom from interference in the home or in the bedroom) to the more abstract right of freedom of choice. Yet the abstract nature of the right, however carefully Blackmun had attempted to delineate it, was the cause of some concern for legal scholars assessing *Roe*.

In an essay published shortly after *Roe* was decided, Yale law professor (and former clerk to Chief Justice Warren) John Hart Ely published a searing criticism of the opinion in the *Yale Law Journal*. Characterizing *Roe* as simply "a very bad decision," Ely lambastes the opinion for its lack of constitutional ground-ing.[108] He criticizes the Court's failure to identify a specific constitutional home for the privacy right and its inability to justify abortion as a privacy issue at all as its fatal flaws. Unlike *Griswold* and other privacy cases that had specifically ad-dressed issues of governmental intrusion into the home, *Roe* was clearly not a case about "governmental snooping."[109] The Court's vague characterization of *Roe* as a privacy case, Ely contends, was unconvincing, and the opinion's posi-tion as a foundation for the abortion right thereby substantially weakened.

Future US Supreme Court Justice Ruth Bader Ginsburg, though not as blunt as Ely, was equally critical in her assessment of *Roe*. Focusing on sex-equality issues as well as constitutional ones, Ginsburg maintains that the far-reaching scope of the *Roe* opinion ultimately detracted from its effectiveness. The sheer breadth of the opinion, Ginsburg states, provoked a greater backlash than would have occurred with a more limited decision.[110] Having indicated a lack of en-thusiasm for the privacy rationale ("personal privacy, somehow sheltered by due process"), she suggests that the Court would have been wiser to pursue an analysis focused on gender-based classifications.[111] She contends,

> The conflict . . . is not simply one between a fetus's interests and a woman's interests, narrowly conceived, nor is the overriding issue state versus private control of a wom-an's body for a span of nine months. Also in the balance is a woman's autonomous charge of her full life's course . . . her ability to stand in relation to man, society, and the state as an independent, self-sustaining, equal citizen.[112]

Furthermore, the successful development of sex-equality jurisprudence in the early- to mid-1970s, she asserts, had set the stage for a far less controversial, and more constitutionally solid, resolution to *Roe*.[113] Additionally, the Court's reliance on a doctrine of individual privacy in *Roe* was ultimately detrimental to the effort to seek public funding for abortions. An analysis that emphasized gender equality—along with its attendant class and economic issues—might have proved more hospitable to the notion of public funding.[114]

Ginsburg recognized that *Roe* was not just about abortion. While her article does not mention domestic violence specifically, her concern for the broader ramifications of *Roe* indicates that the privacy analysis employed by the Court did not necessarily serve the interests of gender equality or of women. Likewise, after *Roe*, as Ely and others suggested, the privacy right itself as well as its poten-tial applications were becoming dangerously malleable. While the outcome of *Roe*—the defense of the abortion right—signaled a definitive victory for wom-en's rights, the shifting and expanding judicial definitions of privacy that culmi-nated in *Roe* cannot be viewed in the same light. At its narrowest, during the

Tileston and *Poe* years, the right to privacy was an instrument of exclusion, serving the interests of only heterosexual, married men and women, and overtly privileging the nuclear family form. In this iteration, the privacy right was extended to married couples at the explicit expense of homosexual and single people. Those who engaged in "adultery, homosexuality, and fornication"[115] formed a convenient Other against whom the Court defined the parameters of the privacy right. Yet even the apparent broadening of this right with the *Eisenstadt* and *Roe* decisions—to include single people, and to disregard marital status—left women in a tenuous position. The abortion right that had been secured came under legislative attack almost immediately,[116] and the privacy rights of homosexuals still remained unarticulated.[117] Likewise, the implications of this newly expansive approach to privacy for the problem of domestic violence remained to be seen.

Interestingly, in the years that preceded *Roe*, feminist activists fighting for reproductive rights defined those rights and the concept of privacy much more expansively than the Court ultimately did. Dr. Alice Rossi, for example, writing on a woman's "Right . . . to Control her own Reproductive Life," framed reproductive and privacy rights as human rights. In particular, she noted that:

[T]here are three specific [topics] which are of most concern to the questions of human rights of women and the means to exercise them in the United States in the late 1960s:

1. The right to decide and the means to achieve it, when and with whom a woman shall engage in sexual intercourse.
2. The right to decide, and the means to achieve it, whether and when sexual intercourse shall be recreative or procreative.
3. The right to decide, and the means to achieve it, whether a given pregnancy shall be brought to term or not.

In all three issues, we can argue that these are matters that pertain to the private right of every citizen over his own person, and the social right of access to those means necessary for the care of his own person. . . . So long as no harm is inflicted upon another person, no legislation should apply to the sex lives of Americans, and no barriers imposed to full access to the means necessary to conduct these sexual lives as one wishes in accord with one's values and beliefs.[118]

Rossi concludes by noting that "in defense of the dignity and the privacy of their own person, every woman must fight for the recognition of her right to control her own reproductive processes."[119] By portraying reproductive and privacy rights as a matter of bodily integrity and personal autonomy, Rossi portrays the privacy right in a much broader, more affirmative light than the one developed in the line of cases leading up to *Roe*.

Likewise, when feminist activist Betty Friedan gave the keynote speech at the First National Conference for Repeal of Abortion Laws in Chicago in 1969, she sounded a similar note, describing "the revolution of American women toward full equality, full participation, human dignity and freedom in our society. . . . [T]here is no freedom, no equality, no full human dignity and personhood possible for women until we assert and demand a control over our own bodies, over our own reproductive process."[120] Furthermore, she notes,

> The right of woman to control her reproductive process must be established as a basic, inalienable, human, civil right, not to be denied or abridged by the state. Just as in American tradition, in the American Constitution, the right of individual conscience, religious conscience, spiritual conscience is considered an inalienable private right not to be denied or abridged by the state . . . [121]

By invoking the language of the Constitution to discuss reproductive and privacy rights as human rights, Friedan underscores a more expansive understanding of privacy and its links to liberty and self-determination. Four years later, just after the *Roe* decision, Mary-Ann Lupa, president of the Chicago chapter of NOW, described women "demand[ing] the right to control their own lives—the right to make decisions that affect their own health and well-being."[122] Like other activists for reproductive rights, she identified those rights as a broader struggle for autonomy and self-determination.

The post-*Roe* years have been marked by deliberate testing of both the abortion right and the privacy right. While the doctrine of stare decisis[123] has been a powerful influence on this series of decisions, the Court has acknowledged that "arguments continue to be made . . . that we erred in interpreting the Constitution"[124] in *Roe* and has often been willing to narrow considerably the scope of both rights. As these rights have continued to contract, the notion of the right to privacy as a tool for securing women's freedom has become increasingly implausible. On the contrary, the Court has been quick to delineate the many freedoms that such a privacy right does *not* entail, such as public funding for abortion.[125]

The privacy right as developed in the line of cases leading up to *Roe* would eventually prove critical to the problem of domestic violence. As MacKinnon and other feminist theorists have since observed,[126] the privacy that reproductive rights advocates sought—and that the Court affirmed—was a negative right, one that encouraged the state *not* to interfere in the private realm. While immediately beneficial to the cause of reproductive rights, this was the same idea that battered women's advocates were actively combating when they urged police to intervene in the domestic sphere.

Yet the battered women's movement did not respond immediately to this problem presented by *Roe*. The lack of immediate response suggests that the two movements, while certainly sharing some common goals related to advancing women's rights, may not have been sharing or comparing legal strategies; indeed, the problem *Roe* presented may not even have been immediately apparent to anti-domestic-violence activists. Marjory Fields, a lawyer-activist within the battered women's movement from its earliest days, notes that "the [reproductive rights and battered women's] movements really were separate" at that time.[127] Zorza concurs, stating that the relationship between the two movements was simply "not as close as it should have been."[128] Likewise, the archives of the NCOWFL and the NBWLP do not reveal any immediate response within the battered women's movement to the privacy paradox that *Roe* presented.

Of course, some activists worked within and were interested in both movements simultaneously. And while the issue of abortion was a politically charged one that some battered women's activists were hesitant to support, others, such as Morgan Plant, viewed it as a priority. In an article for *Aegis* magazine entitled, "Abortion is a Battered Women's Issue,"[129] Plant urged her fellow activists to join the pro-choice struggle, describing the interdependence of the two issues. Overall, however, the movement did not respond directly to the concept of privacy as it had been articulated in the reproductive rights cases.

Instead, throughout most of the 1970s, the battered women's movement continued to work with privacy in the same ways it always had. Activists addressed cultural notions of privacy by raising public awareness of the problem of domestic violence (thereby bringing it out of the private realm), and by providing private (i.e., secret and safe) places for women in danger to live. At the same time, lawyers within the movement addressed privacy within the judicial realm by seeking increased state intervention in violent homes.[130] Eventually, however, as the movement's judicial strategies expanded, battered women's advocates began to consider the implications of *Roe* for domestic violence. When they did, the most obvious response might have been to assume—as feminist legal scholars subsequently have—that the reproductive-rights-style privacy was inherently detrimental to battered women, because it kept the state from interfering in the private sphere (specifically, the home). Such an approach would thus assume that the constitutional right to privacy represented, at best, a double-edged sword for battered women. Instead, the lawyer-activists working on a pivotal domestic violence case of the early 1980s adopted an entirely different approach, one that suggested that such a right—properly construed—might prove beneficial, and even empowering, for battered women.

THE CASE OF PEOPLE V. LIBERTA

In the case that would eventually strike down the marital exemption to New York State's criminal rape statute, feminist attorneys responded pointedly to the reproductive rights privacy litigation of the previous decade and used it to their advantage. In so doing, they inverted the legal paradox that privacy is often thought to represent for feminists, and successfully employed concepts of privacy to secure a critical legal protection for women. Because their efforts were largely accepted by the Court—and served as a model for subsequent marital rape decisions—the strategies employed in the case of *People* v. *Liberta* merit careful consideration as an example of pioneering domestic violence privacy theory and litigation.[131]

The facts of the *Liberta* case are undisputed. Mario and Denise Liberta were married in 1978. Later that year, Mario began physically abusing Denise. In 1980, Denise obtained a temporary order of protection that ordered Mario to stay away from her and their home but allowed him weekly contact with their 18-month-old son. On March 24, 1981, one such visit between Mario and their son took place at the motel where Mario had been living; Mario, Denise, and their now 2½-year-old son were all present. Inside the motel, Mario viciously attacked Denise and threatened to kill her. He forced her to engage in vaginal and oral sex with him in the presence of their son, forcing the toddler to watch and take part in several of the sexual assaults. The next day, Denise swore out a felony complaint against Mario, and, after a jury trial, he was convicted in July of that year of both rape in the first degree and sodomy in the first degree.[132]

Mario Liberta appealed his conviction on two grounds. First, he contended that New York's rape and sodomy statutes did not apply to him. The existing rape law stated that a man was guilty of first-degree rape "when he engages in sexual intercourse with a female . . . by forcible compulsion," and defined female as "any female person who is not married to the actor."[133] The sodomy statute contained a similar marital exemption, referring to "sexual conduct between persons not married to each other."[134] In light of these marital exemptions, Mario asserted, he had committed no crime, because he was still legally married at the time of the assault. While the trial court agreed with Mario and dismissed the indictment, the Appellate Court disagreed, noting that the order of protection that was in effect at the time of the attack rendered the Libertas legally not married for the purposes of the rape and sodomy statutes. Those statutes defined "not married," in part, as "living apart . . . pursuant to a valid and effective . . . order issued by a court of competent jurisdiction which by its terms or in its effect requires such living apart."[135]

Second, Mario suggested that even if the court refused to accept him as legally married (and therefore covered by the marital exemptions), his conviction should nonetheless be overturned on constitutional grounds. He claimed that both laws were unconstitutional violations of the equal protection clause of the Fourteenth Amendment: first, by unfairly burdening only some men (just the unmarried ones), and second, by burdening only men, and not women. While the lower courts all rejected this argument, *Liberta* eventually reached the Court of Appeals, New York's highest-level appellate division. In the opinion written by the Court of Appeals, the constitutional questions would ultimately serve as the basis for the most significant and far-reaching aspects of the decision. In an unusual turn of events, it was the feminist lawyer-activists working on *Liberta* that urged the Court to consider Mario Liberta's constitutional arguments.

The lawyers who chose to fight Mario Liberta did so quite purposefully. Rather than viewing *Liberta* as simply another marital rape case, they perceived it as an opportunity to challenge New York's marital rape exemption. Former Acting US Solicitor General Barbara Underwood was working as an assistant district attorney in Brooklyn at the time. Underwood and her boss, Brooklyn District Attorney (and former US Representative) Elizabeth Holtzman, learned of *Liberta* once it had reached the state Court of Appeals level. Underwood and Holtzman had learned that the District Attorney's office in Erie County, New York, where the case originated, planned to argue that the marital exemption to the state statutes was not unconstitutional, and that Liberta's conviction therefore should stand. Already interested in a variety of women's and other progressive legal issues, Holtzman and Underwood had no desire to see Liberta's conviction overturned. At the same time, they were not comfortable with the Erie team's plan to affirm the marital rape exemption. Given this conundrum, they realized that *Liberta* presented "an interesting legal question . . . We thought, maybe we can make a contribution here. It seemed like a case in which our contribution as a prosecutor's office . . . might make a difference."[136]

While Holtzman, Underwood, and Evan Wolfson (another assistant district attorney in Holtzman's office) relished the opportunity to challenge the marital exemption, their colleagues across the state did not share their enthusiasm. In fact, not one other prosecutor's office in the state of New York would join Holtzman's office as amicus curiae (or "friend of the court," for the purpose of writing an informational brief), leaving the Brooklyn District Attorney's office to file its own amicus brief.[137] Other women's rights advocates, however, from both the legal and grassroots arenas were eager to participate as amici. While some briefs, such as the one filed by Marjory Fields of Brooklyn Legal Services, were rejected as the Court attempted to limit the number of amici,[138] one other brief was accepted by the Court. Filed by the NCOWFL and the Center for Constitutional Rights, the brief also represented scores of other organizations: battered women's shelters, rape crisis centers, Women Against Pornography, both state and local chapters of NOW, several branches of Planned Parenthood, and many others signed on.[139]

The two briefs made similar arguments, and both urged the Court to take the same two-pronged course of action. First, and in a somewhat unusual rhetorical move, the briefs asked the Court to give serious consideration to Mario Liberta's suggestion that the existing marital rape exemptions were unconstitutional. While the defendant complained of the unfairness that resulted from allowing only married men to rape with impunity, however, these briefs instead pointed to the unfair distinction that the exemption made between married and unmarried rape *victims*. This distinction was indeed a violation of the equal protection clause, they argued, and as such, the marital rape exemption portion of the rape and sodomy statutes should be struck down.

Second, these briefs also urged that Mario's conviction should not be overturned. Even if the Court agreed to strike down the marital rape exemption as the briefs suggested, the rape and sodomy statutes under which Mario was convicted would remain intact. Additionally, the briefs argued, Mario was not legally entitled to the marital exemption that was in place at the time of the assault. Because of the order of protection that was in effect at that time, the Libertas were not legally married when Mario attacked Denise. Thus, as an unmarried man, Mario could expect no legal protection from the marital exemption.

Compared to simply advocating for the constitutionality of the statute as grounds for upholding the conviction, such an approach would require some complex legal maneuvering. Holtzman's brief,[140] therefore, detailed for the Court the justification for each of the steps that would make such a ruling possible. Given the complexity of their proposal, and knowing that the Court would be reluctant to strike down an existing statute, Underwood recalls, "We thought, 'Let's see if we can show them a way to do this.'"[141] An important part of the "way to do this," according to Holtzman's office, was to rely on the right to privacy, and specifically on the reproductive rights cases that helped to create it.

Prior to *Liberta*, "there [existed] a prevailing notion that law should protect the privacy of the family unit."[142] Holtzman's brief squarely addressed this notion, observing that this privacy had been used as one form of justification for marital rape exemptions nationwide. Her brief quickly dismissed this rationale. Noting the lack of marital exemptions for aggravated sexual abuse and for assault, Holtzman concluded, "Violence is not a protected part of the marital relationship. New York has simply not removed the criminal sanction from the marital bedroom."[143] Additionally, the brief discounted the suggestion that the marital rape exemption itself promotes domestic harmony and reconciliation, stating, "Marital disharmony is created by the sexual violence, not by a subsequent criminal prosecution."[144] In short, "[M]arital privacy cannot be invoked to justify the exemption for marital rape."[145] The NCOWFL brief adopted a similar approach. Citing the US Supreme Court's abandonment of inter-spousal tort immunity, as well as its rejection of a spousal consent requirement for abortion, the brief declared, "Marital privacy is not inviolate."[146] By refusing to acknowledge the home as a site protected from criminal sanctions—or marriage as a relationship protected from government intrusion—these briefs effectively discredited the conception of privacy as a license for domestic abuse.

Case Resources

Carey v. Population Services International

Findlaw (http://laws.findlaw.com/us/431/678.html) (full text)

Planned Parenthood v. Danforth

Findlaw (http://laws.findlaw.com/us/428/52.html) (full text)

Having rejected a construction of privacy that erased legal recourse for domestic violence (and ultimately protected the batterer), Holtzman's brief went on to assert the battered woman's right to privacy. The marital rape exemption, she argued, unconstitutionally deprived women of that right. The location and nature of this privacy right "came out of the *Roe* v. *Wade* litigation and the idea of bodily autonomy."[147] In fact, the brief drew specifically on a number of reproductive rights cases, including *Roe, Eisenstadt, Carey v. Population Services International*,[148] and *Planned Parenthood v. Danforth*.[149] The selection of cases—all dealing with the individual woman's right to make decisions regarding her own body[150]—linked the privacy right very deliberately with ideas about individual and bodily autonomy. Noting that "Respect for individual autonomy as protected by the privacy right is the very underpinning of the American constitutional scheme,"[151] Holtzman declared that this right remains intact for all women, whether married or not; this right "does not stop at the threshold she crosses as a bride."[152]

At the core of Holtzman's argument was her exploration of two core concepts related to privacy: marriage and individual autonomy. With the marital rape exemption, she argued, "the State forces a woman to choose between two equally fundamental aspects of the right to privacy: the right to marriage and the right to personal autonomy in sexual matters."[153] Choosing one should not have to mean giving up the other, Holtzman contended. By casting the reproductive rights decisions as pertaining to "personal autonomy in sexual matters"[154]—an interpretation certainly invited by the expansive *Roe* opinion—the brief cogently linked the issues of abortion and marital rape under the rubric of a privacy right that is beneficial to women. Drawing explicitly on *Griswold*, the brief further explained that if a woman has no legal power to resist forcible sex within marriage, she also loses "her constitutionally protected freedom of choice in matters of contraception;" the exemption, therefore, "violates profoundly her most intimate constitutional rights."[155] The characterization of constitutional rights as intimate—and subject to violation—underscored the construction of privacy as an individual, corporeal right.

Laurie Woods, in the NCOWFL brief, echoed Holtzman's sentiments. The NCOWFL brief referred to reproductive rights, broadly conceived, as the basis for the right to privacy. Citing cases involving not only abortion[156] and contraception[157] but also sterilization[158] and hysterectomy,[159] Woods contended that these cases share more than a topical similarity. More importantly, each of them affirms the right to make individual decisions about issues affecting bodily integrity.[160] This bodily integrity includes "the right not to be compelled by a third party to use or dispose of one's body or labor against one's will," and enjoys particular recognition in the Thirteenth Amendment, the prohibition against involuntary servitude.[161] This radical revisioning of the privacy right, which affords constitutional protection to notions of individual dignity, personhood, and autonomy, was a substantial departure from the reverence for marital privacy espoused in *Poe* and *Griswold*, the cases that encouraged and initiated the formulation of the privacy right in the latter half of the twentieth century.

In another important way, Holtzman's and Woods's briefs represented a complete reversal of a key element of *Griswold*. *Griswold*, like *Poe* before it, delineated a right to privacy by specifically naming what that right did not include: extramarital sex—in particular, adultery, fornication, and homosexuality. Privileging one form of sexuality to the exclusion of others was central to those earlier conceptions of privacy. Subsequently, however, in the 1980 New York case of *People* v. *Onofre*,[162] the privacy right had been used for the opposite purpose: to extend to homosexual and unmarried couples the right to engage in sodomy (and other private, consensual sexual acts) without fear of prosecution. The New York statute, as written, forbade sodomy only among unmarried couples. The *Onofre* case, in which a man was arrested for engaging in consensual oral sex in his home with another man, challenged this statute. The New York Court of Appeals reversed the conviction, finding the criminal sanctions attached to the sodomy statute in violation of the constitutional right to privacy. Despite the fact that, six years after *Onofre*, the US Supreme Court would rule just the opposite with regard to privacy,[163] the *Onofre* opinion, unchallenged at the time of *Liberta*, nonetheless provided a solid foundation for Holtzman's brief.

Both the NCOWFL brief and, to a lesser extent, the Brooklyn District Attorney's brief in *Liberta* relied upon *Onofre* as a cornerstone of their construction of the right to privacy. As Woods observed in the NCOWFL brief, the same court that was to decide *Liberta* had, in *Onofre*, characterized the right of privacy as "a right of independence in making certain kinds of important decisions" and concluded that this right pertains to "individual decisions as to indulgence of sexual intimacy . . . so long as the decisions are voluntarily made by

adults in a noncommercial, private setting."[164] Holtzman's brief also acknowledged the link between this notion of privacy and the privacy at stake in *Liberta*, placing particular emphasis on the Court's articulation, in *Onofre*, of a
"fundamental right to personal decision" with regard to matters of sexuality.[165]
In both briefs, *Onofre* served as the critical bridge between the privacy of the
early reproductive rights cases (where it was established as a fundamental right,
but only because of its protection of the marital home) and the problem of marital rape that was at issue in *Liberta* (which called for a greater emphasis on
bodily integrity and personal autonomy). By relying on *Onofre* in this way—a
particularly effective strategy, given that the *Onofre* opinion was written by the
Liberta court—these lawyers were able to retain the fundamental status of the
right to privacy, while removing its associations with the marital home.

The innovative and powerful privacy arguments contained in the two briefs
had far-reaching implications for the issues of privacy and domestic violence. In
an effort to strike down the marital rape exemptions, these briefs constructed
an alternative vision of the privacy right. Rather than rejecting wholesale the
existing judicial conceptions of privacy, they used several important aspects of
this right as a foundation for their more progressive conceptualization. Building
on the jurisprudence that declared privacy a fundamental right, they nonetheless rejected its characterization as a license for freedom from government intrusion into the marital home, or as a privileging of marital relationships and
sexuality. Additionally, the privacy right's development in reproductive rights
litigation allowed the attorneys implicitly to link privacy to a broader agenda of
women's rights and equality, shifting the focus onto women's individual autonomy and bodily integrity. Making particular use of the *Onofre* opinion, which
emphasized personal decision-making while specifically decentering marital
sexuality, they created a new vision of privacy that did not depend on marital
status, but rather validated and affirmed notions of dignity and personhood.
The marital rape exemption itself, the product of common law notions about
the supremacy and inviolability of marriage, was quite conceivably defensible
under a *Poe*-like privacy argument that centered on protection of the marital
home. (This exact approach was, in fact, adopted by the Erie County District
Attorney's office, arguing for the People of the State of New York in this case.)[166]
By flatly rejecting such conceptions, however, attorneys from the Brooklyn District Attorney's office and from the other amici such as the NCOWFL and the
Center for Constitutional Rights used their own radical revisioning of the privacy right to help combat the exemption and serve as the basis for the protection
of abused women.

The opinion ultimately issued by the Court in *Liberta* confirms that the
briefs had a significant impact on this case. Judge Sol Wachtler, writing for the
Court, issued the exact disposition recommended by the amici—not the one

sought by either the counsel for the state or by Mario Liberta himself.[167] While Liberta's lawyers had argued for the unconstitutionality of the marital rape and sodomy statutes resulting in the overturning of his conviction, the Erie County District Attorney's office, representing the People, asked the Court to uphold Liberta's conviction by affirming the constitutionality of the statutes. Instead, the Court chose the more complex ruling advocated by the amici: it struck down the marital exemption to the existing statutes, while upholding all other aspects of the statutes (and Liberta's conviction).

Wachtler's opinion echoed that of the amici with regard to three crucial issues: standing, equal protection, and privacy. First, the Court refused to overturn Liberta's conviction, noting the unique role of standing in this case. As the amici had outlined, the temporary order of protection in effect at the time of the attack rendered Liberta legally not married, and therefore immune to the protection of the marital exemption that existed at the time. At the same time, this status—"statutorily 'not married'" for the purpose of the case—granted Liberta standing to challenge the constitutionality of the marital rape exemptions, just as any other unmarried man would have had.[168] This unique set of circumstances afforded the Court the opportunity to review and strike down the marital rape exemption, while simultaneously leaving Liberta's conviction intact.

With regard to Liberta's equal protection claims, the Court's opinion again mirrors that of the amici. Holtzman's brief, for example, had argued that Liberta's constitutional challenge was partially correct: "The State may not lawfully distinguish between married and unmarried men who rape or sodomize women. . . . [M]ore importantly, [the marital exemption] irrationally classifies their victims, thereby denying equal protection to women who are raped or sodomized by their husbands."[169] Noting that a statutory classification based upon marital status must have some rational basis in order to meet equal protection standards, the Court concluded that such a rational basis did not exist in this case.[170] The Court explicitly rejected any such purported rationales, including the suggestion that marriage itself implies consent to all sexual intercourse. The Court here echoes Holtzman's amicus brief (in which she contends that women's rights should continue even beyond "the threshold she crosses as a bride"). Wachtler writes, "[A] marriage license should not be viewed as a license for a husband to forcibly rape his wife with impunity."[171] Likewise, Woods's discussion of the "serious physical and psychological injury" suffered by women who are raped by their husbands urged the Court to reject any notion of marriage as implied consent.[172] Wachtler's opinion agrees: "[Rape] is a degrading, violent act which violates the bodily integrity of the victim and frequently causes severe, long-lasting physical and psychic harm. To ever imply consent to such an act is irrational and absurd."[173]

Finally, the conception of privacy advanced by amici was well received by the Court. Responding to the State's suggestion that the right to marital privacy serves as an appropriate justification for the constitutionality of the exemptions, the Court strongly disagreed. Even citing *Griswold* as the basis for this conclusion, Wachtler wrote, "The marital exemption simply does not further marital privacy because this right of privacy protects consensual acts, not violent sexual assaults."[174] Additionally, the *Liberta* Court observed definitively that "[A] husband cannot invoke a right of marital privacy to escape liability for beating his wife [and] he cannot justifiably rape his wife under the guise of a right to privacy."[175] Relying, as amici did, on *Danforth*, the Court observed, "A married woman has the same right to control her own body as does an unmarried woman."[176] The opinion also discarded the notion of maintaining the exemption as a means of promoting marital harmony,[177] using the logic advanced by the Holtzman brief: "Clearly, it is the violent act of rape and not the subsequent attempt of the wife to seek protection through the criminal justice system which 'disrupts' a marriage."[178] Thus, the *Liberta* court endorsed the conception of privacy advanced by the amici briefs and relied upon this model of privacy in the writing of its opinion. Drawing on the reproductive rights cases to affirm notions of a woman's bodily integrity, while simultaneously rejecting the argument that the right to privacy protects violence in the home, the *Liberta* opinion affirmed the amici's revisioning of privacy.

The effect of the *Liberta* opinion has been substantial. Other states, striking down their own marital rape and forcible sodomy exemptions, have used *Liberta* as a model. An Alabama court, for example, borrowed liberally from the language, reasoning, and constitutional analysis of *Liberta* when invalidating that state's marital sodomy exemption.[179] Likewise, the Wyoming case of *Shunn v. State* deliberately echoed *Liberta*'s equal protection analysis in striking down the state's marital rape exemption.[180] In the midst of a national movement to strike marital rape exemptions from state law books, *Liberta* was a strong judicial voice decrying the existence of such exemptions and advocating for legal recourse for women who were sexually assaulted by their husbands.[181]

Through a concerted, deliberate effort, lawyers and activists in the state of New York placed the issue of the marital rape exemption before the state judiciary and were ultimately instrumental in its invalidation. At the same time, they also shaped the future of privacy jurisprudence: by rejecting a construction of privacy that was based on the privileging of the marital relationship—to the exclusion of other sexual relationships and the detriment of battered women—they constructed an alternative model of privacy. The model they presented to the Court was bolstered by the fundamental nature of the privacy right that had been established in the reproductive rights cases, yet it privileged bodily integrity and personal autonomy over marital status. In this way, they inverted the existing privacy paradigm and used it as a source of legal protection for battered women. Indications that the *Liberta* court—and, subsequently, other state courts as well—accepted or were at least influenced by this revisioning of privacy are plentiful. As feminist legal scholars confronting the problem of domestic violence seek alternative conceptions of privacy, the theoretical strategies and practical successes of *Liberta* may serve as a model for future efforts.

CONCLUSION

During its early years in the early-to-mid-1970s, the US battered women's movement was marked by an emphasis on physically sheltering women from their abusers. As the movement matured through the late 1970s and early 1980s, however, it quickly turned to legislative and judicial remedies as a means of combating domestic violence. The movement's strong ties to the anti-rape effort helped to determine its priorities as well as its strategies, many of them focused on removing domestic violence from the private realm. As in the anti-rape movement, activists used consciousness-raising groups and media campaigns to reduce the shame and stigma of domestic abuse and to raise public awareness about the issue. In these ways, battered women's advocates confronted and challenged cultural notions of privacy. Also, as activists began to organize on regional and national levels, several groups focusing primarily or solely on the legal rights of battered women developed. By encouraging state intervention in violent homes, these groups began challenging concepts of domestic violence and privacy within the judicial realm. These groups would eventually shape the path that domestic violence litigation would take.

At the same time, decades of courtroom activity around the issue of reproductive rights were culminating in the decisions of *Griswold*, *Eisenstadt*, and *Roe*. In the process of securing the right to contraception and abortion, these cases and their predecessors developed a right to privacy that shifted with each new decision. Originally rooted in liberal individualism, the right to privacy as developed in the contraception cases of the 1950s and 1960s began to signify a reverence for the marital home and a privileging of marital relationships. By the early 1970s, however, the privacy right seemed to be expanding in some ways to pertain to nonmarried individuals. While the shape of the right continued to change, however, its fundamental nature did not. This fundamental right to privacy, however construed, represents a potential paradox for battered women's advocates. The privileging of the domestic sphere that featured so prominently in some conceptions of privacy, particularly those related to reproductive rights, often creates dangerous conditions for battered women.

Feminist legal theorists and battered women's advocates today continue to ponder how best to address this paradox. The 1984 New York case of *People v. Liberta* provides one possible answer. The history of *Liberta* reveals a group of feminist lawyers and activists who deliberately used the courts as a mechanism of social change. Sensing an opportunity to effect change, these attorneys (and the activist groups that supported them on their amici briefs) sought to remove the marital exemption from New York's criminal rape statute. Rather than avoiding the potentially problematic issue of the right to privacy, they confronted it directly. Their analysis simultaneously rejected those aspects of the existing privacy right that privileged the marital relationship, and reshaped the right to emphasize women's bodily integrity and autonomy. Their response to *Liberta*, based on their new construction of the privacy right, was clearly reflected not only in the opinion of the *Liberta* court, but subsequently in the opinions of other state appellate courts striking down marital exemptions as well. Their success in advancing a form of privacy that was empowering to victims of domestic violence suggests that these lawyers' theorizing about *Liberta* could well serve as a model for other battered women's advocates confronting the paradox of legal privacy.

NOTES

1. For a detailed history of the anti-rape movement, see Maria Bevacqua, *Rape on the Public Agenda: Feminism and the Politics of Sexual Assault* (Boston: Northeastern University Press, 2000).

2. For a thorough examination of the movement against sexual harassment, see Carrie N. Baker, "Sex, Power, and Politics: The Origins of Sexual Harassment Policy in the United States" (PhD diss., Emory University, 2001).

3. 64 N.Y.2d 152 (1984).

4. 410 U.S. 113 (1973).

5. See Elizabeth Hafkin Pleck, *Domestic Tyranny: The Making of Social Policy Against Family Violence from Colonial Times to the Present* (New York: Oxford University Press, 1987); Catharine A. MacKinnon, *Toward a Feminist Theory of the State* (Cambridge: Harvard University Press, 1989); Martha Albertson Fineman and Roxanne Mykitiuk, eds., *The Public Nature of Private Violence: The Discovery of Domestic Abuse* (New York: Routledge, 1994); Elizabeth Schneider, "The Violence of Privacy," in *The Public Nature of Private Violence: The Discovery of Domestic Abuse*, ed. Martha Albertson Fineman and Roxanne Mykitiuk, (New York: Routledge, 1994): 36–58, and *Battered Women and Feminist Lawmaking* (New Haven: Yale University Press, 2000); Cynthia Daniels, ed., *Feminists Negotiate the State: The Politics of Domestic Violence* (Lanham, MD: University Press of America, 1997); and Reva B. Siegel, "The

Rule of Love: Wife Beating as Prerogative and Privacy," *Yale Law Journal* 105 (1996): 2117–207.

6. *Poe* v. *Ullman*, 367 U.S. 397 (1961): *dissent*, 521.

7. See Catharine A. MacKinnon, "Reflections on Sex Equality Under Law," *Yale Law Journal* 100 (1991): 1281, and *Toward a Feminist Theory of the State* (Cambridge: Harvard University Press, 1989).

8. Patricia Boling, *Privacy and the Politics of Intimate Life* (Ithaca: Cornell University Press, 1996): 34–35.

9. With regard to class, Roberts notes that "the power of privacy doctrine in poor women's lives is constrained by liberal notions of freedom. First, the abstract freedom to choose is of meager value without meaningful options from which to choose and the ability to effectuate one's choice. The traditional concept of privacy makes the false presumption that the right to choose is contained entirely within the individual and not circumscribed by the material conditions of the individual's life." ("Punishing Drug Addicts Who Have Babies: Women of Color, Equality, and the Right of Privacy," *Harvard Law Review* 104 [1991]: 1477–78.)

10. Ibid., 1478.

11. Ibid., 1479–82.

12. Elizabeth Schneider, "The Violence of Privacy," in *The Public Nature of Private Violence: The Discovery of Domestic Abuse*, ed. Martha Albertson Fineman and Roxanne Mykitiuk, 36–58 (New York: Routledge, 1994): 52.

13. Ibid., 53.

14. Elizabeth Hafkin Pleck, *Domestic Tyranny: The Making of Social Policy Against Family Violence from Colonial Times to the Present* (New York: Oxford University Press, 1987): 182–87.

15. Domestic Violence: A National Perspective, 1976, p. 2. Schlesinger Library, Radcliffe Institute for Advanced Study, Harvard University, Yolanda Bako papers (including papers of the National Coalition Against Domestic Violence), 99-M80, Box 1.

16. Elizabeth Hafkin Pleck, *Domestic Tyranny: The Making of Social Policy Against Family Violence from Colonial Times to the Present* (New York: Oxford University Press, 1987); Susan Schechter, *Women and Male Violence: The Visions and Struggles of the Battered Women's Movement* (Boston: South End Press, 1982).

17. Barbara Hart, interview by author, May 1, 2002.

18. Susan Schechter, *Women and Male Violence: The Visions and Struggles of the Battered Women's Movement* (Boston: South End Press, 1982): 55.

19. Linda Gordon has observed the interesting link that alcohol provides between nineteenth- and twentieth-century activism to end domestic violence. Just as temperance advocates took up the cause of domestic violence in the late nineteenth century, the first shelters to house battered women in the twentieth century were founded for wives of alcoholic husbands (*Heroes of Their Own Lives: The Politics and History of Family Violence* [New York: Viking, 1988]: 264).

20. Joan Zorza, interview by author, December 14, 2001.

21. Ibid.

22. Ibid.

23. History of Services Development in Domestic Violence Programs, 1983, p.2. Schlesinger Library, Radcliffe Institute for Advanced Study, Harvard University, Yolanda Bako papers (including papers of the National Coalition Against Domestic Violence), 99-M80, Box 1.

24. Domestic Violence: A National Perspective, 1976, p. 8–9. Schlesinger Library, Radcliffe Institute for Advanced Study, Harvard University, Yolanda Bako papers (including papers of the National Coalition Against Domestic Violence), 99-M80, Box 1; Del Martin, *Battered Wives* (San Francisco: Glide Publications, 1976): 196–213; Susan Schechter, *Women and Male Violence: The Visions and Struggles of the Battered Women's Movement* (Boston: South End Press, 1982): 55–58.

25. Given the informal, grassroots origins of these shelters, no data exist regarding the race, ethnicity, sexual orientation, or other characteristics of their founders. My own interviews with early-movement activists, however, support Schechter's characterization of their diversity in each of these areas. Additionally, while there is no established link between such characteristics and the guiding philosophy of shelters themselves, scholars have noted that members of traditionally marginalized groups are often more likely to reject traditional hierarchical approaches in favor of more innovative and egalitarian models. Patricia Hill Collins, *Black Feminist Thought: Knowledge, Consciousness, and the Politics of Empowerment* (London: Routledge, 1990); Nancy A. Matthews, *Confronting Rape: The Feminist Anti-Rape Movement and the State* (London: Routledge, 1994).

26. Susan Schechter, *Women and Male Violence: The Visions and Struggles of the Battered Women's Movement* (Boston: South End Press, 1982): 57.

27. Zorza, interview, 2001. For a discussion of similar tensions in the anti-rape movement at this time, see Nancy A. Matthews, *Confronting Rape: The Feminist Anti-Rape Movement and the State* (London: Routledge, 1994): 115.

28. Zorza, interview, 2001.

29. Ibid.

30. National Coalition Against Domestic Violence Statement, n.d., Schlesinger Library, Radcliffe Institute for Advanced Study, Harvard University, Yolanda Bako papers (including papers of the National Coalition Against Domestic Violence), 96-M117–96-M137, Box 1. Paradoxically, however, while the existence of shelters themselves held this symbolic power, shelters' practical needs—for providing safety to women via secrecy and anonymity—also complicated efforts to divorce the problem of domestic violence from issues of shame and invisibility.

31. Maria Bevacqua, *Rape on the Public Agenda: Feminism and the Politics of Sexual Assault* (Boston: Northeastern University Press, 2000): 58–60.

32. Domestic Violence: A National Perspective, 1976, p. 2. Schlesinger Library, Radcliffe Institute for Advanced Study, Harvard University, Yolanda Bako papers (including papers of the National Coalition Against Domestic Violence), 99-M80, Box 1.

33. There is some disagreement regarding the founding of the first rape crisis hotline. According to Elizabeth Pleck, the first was established in Berkeley, California, in 1972 (*Domestic Tyranny*, 185). Schechter, however, suggests that the first one opened that same year in Washington, D.C. (*Women and Male Violence*, 35).

34. Del Martin, *Battered Wives* (San Francisco: Glide, 1976): 222.

35. Hart interview, 2002.

36. Domestic Violence: A National Perspective, 1976, p. 7. Schlesinger Library, Radcliffe Institute for Advanced Study, Harvard University, Yolanda Bako papers (including papers of the National Coalition Against Domestic Violence), 99-M80, Box 1.

37. National Coalition Against Domestic Violence Statement, n.d. Schlesinger Library, Radcliffe Institute for Advanced Study, Harvard University, Yolanda Bako papers (including papers of the National Coalition Against Domestic Violence), 96-M117–96-M137, Box 1.

38. Notes from the National Coalition Against Domestic Violence Steering Committee Meeting, May 12–14, 1978, n. pg. Schlesinger Library, Radcliffe Institute for Advanced Study, Harvard University, Yolanda Bako papers (including papers of the National Coalition Against Domestic Violence), 96-M117–96-M137, Box 1.

39. History of Services Development in Domestic Violence Programs, 1983, p. 3. Schlesinger Library, Radcliffe Institute for Advanced Study, Harvard University, Yolanda Bako papers (including papers of the National Coalition Against Domestic Violence), 99-M80, Box 1.

40. Ibid., 3.

41. National Coalition Against Domestic Violence Statement, n.d. Schlesinger Library, Radcliffe Institute for Advanced Study, Harvard University, Yolanda Bako papers (including papers of the National Coalition Against Domestic Violence), 96-M117–96-M137, Box 1.

42. A more detailed analysis of this effort occurs later in this chapter. See "The Case of *People* v. *Liberta*," *infra*.

43. National Coalition Against Domestic Violence Statement, n.d. Schlesinger Library, Radcliffe Institute for Advanced Study, Harvard University, Yolanda Bako papers (including papers of the National Coalition Against Domestic Violence), 96-M117–96-M137, Box 1.

44. Resolutions Adopted by Delegates to the National Women's Conference, 1977. Schlesinger Library, Radcliffe Institute for Advanced Study, Harvard University, Andrea Dworkin papers, 2001-M196, Box 15.

45. Proposed National Plan of Action, 1977. Schlesinger Library, Radcliffe Institute for Advanced Study, Harvard University, Andrea Dworkin papers, M196, Box 15.

46. National Coalition Against Domestic Violence Statement, n.d. Schlesinger Library, Radcliffe Institute for Advanced Study, Harvard University, Yolanda Bako papers (including papers of the National Coalition Against Domestic Violence), 96-M117–96-M137, Box 1.

47. Notes from the National Coalition Against Domestic Violence Steering Committee Meeting, May 12–4, 1978, n. pg. Schlesinger Library, Radcliffe Institute for Advanced Study, Harvard University, Yolanda Bako papers (including papers of the National Coalition Against Domestic Violence), 96-M117–96-M137, Box 1.

48. Thereafter, the directory continued to be updated until seven subsequent editions had been issued.

49. Explaining its interest in the issue of domestic violence, the commission noted, in the publication that resulted from the consultation, that its "jurisdictional basis to study the problems of battered women stems from its statutory mandate to study and collect information regarding the denial of the equal protection of the laws on the basis of sex and, in particular, in the administration of justice. Women who complain of abuse often are treated cavalierly by the police, the courts, and other elements of the criminal justice system. Little effort has been made in most jurisdictions to provide the necessary specialized facilities to serve victims of domestic violence." US Commission on Civil Rights, *Battered Women: Issues of Public Policy* (Washington, DC: January 30–31, 1978).

50. Ibid., iv.

51. History of Services Development in Domestic Violence Programs, 1983, pp. 3–4. Schlesinger Library, Radcliffe Institute for Advanced Study, Harvard University, Yolanda Bako papers (including papers of the National Coalition Against Domestic Violence), 99-M80, Box 1; Susan Schechter, *Women and Male Violence: The Visions and Struggles of the Battered Women's Movement* (Boston: South End Press, 1982): 137–38.

52. Hart, interview, 2002.

53. National Communication Network Herstory, 1977, p. 3. Schlesinger Library, Radcliffe Institute for Advanced Study, Harvard University, Yolanda Bako papers (including papers of the National Coalition Against Domestic Violence), 96-M117–96-M137, Box 2.

54. Hart, interview, 2002.

55. National Communication Network Herstory, 1977. Schlesinger Library, Radcliffe Institute for Advanced Study, Harvard University, Yolanda Bako papers (including papers of the National Coalition Against Domestic Violence), 96-M117–96-M137, Box 2; *Aegis, the Magazine on Ending Violence Against Women*, 1978, Schlesinger Library, Radcliffe College; Susan Schechter, *Women and Male Violence: The Visions and Struggles of the Battered Women's Movement* (Boston: South End Press, 1982).

56. National Battered Women's Law Project Proposal, p. 10. Schlesinger Library, Radcliffe Institute for Advanced Study, Harvard University, National Center on Women and Family Law records, 96-M105, Box 10.

57. Ibid., 12.

58. A detailed discussion of these class-action suits follows in chapter four.

59. National Coalition Against Domestic Violence Statement, n.d. Schlesinger Library, Radcliffe Institute for Advanced Study, Harvard University, Yolanda Bako papers (including papers of the National Coalition Against Domestic Violence), 96-M117–96-M137, Box 1.

60. *Meyer v. Nebraska*, 262 U.S. 390 (1923).

61. *Pierce v. Society of Sisters*, 268 U.S. 510 (1925).

62. *Prince v. Massachusetts*, 321 U.S. 158 (1944).

63. *Poe*, 519.

64. David J. Garrow, *Liberty and Sexuality: The Right to Privacy and the Making of Roe v. Wade* (New York: MacMillan, 1994): 2–3; 15–16.

65. 11 A.2d 856 (1940).

66. Garrow, *Liberty and Sexuality*, 2–78.

67. 318 U.S. 44 (1943).

68. Ibid., 92–95.

69. Ibid., 100.

70. *Tileston*, 45–46.

71. Garrow, *Liberty and Sexuality*, 135–47.

72. 367 U.S. 397 (1961).

73. Garrow, *Liberty and Sexuality*, 166–67.

74. *Poe*, 501, 508.

75. Ibid., 517.

76. Ibid., 521.

77. Ibid., 536; emphasis added.

78. Substantive due process, debated vigorously within the Court during the early decades of the twentieth century, generally refers to the notion that the right to "due process" guaranteed by the Fifth and Fourteenth Amendments is much broader than simply a procedural restraint, and that it instead, as Harlan asserted in *Poe*, "includes a freedom from all substantial arbitrary impositions and purposeless restraints" (*Poe*, 543).

79. Ibid., 550.

80. Ibid., 539; original emphasis.

81. Ibid., 536 and 548; 537; 539; 546; 548. The strength of the link between marriage and privacy in Harlan's dissent is again apparent when he criticizes the Connecticut statute for "punish[ing] married people for the private use of their marital intimacy" (548).

82. Ibid., 552.

83. Ibid., 553.

84. In this same vein, recalling the caveat in *Prince* that "the family . . . is not beyond regulation," he notes that "it would be an absurdity to suggest . . . that the home can be made a sanctuary for crime" (Ibid., 552) thereby placing an important yet often-forgotten restriction on the still-developing right to privacy.

85. Garrow, *Liberty and Sexuality*, 201–207.

86. 381 U.S. 479 (1965).

87. *Griswold*, 483.

88. Ibid., 484.

89. Ibid., 485.

90. Ibid., 487.

91. Ibid., 482.

92. Ibid., 487.

93. Ibid., 494. It is interesting to note that this ostensibly "personal" right was completely dependent upon marital status. *Personal* here can hardly mean *individual*, since individuals only obtained this right via their legal relationship to another individual.

94. Ibid., 495, 496.

95. Garrow, *Liberty and Sexuality*, 320–21.

96. 405 U.S. 438 (1972).

97. *Eisenstadt*, 453.

98. Sarah Weddington, *A Question of Choice* (New York: Putnam, 1992): 35–44.

99. Sarah Weddington, interview by author, November 26, 2002.

100. The other plaintiffs included a married couple, Marsha and David King (referred to in the suit as Jane and John Doe), and a physician, John Hallford, who had two state abortion prosecutions pending against him. Marsha King had just recently suffered an extremely stressful and health-threatening abortion in Mexico due to the lack of availability of abortion in Texas (*Roe*, 113; Weddington, *A Question of Choice*, 50–52, 59; Garrow, *Liberty and Sexuality*, 401).

101. Weddington, *A Question of Choice*, 54; original emphasis.

102. Weddington, interview, 2002.

103. Once the case reached the US Supreme Court, the Does were denied standing because their claim was based on the possibility of future pregnancies, not a pregnancy that actually existed at the time of the filing of the original suit. Dr. Hallford was also denied standing, but Roe was granted standing. At the same time, a companion case, filed in Georgia, was decided alongside *Roe*. (See *Doe v. Bolton*, 1973, http://laws.findlaw.com/us/410/179.html [full text].)

104. *Roe*, 129.

105. Ibid., 153.

106. Ibid., 153.

107. Ibid., 153–54.

108. John Hart Ely, "The Wages of Crying Wolf: A Comment on *Roe v. Wade*," *Yale Law Journal* 82 (1973): 947.

109. Ibid., 930.

110. Ruth Bader Ginsburg, "Some Thoughts on Autonomy and Equality in Relation to *Roe v. Wade*," *North Carolina Law Review* 63 (1985): 381.

111. Ibid., 380, 377.

112. Ibid., 383.

113. When I interviewed Weddington, we discussed Ginsburg's criticism of the *Roe* opinion, and Weddington noted that while the sex-equality cases were in process as she prepared for *Roe*, they had not yet been decided. Specifically, she pointed out that when she first filed *Roe* in 1970, the landmark sex-equality case *Reed v. Reed* (404 U.S. 71 [1971]), http://laws.findlaw.com/us/404/71.html (full text), http://www.oyez.org/cases/case?case=1970-1979/1971/1971_70_4 (audio), had not yet been decided. Thus, she did not feel assured about the potential success of an equal protection argument: "I felt, while I did put in the gender equity argument, that . . . I still don't think we could've gotten the court to go on that basis at that particular time. So if Ruth Bader Ginsburg ends up taking the court in that direction, it would certainly be fine with me, but I don't think we could've won with that at that particular spot in time" (Weddington, interview, 2002). Weddington echoes this idea in *A Question of Choice*, 117.

114. Ruth Bader Ginsburg, "Some Thoughts on Autonomy and Equality in Relation to *Roe v. Wade*," *North Carolina Law Review* 63 (1985): 384–85.

115. *Poe*, 552.

116. See, for example, *Planned Parenthood of Central Missouri* v. *Danforth*, 428 U.S. 52 (1976), http://laws.findlaw.com/us/428/52.html (full text); *Bellotti* v. *Baird*, 428 U.S. 132 (1976), http://laws.findlaw.com/us/428/132.html (full text); *Beal* v. *Doe*, 432 U.S. 438 (1977), http://laws.findlaw.com/us/432/438.html (full text), http://www.oyez.org/cases/case?case=1970–1979/1976/1976_75_554 (audio); and *Maher* v. *Roe*, 432 U.S. 464 (1977), http://laws.findlaw.com/us/432/464.html (full text), http://www.oyez.org/cases/case?case=1970–1979/1976/1976_75_1440 (audio).

117. The failure to articulate the position of homosexuals with regard to this privacy right was not merely an oversight. This right was explicitly denied to homosexuals by the Court in 1986 in *Bowers* v. *Hardwick*, 478 U.S. 186 (1986), http://laws.findlaw.com/us/478/186.html (full text), http://www.oyez.org/cases/case/?case=1980–1989/1985/1985_85_140 (audio). The implications of this decision are discussed in greater detail in chapter five.

118. Dr. Alice Rossi, "Sociological Argument in Support of Effect of Denial of Right to a Woman to Control her own Reproductive Life," 1967, p. 1–2. Schlesinger Library, Radcliffe Institute for Advanced Study, Harvard University, National Organization for Women records, MC 496, Box 49, Folder 16.

119. Ibid., 13.

120. Betty Friedan, "Abortion: A Woman's Right," Keynote Speech, First National Conference for Repeal of Abortion Laws, Chicago, Illinois, February 14, 1969. Schlesinger Library, Radcliffe Institute for Advanced Study, Harvard University, National Organization for Women records, MC 496, Box 49, Folder 16.

121. Ibid.

122. Press Release, August 16, 1973. Schlesinger Library, Radcliffe Institute for Advanced Study, Harvard University, National Organization for Women records, MC 496, Box 49, Folder 27.

123. Latin for "to stand by that which is decided," the doctrine of *stare decisis* states that courts apply the same reasoning when deciding cases as has been used in previous, similar cases.

124. *City of Akron* v. *Akron Center for Reproductive Health, Inc., et al.*, 462 U.S. 416 (1983), 419, http://laws.findlaw.com/us/462/416.html (full text), http://www.oyez.org/cases/case?case=1980–1989/1982/1982_81_746 (audio).

125. See, for example, *Maher* v. *Roe*, 432 U.S. 464 (1977), http://laws.findlaw.com/us/432/464.html (full text), in which the court held that Connecticut's state Medicaid program was constitutionally justified in excluding nontherapeutic abortions, and that this regulation "does not impinge on the fundamental right of privacy recognized in *Roe*. . . . That right implies no limitation on State's authority to make a value judgment favoring childbirth over abortion and to implement that judgment by the allocation of public funds" (471–74).

126. See, e.g., Catharine A. MacKinnon, *Toward a Feminist Theory of the State* (Cambridge: Harvard University Press, 1989); Dorothy Roberts, "Punishing Drug Addicts Who Have Babies: Women of Color, Equality, and the Right of Privacy," *Harvard Law Review* 104 (1991); Elizabeth M. Schneider, "The Violence of Privacy," in

The Public Nature of Private Violence: The Discovery of Domestic Abuse, ed. Martha Albertson Fineman and Roxanne Mykitiuk (New York: Routledge, 1994): 36–58.

127. Marjory Fields, interview by author, January 22, 2002.

128. Zorza, interview, 2001.

129. Morgan Plant, "Abortion is a Battered Women's Issue," *Aegis* 33 (1982): 32–35.

130. Chapter four provides a thorough discussion of these legal efforts.

131. The *Liberta* model, while undeniably innovative, bears some significant limitations. Given that the case itself pertains to a marital rape exemption, the successful strategies here apply to and assume a heterosexual, marital definition of domestic violence. Vast numbers of battered women, of course, fall outside the scope of this definition. The limitations and implications of such assumptions will be discussed in greater detail in chapter five.

132. *Liberta*, 158–59.

133. Ibid., 159.

134. Ibid., 159.

135. Ibid., 159–60.

136. Barbara Underwood, interview by author, December 20, 2001.

137. Elizabeth Holtzman, interview by author, December 21, 2001.

138. Fields, interview, 2002.

139. Schlesinger Library, Radcliffe Institute for Advanced Study, Harvard University, National Center on Women and Family Law records, 96-M105, Box 33. While this brief is the product of a collaborative effort, for the purpose of consistency, I will refer to this brief as "the NCOWFL brief" and will attribute its authorship to Laurie Woods, executive director of the NCOWFL.

140. Schlesinger Library, Radcliffe Institute for Advanced Study, Harvard University, National Center on Women and Family Law records, 96-M105, Box 32. Although both Holtzman and Underwood acknowledge that Underwood and Wolfson are responsible for primary authorship of the brief, it was submitted in Holtzman's name as the District Attorney of Brooklyn. Holtzman, who was in full agreement with the theory and approach of the brief, authorized its preparation and fully supported the efforts of Underwood and Wolfson. The brief is referred to in the NCOWFL files as "Holtzman's brief," and this is the usage I employ. Likewise, for the sake of consistency, I attribute its authorship to Holtzman.

141. Underwood, interview, 2001.

142. Ibid.

143. *Brief Amicus Curiae* of Elizabeth Holtzman, Kings County District Attorney, October 30, 1984: 23 [hereafter referred to as Holtzman Brief]. Schlesinger Library, Radcliffe Institute for Advanced Study, Harvard University, National Center on Women and Family Law records, 96-M105, Box 33.

144. Ibid., fn 18.

145. Ibid., 23.

146. *Brief Amicus Curiae* of National Center on Women and Family Law, Inc., and Center for Reproductive Rights, et al., September 18, 1984: 34 (hereafter referred to as NCOWFL Brief). Schlesinger Library, Radcliffe Institute for Advanced Study,

Harvard University, National Center on Women and Family Law records, 96-M105, Box 33.

147. Holtzman, interview, 2001.

148. 431 U.S. 678 (1977).

149. 428 U.S. 52 (1976).

150. *Eisenstadt*, for example, affirmed "the right of the individual . . . to be free from unwarranted governmental intrusion into matters so fundamentally affecting a person as the decision whether to bear or beget a child" (*Eisenstadt*, 453). *Carey* protected "individual decisions in matters of procreation and contraception" and "the freedom to choose contraception" (*Carey*, 688). And *Danforth* declared parental- and spousal-consent provisions to be unconstitutional, asserting instead the primacy of the pregnant woman's decision, "inasmuch as it is the woman who physically bears the child and who is the more directly and immediately affected by the pregnancy" (*Danforth*, 81).

151. Holtzman Brief, 28. Schlesinger Library, Radcliffe Institute for Advanced Study, Harvard University, National Center on Women and Family Law records, 96-M105, Box 33.

152. Ibid., 30.

153. Ibid., 29.

154. Ibid., 29.

155. Ibid., 29.

156. *Danforth, supra.*

157. *Zagarow v. Zagarow*, 105 Misc. 2d 1054 (1980); *Griswold, supra.*

158. *Ponter v. Ponter*, 135 N.J. Super. 50 (1975).

159. *Murray v. Vandevander*, 522 P.2d 302 (1974).

160. NCOWFL Brief, 20–21. Schlesinger Library, Radcliffe Institute for Advanced Study, Harvard University, National Center on Women and Family Law records, 96-M105, Box 33.

161. Ibid., 21–22.

162. *People v. Onofre*, 51 N.Y. 2d 485 (1980).

163. *Bowers* and its implications for the right to privacy will be discussed in further detail in chapter five.

164. *Onofre*, 486, 488; qtd. in NCOWFL Brief, 19–20. Schlesinger Library, Radcliffe Institute for Advanced Study, Harvard University, National Center on Women and Family Law records, 96-M105, Box 33.

165. *Onofre*, 486; qtd. in NCOWFL Brief, 27. Schlesinger Library, Radcliffe Institute for Advanced Study, Harvard University, National Center on Women and Family Law records, 96-M105, Box 33.

166. *Liberta*, 164–65.

167. Of the six other justices on the court, five concurred with Wachtler's opinion, and one did not participate.

168. Ibid., 161.

169. Holtzman Brief, 3–4. Schlesinger Library, Radcliffe Institute for Advanced Study, Harvard University, National Center on Women and Family Law records, 96-M105, Box 33.

170. *Liberta*, 163–64.

171. Ibid., 164.

172. NCOWFL Brief, 25. Schlesinger Library, Radcliffe Institute for Advanced Study, Harvard University, National Center on Women and Family Law records, 96-M105, Box 33.

173. *Liberta*, 164.

174. Ibid., 165.

175. Ibid., 165.

176. Ibid., 164.

177. The "marital harmony" argument, popular since at least the nineteenth century, had found expression in cases such as *Bradley* v. *State*, 1 Miss. (1 Walker) 158 (1824); *State* v. *Black*, 60 N.C. (Win.) 268 (1864); *State* v. *Rhodes*, 61 N.C. (Phil. Law) 453 (1868); and *State* v. *Oliver*, 70 N.C. 60 (1874), discussed in chapter two.

178. *Liberta*, 165.

179. *Williams v. State*, 494 So.2d 819 (1986).

180. 742 P.2d 775 (1987).

181. For more on the state-by-state reversals of marital rape exemptions, see Jill Elaine Hasday, "Contest and Consent: A Legal History of Marital Rape," *California Law Review* 88 (2000): 1373.

4. FROM *BRUNO* TO *GONZALES*

Patriarchal Privacy and the Failure to Protect

INTRODUCTION

While *People* v. *Liberta*[1] represented a considerable success for battered women bringing criminal cases, the movement's more common judicial victories during the 1980s took place in a different arena: civil litigation. The deluge of civil cases at this time represented a concerted strategy on the part of battered women's legal advocates. The growth of national organizations dedicated to addressing domestic violence throughout the 1970s had facilitated increased communication among victims and activists, who began to realize that the problem of police noninterference in "domestic disputes" was widespread and pervasive. Just as the movement was considering how best to address this problem, the US Supreme Court ruled, in 1978, that municipalities could be held liable in civil court for their actions.[2] This increased awareness of police negligence in cases of domestic abuse, along with the availability of a new remedy, contributed to a wave of civil suits targeted at the problem of police negligence. These kinds of suits also provided another legal option for battered women and their advocates to pursue when the criminal law proved inadequate.

Unlike criminal cases, in which the state served as prosecutor and plaintiff against batterers, these civil cases usually placed the state (or its agents) in the role of respondent. Battered women themselves were the plaintiffs in these cases, and police departments, most often, were the defendants.[3] In these lawsuits, often referred to as "Section 1983 cases," victims of domestic violence sought financial awards from police and other government entities based on Section 1983 of the Civil Rights Act of 1871, which provides a federal cause of action for individuals whose constitutional rights are violated by state actors.[4] Specifically, the constitutional bases of these suits lay primarily in the substantive due process and equal protection clauses of the Fourteenth Amendment and the notion that the state had a duty to protect battered women from violence. When police systematically refused to arrest abusive partners, they failed to protect battered women to the same extent that they protected men or victims of non-domestic (i.e., "stranger") violence.

At the root of this failure to protect battered women was the patriarchal notion of privacy: respect for the nuclear, familial home and the man's dominance therein. By challenging in court existing law-enforcement policies and procedures of noninterference in violent homes, battered women and their lawyers tested judicial notions of privacy, asking whether courts would refute or uphold the antiquated ideal of "a man's home as his castle." Thus, while these cases were primarily argued on equal protection or substantive due process grounds, they simultaneously attempted to chip away at patriarchal ideas about privacy and gender roles. In so doing, they articulated rights for women that superseded the presumed right of men to behave with impunity in their homes regardless of the welfare of others.

Two issues that would prove critical to many of these cases were the doctrines of "special relationship" and "qualified immunity." Unlike equal protection and due process, which are constitutional grounds on which to bring a wide range of cases, these are two doctrines developed through case law that help to define the responsibility of state actors to individuals. The first of these, special relationship, delineated the particular circumstances, such as the existence of a restraining order, in which police might owe battered women a special duty of protection. The second, qualified immunity, outlined those situations in which individual officers might be exempt from just such a responsibility. The courts' wide-ranging interpretations of these issues, discussed in further detail in this chapter, helped to shape the outcome of battered women's civil cases.

This chapter will explore the influence of these two issues while tracing the major developments of this period of civil litigation. I will begin with a brief examination of the precursors to this judicial trend, followed by a more detailed explanation of the first two landmark class-action civil lawsuits battered women brought against police: *Bruno v. Codd*[5] and *Scott v. Hart*.[6] After discussing the effects of *Bruno* and *Scott*, I will then turn to the individual lawsuits of the early- to mid-1980s (a fairly fruitful period for battered women plaintiffs), when the issues of special relationship and qualified immunity first became salient. The next section of the chapter will explore the ways in which these individual civil suits against police faced increasing difficulty in the courts during the latter half of the decade.

In 1989, the judicial landscape changed dramatically. In a landmark child abuse case entitled *DeShaney* v. *Winnebago County Department of Social Services,*[7] the United States Supreme Court declared that "a State's failure to protect an individual against private violence simply does not constitute a violation of the Due Process Clause,"[8] except in cases in which the individual was either physically in state custody at the time of the assault, directly exposed to increased danger by a state actor, or injured due to inadequate police training.[9] These new, strict requirements for seeking civil redress rendered future "failure to protect" litigation on behalf of battered women exceedingly difficult. In the next section of the chapter, I will examine the *DeShaney* case and its aftermath, paying particular attention to the judicial reasoning of the majority opinion and the dissents, as well as the implications of this case for battered women's civil litigation against police and other state entities.

In the decade that followed *DeShaney,* civil suits against police departments for their failure to protect battered women seemed all but impossible. In fact, it was not until 2002 that the movement had any indication that such suits might see real success again. In the Tenth Circuit's 2002 opinion in the case of *Gonzales* v. *Castle Rock,* the court accepted the plaintiff's argument that *DeShaney* had closed off only substantive, but not procedural, due process claims.[10] As such, the court found, battered women did have another option available to them, even after *DeShaney.* Unfortunately, the circuit court's opinion was not the final word in *Gonzales,* and the ultimate outcome of this case at the US Supreme Court level has come to signify a strengthening of the *DeShaney* ruling, and a bleak future indeed for battered women's civil litigation. The final section of this chapter therefore explores the *Gonzales* case and reflects on the future of battered women's civil suits against police and other state actors in light of its outcome.

The history of these civil cases provides a valuable vantage point on the utility of privacy for battered women's activists. The "failure to protect" cases were predicated in many ways on a paternalistic model of the state as protector. While this strategy was undeniably successful on several levels—bringing justice to individual victims or their surviving family members, sending a powerful message about domestic violence, and raising public awareness of the issue—it had some serious limitations, as well. Lawyers advocating for battered women in the post-*DeShaney,* post-*Gonzales* era have continued to find themselves in the difficult position of having to prove their clients worthy of state protection and state intervention in their homes. The significantly decreased chance of success with such suits today suggests that this model may have run its course. Instead, the greatest use of privacy for battered women may be its role in the assertion, *Liberta*-style, of an affirmative right to bodily integrity and self-determination.

SIGNIFICANCE OF THE "FAILURE TO PROTECT" ERA

The proliferation of the "failure to protect" cases during the 1980s indicated a critical moment in the battered women's movement. Primarily, this abundance of cases signaled that battered women's advocates of this era were specifically and deliberately pursuing a judicial strategy to combat domestic violence. A memo entitled "Action Programs in Domestic Violence" from the 1978 National Conference of the National Organization for Women, for example, suggested that one way to take action was the following:

> LITIGATION: Where there are laws, there is often a grave lack of enforcement. This is particularly true on an issue involving the privacy of the family. Perhaps you have a county prosecutor who refuses to take domestic violence cases—perhaps you should take HIM/HER to court.[11]

Using the courts to effect social change in the arena of domestic violence made good sense at this time, given the support that had recently become available with the formation of the National Battered Women's Law Project (NBWLP) in the mid-1970s. Unlike criminal cases (such as *Liberta*) that were initiated by an obvious violation of criminal law against a particular individual, each element of these civil cases had to be carefully formulated, from the selection of plaintiffs to the selection of judicial grounds on which to proceed. As a result, battered women's advocates bringing civil lawsuits could more easily shape their cases for the benefit of not only the named plaintiffs, but the movement itself.

In addition to combating domestic violence, some of the lawyer-activists who brought these cases were purposefully battling broader societal attitudes as well. Meeting minutes from an early litigation strategy session for *Bruno v. Codd*, one of the first two class-action suits against police, note that the "purpose and effect of the lawsuit was discussed. It was agreed that the underlying problem being confronted is sexism. . . . [W]e should not lose sight of the fact that the problem is larger than framed by our lawsuit."[12] The filing of class-action and other civil suits as a means of confronting sexism as well as domestic violence indicates that the battered women's movement was very deliberately choosing judicial paths to effect social change.

Having chosen this judicial strategy, battered women's activists pursued it vigorously. Shortly after the initiation of the *Bruno* and *Scott* lawsuits, scores of similar cases were brought on behalf of battered women around the country. The surge in activity between 1979 and 1989 was so vast that the NBWLP produced several publications tracking this new arena of battered women's litigation.[13] These reports detailed an array of civil suits against police and prosecutors in numerous states, including Alaska, Oregon, Connecticut, Texas, South Carolina, Tennessee, Michigan, Washington, Arizona, Kansas, Illinois, Pennsylvania, New York, and California. The multitude of similar cases brought within the same time period, combined with the communication afforded by the NBWLP, gave activists the opportunity to learn from and build on each other's strategies and successes. This series of cases, therefore, signaled a concerted, nationwide effort to use the judicial system to uphold the rights of battered women.

In addition, the nature of the rights being asserted at this time diverged significantly from those usually at issue in the more common criminal cases. Whereas criminal cases were brought by the state on charges of assault and battery or other violations of the state's criminal code, these civil cases were brought by and on behalf of battered women themselves. This formulation was particularly empowering for battered women, as it afforded them an active role in the pursuit of justice. As plaintiffs, women were able to move beyond the role of victim and participate as agents in the judicial process. These suits were brought on state or federal constitutional grounds, or both, enabling plaintiffs the opportunity to succeed and to effect change on several levels.

Most cases were brought on the basis of equal protection and/or due process clauses, via Section 1983. The specific nature of the claims varied, but most asserted that the plaintiffs were being denied the equal protection of the laws in some way. Some claims were based solely on gender, arguing that women did not enjoy the full protection of the laws relative to men. Others included a racial analysis, noting that battered women of color were not protected equally relative to white women and men. Others claimed that battered women received less protection than non-battered women, or than all victims of non-domestic crimes. By asserting the battered woman's right to equal protection of the laws, particularly with regard to her gender and her race, these suits emphasized an affirmative right that extended beyond basic criminal remedies. Likewise, by seeking financial damages as well as policy changes from state entities, these cases implicitly urged courts to recognize the economic component of domestic abuse as well as the intrinsic value of its victims. The resulting financial awards provided a crucial affirmation of women's agency, serving as a formal, tangible recognition of women's suffering.

Many of the civil cases brought on behalf of battered women during this era achieved success in the courtroom. In some cases, courts flatly rejected police officers' defenses that they should be immune from such litigation by virtue of the discretionary judgment necessary to fulfilling their official roles.[14] At other times, courts affirmed battered women's equal protection and due process claims, finding, for a variety of reasons, that police officers did have a specific affirmative duty to protect battered women, and that they could therefore be held liable under §1983 when they failed to provide this protection.[15] The most highly publicized of these cases was *Thurman* v. *City of Torrington*,[16] in which a Connecticut District Court found that city officials and police officers "are under an affirmative duty to take reasonable measures to protect the personal safety of . . . women whose personal safety is threatened by individuals with whom they have or have had a domestic relationship," and that "failure to perform this duty would constitute a denial of equal protection of the laws."[17] This case also resulted in an unusual degree of financial remuneration for the plaintiff, with a federal jury eventually awarding Thurman significant compensatory damages.

While several of these suits succeeded in court and resulted in financial awards to plaintiffs, the success of this strategy could also be gauged by the degree to which they raised awareness about the problem. Local media, for example, often provided supportive coverage even to those cases whose outcomes did not strictly favor the battered women plaintiffs, thereby generating a great deal of publicity for the issue of domestic violence and engendering public pressure on police departments and other state entities.[18] At the same time, such cases served as models for other lawyer-activists around the country. As the National Center on Women and Family Law (NCOWFL) began tracking the strategies and judicial successes and failures of each case, battered women's advocates were able to more effectively tailor and refine their approaches to subsequent cases.

Neither of the two major class-action suits that ushered in this era—*Bruno* v. *Codd* and *Scott* v. *Hart*—achieved unequivocal success in the courtroom. The damages plaintiffs sought were not awarded, and the courts, for the most part, did not accept the arguments of the plaintiffs. Yet the settlements in which both cases ended ultimately provided the critical first steps toward improving police departments' policies and procedures regarding domestic violence. After the filing of these and similar cases prompted modifications to official procedures, battered women's advocates succeeded in effecting similar policy changes without litigation in several cities, including Atlanta, Chicago, New Haven, and San Francisco.[19]

At the same time, lawyers and activists were aware that such developments, while undeniably important, would never solve the problem entirely. They noted that "legal advocacy [was not] sufficient by itself either to combat woman battering or completely aid one woman."[20] Success within the courtroom would need to be accompanied by attitudinal change. Laurie Woods, Executive Director of the NCOWFL, observed that "the attitudes which originally gave rise to the practice of arrest-avoidance in wife-assault cases are independently and deeply ingrained in members of the police force. They are not likely to be eliminated by a mere change in regulations."[21] Nonetheless, such policy changes were a significant first step in altering police attitudes and practice, and the lawsuits which gave rise to them also allowed for compliance measures, including monitoring by battered women's advocates. Thus, cases that appeared unsuccessful by purely judicial measures often served the larger goals of the movement to some extent.

BATTERED WOMEN'S CIVIL LITIGATION IN THE PRE-*DESHANEY* ERA

PRECURSORS TO BRUNO AND SCOTT

While this civil litigation on behalf of battered women proliferated during the 1980s, it did not originate then. In fact, several similar cases had achieved various degrees of success in prior decades. As early as 1956, for example, the Supreme Court of New York held the city of Watertown liable for the injuries of a battered woman and the death of her husband as a result of the negligent actions of the city's police force.[22] In this case, the Watertown police had prior knowledge that the husband had threatened to kill his wife and others with his unlicensed gun, for which he did not have a permit. The police nevertheless returned the gun to the husband, thus enabling him to use it to shoot his wife and himself shortly thereafter. Eight years later, a California court held that a municipality could be liable when its police department failed to inform a battered woman, as promised, when her abusive husband had been released from jail.[23] In several other early cases, courts found potential liabilities for those municipalities whose police had failed to provide adequate protection to battered women who had previously reported domestic threats and assaults,[24] including municipalities that had withdrawn existing police protection[25] or that had released batterers from police custody despite the batterers' threats of murder.[26] These early cases, still too isolated and few in number to signify a cohesive strategy for battered women's legal advocacy, nevertheless paved the way for the surge of civil litigation that was to come. Having succeeded in various courtrooms, these cases precipitated the next major judicial strategy of the battered women's movement.

THE CLASS-ACTION LAWSUITS: BRUNO AND SCOTT

The first indication that the movement's lawyer-activists were using civil litigation as a coordinated judicial strategy came in the form of two class-action lawsuits filed almost simultaneously on opposite coasts: *Scott v. Hart* in California, and *Bruno v. Codd* in New York. Both cases were filed in late 1976, as the battered women's attorneys for both cases were in contact with each other.[27] While they differed from each other in several significant ways, both cases proved instructive to battered women's advocates and opened the door for the series of civil litigation that would soon follow.

Scott v. Hart was filed in Oakland, California in October, 1976. The class-action suit named five battered women plaintiffs, four African-American and one white, on behalf of all women in Oakland who had received inadequate police response to domestic violence. The original complaint details a slew of offenses committed against these five women by the Oakland police, including failure to respond to a domestic assault for which one woman was hospitalized; forcing a female victim to leave her own home after an assault (out of refusal to believe that she lived and paid rent there); encouraging assailants to press charges against victims; falsely informing battered women that they had no legal recourse; threatening to arrest victims; refusing to arrest batterers; failing, despite their promises to do so, to follow up on a victim's attempt to make a citizen's arrest;[28] and providing a batterer with keys to his victim's home and vehicle.[29] In this last case, officers were called to a hospital where the plaintiff was taken after her husband severely beat and threatened to kill her. After locating the assailant, police refused to arrest him, instead providing him the keys to the plaintiff's home and car. Thus deprived of transportation, the plaintiff was forced to walk home from the hospital at 4:00 a.m. Police refused her request for a ride home by noting that they "were not a taxi service" and suggested that in the event the husband did in fact wait at her home to carry out his threats to kill her, she should call them again. The defendants named in the *Scott* suit were George Hart, chief of the Oakland Police Department (OPD), and the Oakland City Council, the governing body responsible for establishing city policy and overseeing the OPD.[30]

The *Scott* case was brought on both state and federal grounds, thus allowing the plaintiffs the flexibility of attempting to prove their case in several different ways simultaneously. On the federal level, plaintiffs first charged that their equal protection rights under the Fourteenth Amendment were being violated, given that assaulted black women were not protected equally relative to assaulted white women and white men, and that women assaulted at home were not protected equally relative to victims of nondomestic assaults. They alleged that the inaction of Hart, the OPD, and the city council amounted to an unconstitutional policy actionable under Section 1983.[31] They also charged that the OPD, a federally funded program, unlawfully perpetuated a policy of race and sex discrimination.[32] On the state level, plaintiffs charged the OPD with breaching their duty to arrest as established in the California Penal Code.[33]

Two months later, in December 1976, battered women and their advocates in New York City filed a similar suit against the New York City Police Department (NYPD), the New York City Department of Probation, and the clerks of the New York Family Court. *Bruno* v. *Codd* contained twelve named plaintiffs, all battered women, suing on behalf of all women in New York City who were similarly situated with regard to domestic violence.[34] The plaintiffs claimed that the NYPD consistently denied protection to victims of domestic abuse on the basis of their marital status, a practice readily admitted by individual officers and disclosed in the New York Police Patrol Guide.[35] Like the *Scott* plaintiffs, they charged police with refusing to arrest assailants and providing battered women with misinformation about their options for legal recourse.[36] The *Bruno* plaintiffs also accused police of overtly favoring batterers at the scene of domestic crimes by verbally supporting abusive husbands with such statements as, "Maybe if I beat my wife, she'd act right too."[37]

In addition to their complaints against the NYPD, the *Bruno* plaintiffs charged both the department of probation and the family court clerks with effectively preventing battered women from obtaining legal recourse through pro se orders of protection.[38] As Laurie Woods, an attorney for the plaintiffs and the future Executive Director of NCOWFL, explained, it was crucial to confront all three entities (the NYPD, the department of probation and the family court clerks) in one suit. Plaintiffs' affidavits revealed that each agency tended to shift responsibility for the protection of battered women onto the other two agencies, resulting in a circle of blame and no real protection for victims. As Woods explained, the attorneys observed

> a pervasive pattern of police sending women to family court, and of probation and clerk officials at the family court sending women to the police. Employees in each agency tended to blame those in the other for the battered woman's inability to get protection. It became apparent that we would have to join all defendants in one suit in order to prevent any one agency from attempting to escape responsibility for its own practices by pointing the finger of guilt at non-party agencies.[39]

For this reason, the *Bruno* plaintiffs named the city and state directors of probation and the chief clerk of family court as well as the police commissioners as defendants in their suit.

Unlike *Scott*, which was brought in federal district court on both state and federal grounds, *Bruno* was brought in state court and made no federal claims.[40] Instead, the *Bruno* plaintiffs charged that police patterns of failure to respond to domestic violence calls, failure to arrest abusive husbands, and failure to notify battered wives of their right to make citizens' arrests were violations of both state and city law. These laws, including the New York City Charter and Code and the New York State Criminal Law, require police officers to enforce the law and to arrest where "reasonable cause" exists, but do not authorize them to use marital status as a basis for denying that protection to one group of victims.[41] Additionally, the *Bruno* plaintiffs charged the department of probation and family court defendants with denying their right of access to court as outlined in the State Family Court Act and the city rules governing the department of probation and the family court.[42]

In addition to the differing legal grounds on which the cases were brought, the selection of plaintiffs also differed radically between the two cases. Because New York Family Court did not have jurisdiction over unmarried battered women, all of the *Bruno* plaintiffs were, by necessity, married women. The *Scott* lawyers, unrestricted by such jurisdictional issues, ensured that their plaintiffs covered a range of marital situations, including married, unmarried and living with boyfriends, and married but in the midst of divorce. In addition, while the *Bruno* case did not mention race or ethnicity,[43] the *Scott* lawyers ensured that their named plaintiffs included African-American as well as white women, a decision that only seemed natural to plaintiffs' lawyers Pauline Gee and Eva Jefferson Paterson, given the racial diversity of the population they were serving.[44] In *Scott*, the African-American plaintiffs initially sued on behalf of all black women in Oakland who had received inadequate police protection relative to their white counterparts.[45]

Interestingly, this race-based claim was quickly dropped. As Gee explains, she and Paterson decided to abandon the racial claim in their amended complaint in response to feedback they had received from women in the community. Some of this feedback came from white women in higher-income neighborhoods, who thanked them for bringing the suit and asked them to broaden the class, given that domestic violence affected them as well, and they too were in need of police protection. As a result, the amended complaint continued to call attention to the race of the named plaintiffs, but did not explicitly bring any racial discrimination claims.[46]

Gee later explained that having a diverse range of plaintiffs was not only meant to represent accurately the population of women, but served another important function as well. She urged attorneys bringing similar suits to "choose named plaintiffs who represent a cross-section of society in terms of ethnicity and socio-economic background to dispel the myth that domestic violence only occurs in the low income and minority population."[47]

While Gee's observation about the importance of racial and class diversity among plaintiffs had not been specifically articulated by the *Bruno* lawyers, the underlying premise of her statement—that such suits could be used as educational tools—certainly was. In fact, lawyers for both cases approached the suits not merely as a means of achieving justice for their plaintiffs, but also as a means of raising awareness about domestic violence. As Gee observed, *Scott* was filed "with two primary goals in mind: (1) to obtain effective police protection for battered women and (2) to educate not only the criminal justice system, but also the public as to the problem of domestic violence."[48] The *Bruno* attorneys concurred. Marjory Fields, currently a justice on the civil branch of the New York State Supreme Court, was one of the six attorneys who represented the *Bruno* plaintiffs. Fields recalled that *Bruno* was "part of our initial attempt to get judges and legislatures to look at [domestic violence] as a valid legal issue, [and] to listen to women the same as other crime victims."[49] Minutes from a litigation strategy session held five months before the filing of the *Bruno* suit observe that "the lawsuit has potential for improving the [problems of domestic violence and sexism]. It would publicize the problem, educate persons as to the extent and the nature of the problem."[50] Likewise, discussing the role of affidavits in the attorneys' preparation of the *Bruno* suit, Laurie Woods recalled, "We felt that these statements were important for two reasons. First, as a technical matter, [and] [m]ore broadly . . . to address the myths and misconceptions about battered women. . . . This was designed to educate the court from the outset by indirectly dispelling certain notions about battered women."[51] From the beginning, then, the lawyers advocating for battered women in both cases clearly understood and intended that the influence of these suits would extend far beyond the courtroom. Rather than pursuing strictly judicial victories, they explicitly planned that these cases would serve as vehicles to change the thinking of police, judges, and the general public about the problem of domestic violence.

To that end, both sets of attorneys garnered plenty of public attention for these suits. Working closely with shelter workers and other battered women's activists, they continually challenged the notion of domestic violence as a private issue. The *Bruno* attorneys, for example, held several press conferences related to the filing of the suit and maintained close contact with various representatives from print, radio, and television media. Both prior to and following the filing of the initial complaint, the *Bruno* attorneys shared media contacts with each other, solicited publicity help from the National Organization for

Women (NOW), and continually invited reporters to cover the issue.[52] Indeed, Marjory Fields initiated such publicity a full two years before *Bruno* was filed, when she was quoted in a *New York Times* article addressing the need for a stronger police response to domestic violence—one of the first stories in any major media outlet addressing the problem of domestic abuse at all.[53] Similarly, the NCOWFL issued a triumphant press release entitled, "Batterers Beware! Oakland Police Department to Afford Better Police Protection to Battered Women" after the settlement of the *Scott* suit, outlining in detail the terms of the settlement and the ways in which police would be held accountable.[54] By continually and deliberately bringing domestic violence into the public realm, these lawyer-activists were able to challenge the cultural notion of domestic violence as a strictly private matter, while simultaneously educating the public about the issue and informing battered women about the new level of protection they could and should expect from state entities.

Both the *Bruno* and *Scott* cases were terminated by agreement between the plaintiffs and the defendants:[55] *Scott* resulted in a settlement decree, and *Bruno* concluded with a consent judgment.[56] While the technical nature of these documents differed, their content was remarkably similar. Both settlements barred police from engaging in arrest-avoidance policies with regard to crimes of domestic violence.[57] Specifically, they required the police to treat domestic violence as a criminal act, by responding quickly to calls for assistance and proceeding with making arrests in domestic situations just as they would in crimes of stranger violence.[58] They also obligated officers to inform battered women of their right to make citizens' arrests and to help them to pursue those arrests when requested to do so.[59] Furthermore, both agreements required explicit changes in the written police policy that, in both New York and Oakland, had encouraged officers to engage in mediation between victim and perpetrator as a means of avoiding arrest.[60] Instead of mediation, the change in policy mandated by these settlements required police to presume that arrest was indeed an appropriate response to domestic violence, and that it was required if the facts at the scene established probable cause.[61] This aspect of the agreements was immeasurably significant, for it went to the very heart of the police attitudes (and the resulting lack of protection) that had inspired the lawsuits. As Woods observed, "mediation is an invitation to the police officer to discourage the victim from pursuing her legal remedies and often to encourage future violence."[62] By mandating arrest instead of mediation in cases of domestic abuse, these provisions directly challenged existing notions that abusive men were immune from state sanction within the private sphere of the home.

In addition to requiring police to respond quickly and arrest as necessary, both settlements also forbade officers from using their most common excuses for refusing to arrest batterers. First, the relationship of the perpetrator to the victim had long been used as a justification for inaction. In the *Scott* lawsuit, for example, plaintiffs reported having to misrepresent their abuse as stranger violence in order to get police to respond at all.[63] Both agreements specifically prohibited the practice of distinguishing between domestic and stranger assaults when determining probable cause for arrest.[64] Second, the victim's previous history of seeking or not seeking police assistance for domestic violence often prejudiced officers' decisions to arrest or not.[65] According to the settlements, a woman's previous calls to police for assistance or decisions whether or not to secure orders of protection could not determine police response to a new incidence of violence.[66] The agreements also prevented police from considering either the victim's stated or perceived preference to pursue the matter in a particular court (*Bruno* only),[67] or the perpetrator's promises to cease the violence (*Scott* only),[68] when assessing probable cause.

By eliminating each of these justifications, the settlements placed the responsibility for punishing batterers, and condemning domestic violence, in the hands of the state. This shift in responsibility represented both a symbolic and a practical departure from the pre-*Bruno* and -*Scott* days, in which battered women were left to defend themselves from assault, often with little or no assistance from local law enforcement. At the same time, by insisting that batterers receive no further protections or consideration than other assailants, these provisions helped to support the characterization of domestic violence as a crime deserving of punishment, not merely a private, family matter unworthy of state intervention.

Finally, both settlements included provisions regarding compliance with their terms. The *Scott* agreement, for example, outlined numerous measures required of the city of Oakland and the OPD. Because the OPD was required to change its police training to reflect the terms of the settlement decree, police agreed to develop, with plaintiffs, a domestic violence training protocol with which to educate current and future officers.[69] Additionally, the OPD worked together with a coalition of plaintiffs and other battered women's advocates to educate judges and district attorneys about the proper handling of domestic violence cases.[70] The *Scott* settlement also required the city of Oakland to apply for federal funding to obtain support services for victims of domestic abuse.[71] The *Bruno* consent judgment, perhaps because of its higher level of judicial enforceability, provided fewer specific instructions regarding compliance. It did, however, require the NYPD to amend all of its official documents, including regulations, memoranda, and training materials, to reflect the terms of the agreement.[72] The agreement further obligated the police commissioner and his successors to inform all NYPD employees of its terms.[73] Additionally, the document mandated that any complaint lodged by a battered woman against an officer for violating the terms of the consent judgment must be investigated and addressed by a supervising officer as soon as possible.[74]

Ultimately, while neither *Bruno* nor *Scott* achieved unqualified success in the courtroom—the plaintiffs were not awarded the damages they sought, and both cases were settled by agreement—their significance to the battered women's movement should not be underestimated. Not only did these cases yield considerable short- and long-term results, but they also established a significant model for subsequent litigation, thereby initiating an era of litigation activism within the movement. Together, *Bruno* and *Scott* signaled the first truly coordinated litigation strategy within the movement, as the lawyers on both coasts shared information and resources with each other and with the NCOWFL.[75] Both were designed to be "impact cases," intended not just to achieve greater legal protection for battered women, but also to raise awareness among police, judges, and the general public about domestic violence and gender inequality.[76]

The long-term effects of the cases have been substantial. At the most practical, local level, the settlements that the *Bruno* and *Scott* plaintiffs reached with police departments dramatically improved the legal protection available to the battered women of Oakland and New York City. In particular, the accountability provisions included in the agreements and the monitoring efforts undertaken by battered women's advocates helped to ensure that the litigation produced genuine and lasting procedural changes. These efforts then resulted in the development of model police protocols that were eventually replicated across the nation, whether as a result of similar litigation or in response to pressure from battered women's advocates.[77]

In addition to securing increased physical protection for battered women, this litigation also effected change of a less tangible, though no less important, nature. The publicity generated by these lawsuits—including some of the very first major newspaper coverage about the scope of the problem of domestic violence[78]—did much to raise awareness among the general public. In addition, anecdotal evidence in the months following the settlements suggested that the suits had begun to affect the attitudes and behaviors of batterers as well as police. Woods observed that, following the *Bruno* settlement,

> [local activists] received telephone calls from women informing them that their husbands had stopped beating them; conversations with clients indicate that a few certain precincts are making arrests and that some officers are informing women that while they could not help them last month, they can now in response to the consent judgment. Conversations also indicate that some husbands have ceased their beating as a consequence of reading about the consent judgment in the newspapers . . . ; others because they have been arrested pursuant to the terms of the agreement.[79]

Thus, while the lawyer-activists involved in these suits were certainly aware of their inability to mandate attitudinal changes via litigation—a natural limitation of the judicial system—it seems clear that the combination of the lawsuits and the ensuing publicity yielded results that extended beyond mere policy changes.

Overall, the *Bruno* and *Scott* suits suggested—on both formal, procedural levels and informal, attitudinal levels—that domestic violence was not simply a private, family matter. By demanding police intervention in violent homes, this litigation directly challenged existing notions that abusive men were immune from state sanction within the private sphere of the home. In fact, the rejection of domestic privacy as a refuge from criminal punishment and the refusal to privilege the marital home as the domain of masculine rule at all costs were at the core of these suits. The impact of this litigation strategy would be felt for years to come, as battered women's advocates proceeded to pursue *Bruno*- and *Scott*-inspired suits for the next ten years.

CIVIL LITIGATION IN THE AFTERMATH OF BRUNO AND SCOTT

The decade following the highly publicized *Bruno* and *Scott* settlements was initially marked by several additional class-action suits in other parts of the country that resulted in settlements similar to those in New York and Oakland.[80] However, class-action lawsuits also contained several inherent disadvantages, including the difficulty involved in securing class-action status, the extra time and resources demanded by such large-scale suits,[81] and the potential of such suits to establish negative judicial precedent for other plaintiffs if they failed.[82] Perhaps because of these potential pitfalls, battered women and their advocates turned increasingly toward individual lawsuits during the 1980s. This development within the movement also reflected a larger national trend of decreasing reliance on class-action lawsuits at this time.[83]

While the level of success attained by the plaintiffs varied greatly in these cases, the outcomes did exhibit a chronological pattern (see Table 4.1: Success of Battered Women's Civil Suits Against Police). In general, those cases that were tried earlier in the decade were decided more favorably, with the most notable and well-publicized financial successes for battered women peaking in the middle of the decade. The latter part of the 1980s was less kind to battered women, as plaintiffs began losing most of their cases in the two years leading up to the *DeShaney* case. *DeShaney*, then, represented the culmination of these losses and was a major judicial defeat for battered women.

While all of these civil cases of the 1980s were brought against local police departments and/or prosecutors, the specific grounds for the proposed remedies varied: while many were brought as federal Section 1983 claims, several were brought on state grounds. Almost all of the cases charged that police failure to protect the plaintiffs from domestic violence (or, in some cases, prosecutors' failure to pursue their cases) violated their rights to equal protection and/or substantive due process. Finally, the outcomes of most of these lawsuits ultimately hinged on at least one of two critical issues: "special relationship" and "qualified immunity," the former of which would factor prominently in the *DeShaney* case at the decade's end.

The basic elements of a Section 1983 claim include consideration of two questions. First, was the person responsible for the offending conduct acting under color of state law? In other words, was the responsible party acting in an official capacity as a representative of the state? Second, did the conduct in question deprive the plaintiff of rights, privileges, or immunities guaranteed by the constitution or laws of the US? While these questions pertain specifically to federal Section 1983 claims, very similar issues govern battered women's state claims against police, as well. Claims based on state law generally referred to state statutes such as Oregon's 1977 Abuse Prevention Act, which included provisions for warrantless arrest based on probable cause for the violation of a protective order.[84] A state case might consider, for example, whether police officers who knowingly failed to enforce such a statute could be held liable for the harm that befell the plaintiff as a result.[85] The civil cases brought by battered women during this era, therefore, whether on federal or state grounds, generally revolved around the issues of who should be held responsible for the offending actions, and to what extent those actions violated statutory or constitutional rights.

For judges deciding these cases, answering these two questions involved consideration of several factors. One of the most significant of these factors was the "special relationship" test. The special relationship concept originated in a series of cases that questioned whether the due process clause of the Constitution implied an affirmative duty on behalf of police officers to protect the public. These cases explored the contours of this duty by examining levels of police responsibility in a variety of situations not related to domestic violence. In one case, for example, a black man had been beaten to death by a gang of white youths. Plaintiffs claimed that police were responsible for generally failing to protect black people on the public streets, an argument that the court rejected.[86] In another case, however, officers who witnessed but did not intervene in a brutal beating were found liable under Section 1983 for failing to perform the duties of their office.[87] As this line of cases developed, courts agreed that police could not be held liable for all citizens' injuries under Section 1983 unless police actions (or failure to act) constituted a specific breach of their stated duties that could be shown to have directly caused the injury.

Eventually, this line of judicial reasoning was narrowed even further, as judges began to suggest that state actors could only be held liable for injury to those who were directly in state custody, such as prisoners and patients in state mental institutions—in essence, only when the state had a "custodial relationship" with particular individuals.[88] Shortly thereafter, courts were asked to consider whether child and family services agencies could be held liable for the deaths of children whose families they were ostensibly supervising. Because these deaths occurred in private homes, but under the supervision of an agency meant to prevent such incidents, courts jettisoned the overly restrictive custodial relationship model. They replaced it with the special relationship model, on the grounds that

> the due process clause of the Constitution provides no basis for imposing liability . . . on state officers who either negligently or even recklessly facilitate the criminal actions of a third party, absent some special relationship between the victim and . . . the state officer.[89]

This special relationship approach allowed for broader interpretation of the due process clause than the custodial model had. Courts considered a variety of factors to determine the presence of a special relationship, including

> 1) whether the state created or assumed a custodial relationship toward the plaintiff; 2) whether the state was aware of a specific risk of harm to the plaintiff; 3) whether the state affirmatively placed the plaintiff in a position of danger; or 4) whether the state affirmatively committed itself to the protection of the plaintiff.[90]

This model, which allowed for the liability of child and family services agencies in child abuse cases, could also apply to police officers in domestic violence cases.

The second potentially mitigating factor in the determination of Section 1983 claims was the concept of "qualified immunity." The qualified immunity doctrine takes into consideration that state agents such as police officers must perform certain discretionary functions as part of their official duties (for example, they must exercise discretion when determining probable cause for arrest, deciding how to proceed in a volatile situation, etc.).[91] Given the inherently discretionary nature of some aspects of the job, this doctrine provides that state actors are immune from liability for damages incurred while performing those discretionary functions.[92] This immunity from liability applies only to those specific actions undertaken as discretionary functions, and only when those actions do not violate "clearly established statutory or constitutional rights of which a reasonable person would have known."[93]

Although this potential for immunity was subject to significant restrictions, it nonetheless represented a considerable obstacle for battered women bringing civil suits against police. Throughout the 1980s, courts considered questions of immunity and police liability in a variety of arenas, including, but certainly not limited to, issues of domestic violence.[94] In addition to the domestic violence cases discussed here, these cases also considered subject matter ranging from duties of police at the scene of traffic accidents[95] to police obligation to protect a rape victim from future assaults from the same assailant[96] to police role in preventing a shootout at a bar,[97] and more.[98]

In the course of these deliberations, judges developed several standards to determine which duties could be considered discretionary and therefore deserving of immunity. At one point, courts noted that officials could be granted qualified immunity "if reasonable officials in the defendants' position at the relevant time could have believed, in light of clearly established law, that their conduct comported with established legal principles."[99] In other words, this standard granted immunity based on what the average or "reasonable" officer would have done in a given situation based on his or her understanding of currently existing law. Ultimately, courts developed an even broader application of this doctrine, leaving only a few instances in which an officer might *not* be granted qualified immunity.[100] In a reflection of the increasingly conservative judicial tenor of the Reagan years, the discretion and immunity afforded to police officers increased as the 1980s progressed.[101] As a result, by requiring plaintiffs to meet such difficult standards, the qualified immunity doctrine provided a potent defense for police officers toward the end of the decade, making Section 1983 cases all the more challenging for battered women.

Despite the potential difficulties posed by the special relationship and qualified immunity doctrines, several courts issued rulings favorable to battered women, most often in the earlier years of the decade. In 1983, the Supreme Court of Oregon found that police officers who violated that state's Abuse Prevention Act by failing to enforce an order of protection could be held liable for the harm that befell battered women and their children as a result.[102] The court flatly rejected the officers' defense of discretionary immunity, noting that the language of the statute mandated a course of action so clearly that it left no room for discretion. As such, the *Nearing* v. *Weaver* court found that the officers undoubtedly had "a duty specifically towards these plaintiffs,"[103] and reversed the lower court's summary judgment as a result.

Two years later, a district court in Pennsylvania ruled in favor of the administrator of the estate of a woman who had been killed by her batterer.[104] The plaintiff in *Dudosh* v. *Allentown* brought a federal Section 1983 claim based primarily on the denial of Kathleen Dudosh's equal protection and due process rights. The court weighed Dudosh's repeated requests for police assistance heavily when determining the existence of a special relationship. In addition, the opinion noted that the protective order secured by Dudosh and served by the police gave the defendants notice of the batterer's violent conduct and "placed an affirmative duty upon the police department to protect the deceased."[105] Given these facts, the court asserted that

> [T]he deceased was not just a member of the public at large who through fate and misfortune becomes a victim of crime in a situation over which the police had no control or notice. She was a specific individual who had been subjected to particularized assaults and threats of murder. For these reasons, . . . we conclude that a special relationship did exist between the deceased and the defendants such that would vest in Ms. Dudosh a right to adequate police protection.[106]

This special relationship, the court concluded, rendered the plaintiffs' equal protection and due process claims viable and subject to relief under Section 1983. Both the *Nearing* and the *Dudosh* courts, therefore, found that protective orders secured by the plaintiffs established an affirmative duty on the part of police to protect them from domestic violence. These opinions plainly signaled that battered women, having deliberately sought legal protection, deserved the full benefit of that protection.[107]

Even in cases that did not primarily turn on issues of special relationship or immunity, courts accepted evidence of police inaction as validation of battered women's equal protection arguments. Police defendants in the 1986 case of *Bartalone* v. *Berrien*[108] had promised plaintiff Sandra Bartalone that they would arrest her assailant husband, but never even attempted to do so.[109] Several days later, the husband threatened Sandra with a shotgun at her workplace; in the ensuing struggle, Sandra was shot in the leg and abdomen.[110] A Michigan district court accepted her argument that the police denied her equal protection "based on her sex, or marital status, or both,"[111] noting that "if a police officer is under a duty to protect persons within the area of his authority, he must do so on a fair and equal basis. The equal protection clause requires him to perform his duties without intentionally discriminating on an irrational basis."[112]

Likewise, in the Tenth Circuit case of *Watson* v. *Kansas City*,[113] plaintiff Nancy Watson detailed a lengthy history of police failure to arrest her abusive husband—himself a police officer—despite her repeated requests for his arrest and the copious physical evidence of his violence toward her. These refusals to arrest were often accompanied by police comments such as, "If you ever call the police again, I will see to it that you are arrested and you'll never see those . . . kids again,"[114] and (after an incident in which her husband beat, stabbed, and raped her) remarks to the effect that "the whole situation was her fault because she had married [him]."[115] Citing the *Bartalone* opinion, the circuit court found Watson's evidence sufficient to support her claim that Kansas City unconstitutionally provided less protection to victims of domestic violence than to victims of stranger violence.[116] By affirming these equal protection claims, opinions such as *Bartalone* and *Watson* gave credence to the concept that the battered women's movement had been promoting for years: namely, that the privacy of the home should not protect violent crimes from punishment.[117]

Two cases that made this point more definitively and successfully than any of their predecessors were *Thurman* v. *Torrington*[118] and *Sorichetti* v. *New York*.[119] The substantial financial awards and the resulting publicity associated with these cases, both decided in the mid-1980s, distinguished them as landmark victories for the battered women's movement as well as for the plaintiffs themselves. In the first case, plaintiff Tracey Thurman brought a federal Section 1983 equal protection case against the city of Torrington, Connecticut for their failure to provide equal police protection to victims of domestic violence (relative to victims of non-domestic violence). She demonstrated an eight-month-long record of failure on the part of the Torrington city police to respond to her requests for protection from her violent husband, Charles Thurman. This detailed history revealed repeated police refusals to help her obtain a criminal warrant against her husband, numerous refusals to arrest (or even attempt to locate) her husband even after he had violated a restraining order, and failure to apprehend the husband even after watching him physically injure her.[120] The incident for which Charles Thurman was finally arrested took place in June 1983. After repeatedly stabbing Tracey in the chest, neck, and throat, Charles was holding a bloody knife when police arrived at the scene. In their presence, he kicked Tracey in the head twice, dropped their infant son onto her bloody body, and continued to verbally threaten her, while police refused to intervene. As she lay on a stretcher being lifted into an ambulance, Charles approached her again. Only at that point was he finally arrested and taken into custody.[121]

While Charles received a twenty-year prison term for attempted murder, Tracey remains partially paralyzed and permanently disfigured as a result of his assaults. Her lawsuit succeeded in two important ways: first, a jury awarded her $2.3 million from the city in compensatory damages, the largest settlement yet received by a battered woman plaintiff in this type of suit. In addition, Thurman's case produced some of the most strident judicial support for battered women in all of the civil cases. Ruling on a 1984 motion by the City of Torrington to dismiss the case, Senior District Judge Blumenfeld noted,

> City officials and police officers are under an affirmative duty to preserve law and order, and to protect the personal safety of persons in the community. . . . This duty

applies equally to women whose personal safety is threatened by individuals with whom they have or have had a domestic relationship as well as to all other persons whose personal safety is threatened, including women not involved in domestic relationships. . . . Failure to perform this duty would constitute a denial of equal protection of the laws.[122]

By affirming the equal protection claim, Judge Blumenfeld also provided significant judicial support for the notion that women deserve protection from violence regardless of whether it is committed in public or in private.

Furthermore, Blumenfeld stated that the relationship of a crime victim to her assailant should have no bearing on the conduct of responding police officers. Citing *Bruno* v. *Codd*, he reiterated that police inaction on the basis of marital status was entirely unacceptable. In addition, he emphatically rejected the persistent argument that failure to act might promote "domestic harmony" (aided, perhaps, by the sheer incongruity of discussing domestic harmony in light of multiple stab wounds):

A man is not allowed to physically abuse or endanger a woman merely because he is her husband. Concomitantly, a police officer may not knowingly refrain from interference in such violence, and may not "automatically decline to make an arrest simply because the assaulter and his victim are married to each other" (*Bruno* 1976, at 1049). . . . Such inaction on the part of the officer is a denial of the equal protection of the laws.

In addition, any notion that defendants' practice can be justified as a means of promoting domestic harmony by refraining from interference in marital disputes, has no place in the case at hand.[123]

This forceful opinion regarding the rights of battered women and the obligations of police officers was a substantial victory for battered women seeking redress via the equal protection doctrine.

Unlike the *Thurman* case, *Sorichetti* v. *City of New York* was not a federal action; the case was brought in state court in response to the city's violation of a state family court act.[124] In addition, the violent acts around which this case centered were committed against an infant rather than an adult woman. (The case was brought by Josephine Sorichetti on behalf of her infant daughter Dina and herself.) Nonetheless, much of the *Sorichetti* case also depended greatly on the assailant's history of violence against his wife, and its outcome, like that of *Thurman*, held considerable promise for future battered women's litigation. The facts of the case detail Frank Sorichetti's history of violence toward his wife Josephine, as well as her repeated attempts to seek help. In November 1975, an order of protection that Josephine had secured was extended for one year, granting Frank weekly visitation rights with Dina.[125] The first such visit resulted in the violence that formed the basis of the lawsuit.

Immediately after picking Dina up, Frank directly threatened Josephine's life, stating, "You, I'm going to kill you."[126] Josephine reported this threat in person at the police station, showing the officer a copy of the order, recounting Frank's violent history, and urging the officer to arrest him. The officer responded that there was nothing he could do and sent her home.[127] The next day, Josephine returned to the station, where, fearing for Dina's safety, she repeatedly begged and demanded that Frank be arrested. Officers repeatedly told her to "just wait" but took no action, even after the time had passed when Frank was obligated by the order of protection to return Dina to her mother.[128] An hour after this deadline had passed, Frank's sister found him passed out on her apartment floor, having just attacked Dina brutally enough to send her into a coma. The injuries Dina sustained as a result of this attack resulted in a forty-day period of hospitalization and permanent disability. Specifically, Frank attacked the infant repeatedly with a fork, knife, and screwdriver and attempted to saw off her leg.[129]

Josephine Sorichetti initiated her civil suit against the city and the police after this last assault. Ultimately, like Tracey Thurman, the *Sorichetti* plaintiffs won significant financial awards: Dina was awarded two million dollars,[130] and Josephine was awarded forty thousand dollars, from the city defendants.[131] Ruling on appeal to uphold these awards, the Supreme Court of New York concluded that the City of New York (via the NYPD) had an affirmative duty to protect Josephine and Dina owing to the special relationship that existed between the City and the plaintiffs.[132] While the court acknowledged that the existence of such special relationships is rare, it held that just such a relationship did exist in this case, based on four factors. The first of these was the order of protection itself, which, as in *Dudosh*, played a critical role in establishing this special relationship.[133] The second factor was the police department's previous knowledge of Frank's history of violence (gained through its dealings with Frank and the information provided by Josephine).[134] Third, the court cited the police department's response to Josephine's requests for help on the day of the incident; and fourth, simply "Mrs. Sorichetti's reasonable expectation of police protection."[135] These elements of the court's decision are significant, for they indicate that, given knowledge of a violent or potentially violent domestic situation—particularly, but not exclusively, via a protective order—police are required to act to protect the victim. Likewise, victims of domestic violence, having sought police assistance, can "reasonably expect" police protection from further violence. Police departments that choose to ignore these requests after the *Sorichetti* ruling do so with full awareness of their own potential for liability.

While the financial awards of the *Thurman* and *Sorichetti* cases were undeniably meaningful for the individual plaintiffs, they also held great significance for the battered women's movement overall. Unprecedented in their magnitude, these awards sent a powerful message that battered women were being recognized and compensated in the courtroom, and that police departments were being held accountable for their willful refusal to assist in cases of domestic abuse. The financial component of the cases, coupled with the court's logic and language on behalf of battered women, also generated a great deal of publicity for the movement and the issue itself. Newspapers and law reviews alike reacted strongly to the *Thurman* and *Sorichetti* cases,[136] and Tracey Thurman's story was even made into a Lifetime Original Movie.[137] The heightened awareness generated by these cases, in addition to their more tangible financial and judicial implications, established *Thurman* and *Sorichetti* as critical judicial successes for the battered women's movement.

Regrettably, the civil litigation of the 1980s did not always bring relief to battered women plaintiffs. As the decade progressed, the doctrines of qualified immunity and special relationship became increasingly greater obstacles for battered women plaintiffs, and several cases resulted in rulings that supported police inaction in violent domestic situations. In a 1987 case heard by the Court of Appeals of Washington, the mother and children of Eleanor Collins sued the local police, the county, and the Victim Assistance Unit of the county prosecutor's office.[138] After an incident in which her husband Dennis assaulted her with a gun and threatened to kill her, officials from these agencies had promised Eleanor that he would be arrested. Although Eleanor relied on this promise, defendants willfully did not arrest Dennis, and several days later he shot and killed her, and shot and assaulted their children. The court ruled for the defendants, dismissing the case altogether by affirming "[t]he absolute immunity [from civil suit] enjoyed by prosecuting attorneys."[139] The institution of prosecutorial immunity, which allows prosecutors to perform their public duties objectively, could not be undermined by the facts of this case, the court concluded. Assessing the competing priorities of defending this immunity and compensating the victims in this case, the court chose the former. In short, the court declared that "the public's need for an independent prosecutor must outweigh the concern over individual wrongs." The other defendants also enjoyed this immunity, although briefly. [140]

In some cases, courts relied on both the special relationship and qualified immunity doctrines in order to find for the defendants. In the 1987 case of *Turner v. North Charleston*,[141] a South Carolina district court granted qualified immunity to defendants on the basis that no "special relationship between the plaintiffs and the city existed that created an affirmative duty of protection."[142] Absent an affirmative obligation, the court reasoned, defendants could not be held liable for failing to provide protection. The facts of the case were undisputed: plaintiffs Janice Turner and her son had contacted police repeatedly during the day to notify them of batterer Vernon Fair's violation of a permanent restraining order and to ask for his arrest. Police ignored the calls, however, until after Fair had entered Turner's home, shot Janice numerous times in the head, and attempted to shoot her son.[143] Nonetheless, the court found that none of the police defendants could be held liable for these injuries, not even the officer who "was apparently aware of the relationship between Turner and Fair, and of Fair's criminal record, but . . . did not return Turner's telephone calls for assistance," because "it is not clear that a reasonable official would understand that he is violating someone's constitutional right by failing to return phone calls."[144] In this case, as in *Collins*, the court found that protection of state actors' discretionary freedom superseded the physical protection of battered women.

One of the broadest interpretations of qualified immunity—and therefore one of the most problematic, for battered women's litigation—came from the Third Circuit (which includes Delaware, New Jersey, Pennsylvania, and the Virgin Islands). The 1988 case of *Hynson* v. *City of Chester*,[145] like the *Collins* case, was brought by the mother and children of a woman killed by her batterer. Alesia Hynson's family brought this Section 1983 case on equal protection grounds, claiming that the Chester police department treated victims of domestic violence differently than victims of non-domestic violence. The *Hynson* court seized this opportunity to respond to what it perceived as "a growing trend of plaintiffs relying upon the due process and equal protection clauses . . . to force police departments to provide women with the protection from domestic violence that police agencies are allegedly reluctant to give."[146]

Here, the court established a very specific standard of qualified immunity, thereby rejecting Hynson's claims:

> [W]e conclude that a police officer loses a qualified immunity to a claim that a facially neutral policy is executed in a discriminatory manner only if a reasonable police officer would know that the policy has a discriminatory impact on women, that bias against women was a motivating factor behind the adoption of the policy, and that there is no important public interest served by the adoption of the policy.[147]

Several factors were enunciated in this standard. First, the court implicitly favored police officers by starting with the presumption that officers *do* have immunity and delineating only those unique circumstances in which such immunity would be lost. In addition, the court stated that, in order for an officer to "lose" this immunity, all three of its stated conditions must be met. First, the "reasonable" officer must be aware of the policy's discriminatory effect on women. Second, the plaintiff must prove that the policy was adopted at least in part with an intentional bias against women. Finally, the plaintiff must prove that the policy serves "no important public interest." Only if a battered woman plaintiff could prove that each of these three conditions were true in her case would the officers in question then lose the immunity that otherwise would shield them from liability.

This multifaceted standard, including the particularly difficult to prove "bias-as-motivator" component, rendered battered women's suits against police officers exceedingly difficult. Ultimately, despite the successes achieved by battered women plaintiffs in the earlier part of the 1980s, their efforts in the latter half of the decade were increasingly stymied by the doctrines of special relationship and qualified immunity. In general, courts had been more receptive to battered women's equal protection and due process claims at the beginning of the decade. Just as these successes seemed to signal a "growing trend," however, courts began to expand the basis for immunity for police officers in a wide variety of circumstances,[148] while continually narrowing the parameters for a special relationship between police and battered women. At the same time, the composition of the nation's highest court became increasingly conservative (and therefore less amenable to the notion of civil litigation as a path to justice) during the 1980s, as President Reagan appointed several new members to the Court and Justice Rehnquist assumed the role of chief justice. The combination of these factors resulted in an increasingly hostile climate for battered women's civil litigation in the years leading up to the *DeShaney* case.

DESHANEY V. WINNEBAGO COUNTY DEPARTMENT OF SOCIAL SERVICES

The case that would ultimately have the greatest impact on battered women's civil litigation was not primarily a battered woman's case. While *DeShaney* v. *Winnebago County Department of Social Services* did pertain to domestic violence, broadly construed—that is, violence committed in the home—it centered on a horrific case of child abuse. The issues of private violence and police liability that were salient in the *DeShaney* case, however, closely echoed those that had been addressed by the battered women's movement in their civil litigation of the past ten years. As such, battered women's advocates immediately understood the US Supreme Court's holding in *DeShaney* to be a tremendous setback to their efforts. In an article for the NCOWFL entitled "Suing the Police After *DeShaney*," Joan Zorza wrote, "[B]efore the *DeShaney* decision, battered women had a much easier time suing the police and municipalities in federal court for failing to protect them . . . Because of the *DeShaney* decision, a battered woman can no longer expect to win a substantive due process civil rights case for failure to act to protect her . . ."[149]

The facts of the *DeShaney* case detail a brutal history of child abuse. Born in 1979, Joshua DeShaney was still an infant when his parents divorced the following year. Joshua's father, Randy DeShaney, was granted custody of him, and the two of them moved to Winnebago County, Wisconsin. In January 1982, Randy's second wife notified the police that Randy had "hit the boy causing marks and [was] a prime case for child abuse."[150] When interviewed by the Winnebago County Department of Social Services (DSS), Randy denied these accusations, and DSS dropped the matter. In January of the following year, Joshua was admitted to the hospital with bruises and abrasions consistent with child abuse. After notifying DSS, the hospital assembled a "Child Protection Team" consisting of several physicians, DSS staffers, a lawyer, and others to examine Joshua's case. Although DSS obtained an order from a Wisconsin juvenile court placing Joshua in temporary custody of the hospital, the "team" subsequently determined that there was insufficient evidence to keep Joshua in state custody. Instead, they recommended several informal measures for his protection, such as enrolling him in a preschool program.

The following month, Joshua returned to the emergency room with more injuries. DSS found no basis for immediate action, but made monthly visits to the DeShaney residence for the next six months. The DSS caseworker responsible for these visits recorded numerous head injuries to Joshua during the course of the six months, but took no further action. In November of that year, Joshua returned to the emergency room, again with "suspicious injuries."[151] DSS continued to take no action, even when, during the caseworker's next two visits to the DeShaney residence, she was told that Joshua was "too ill to see her."[152] Several months later, in March 1984, when Joshua was four years old, his father beat him so brutally that he fell into a coma. His life-threatening condition necessitated emergency brain surgery, which revealed "a series of hemorrhages caused by traumatic injuries to the head inflicted over a long period of time."[153] Joshua did not die, but suffered brain damage so extensive that he will spend the rest of his life in an institution for the severely mentally disabled.[154]

While Randy DeShaney was tried and convicted of child abuse, Joshua and his mother, Melody DeShaney, brought a federal Section 1983 lawsuit against the DSS and Winnebago County. They based their lawsuit on substantive due process grounds, claiming that the defendants deprived Joshua of his Fourteenth Amendment liberty rights by failing to protect him from his father's violence, despite their knowledge of that violence. The *DeShaney* case eventually made its way to the US Supreme Court in 1989. Explaining its rationale for reviewing the case, the high court cited "the inconsistent approaches taken by the

lower courts in determining when, if ever, the failure of a state or local governmental entity or its agents to provide an individual with adequate protective
services constitutes a violation of the individual's due process rights."[155] By con-
struing the issue broadly enough to pertain not only to child abuse cases, but to
all cases of state protective services, the Court guaranteed that its resolution
would have a significant impact on battered women's civil litigation, as well.[156]

Case Resources

DeShaney v. *Winnebago County Department of Social Services*

Findlaw (http://laws.findlaw.com/us/489/189.html) (full text)

Oyez (http://www.oyez.org/cases/case/?case=1980-1989/1988/1988_87_154) (oral
arguments)

Harris v. *McRae*

Findlaw (http://laws.findlaw.com/us/448/297.html) (full text)

Oyez (http://www.oyez.org/cases/case?case=1970-1979/1979/1979_79_1268) (oral
arguments)

The majority opinion in *DeShaney* was authored by Chief Justice Rehnquist
and joined by five other justices, representing the Court's more conservative side:
White, Stevens, O'Connor, Scalia, and Kennedy. The Court flatly rejected the
DeShaneys' due process claim by describing the due process clause as "a limitation on the State's power to act, not as a guarantee of certain minimal levels of
safety and security;"[157] in other words, an expression of negative rather than positive rights. Evoking the rhetoric of the right to privacy, Rehnquist's opinion characterized the due process clause as a means of protecting individual citizens from
excessive state intervention: "Its purpose was to protect people from the State, not
to ensure that the State protected them from each other."[158] The opinion also
cited the controversial 1980 abortion case of *Harris* v. *McRae*[159]—which held
that the government had no obligation to fund abortion services for indigent
patients—to assert that the due process clause confers only negative rights, not
"entitlements."[160] Having painted the due process clause with this brush, the
Court readily concluded that "a State's failure to protect an individual against private violence simply does not constitute a violation of the Due Process Clause."[161]

The majority opinion conceded that an affirmative obligation to protect
individual citizens arises when a special relationship exists between state
agents and those citizens. Nonetheless, the Court construed the nature of
such special relationships even more narrowly in *DeShaney* than it had previously interpreted the much more restrictive "custodial relationships."[162] Specifically, the Court rejected the DeShaneys' argument that the state's knowledge of the violent situation, coupled with its stated intention to protect Joshua,

was sufficient to establish a special relationship and an affirmative duty of care. Instead, the opinion acknowledged only that "when the State takes a person into its custody and holds him there against his will, the Constitution imposes upon it a corresponding duty to assume some responsibility for his safety and general well-being."[163] According to this analysis, the due process clause is a viable source of protection only when the state detains a person involuntarily and then deprives him or her of "basic human needs."[164] As Rehnquist explained, "The affirmative duty to protect arises not from the State's knowledge of the individual's predicament or from its expressions of intent to help him, but from the limitation which it has imposed on his freedom to act on his own behalf."[165]

Unfortunately for the DeShaneys, the Court's analysis rested largely on the presumption of individual citizens who are capable of acting on their own behalf. The majority opinion thereby failed to address the issue at the heart of the *DeShaney* case: that as a four-year-old, Joshua's "freedom to act on his own behalf" was essentially nonexistent.[166] By focusing solely on the negative rights aspect of the due process clause, however—the freedom of the individual from excessive government intervention—the opinion rendered this fact irrelevant to its analysis. Yet Joshua's need for assistance from government agencies was not irrelevant here, and he was harmed as a result of the state's failure to intervene—in the same way that battered women suffer when the privacy right is construed solely as a negative right of freedom from state interference. In both cases, the overemphasis on protection *from* the state, rather than protection *by* the state, removes accountability for state actors who fail to fulfill their duty of protecting individuals in danger.

Justices Brennan, Marshall, and Blackmun dissented from the majority opinion in *DeShaney*. In keeping with their voting on other cases the Court was hearing at this time, this core group represented a more liberal political orientation than that exhibited by Rehnquist and Scalia (and, to varying degrees, several of the other justices).[167] In contrast to their colleagues' more conservative rhetoric, the opinions authored by Brennan, Marshall, and Blackmun seemed to be informed by social justice approaches that often benefited traditionally disadvantaged groups. In *DeShaney*, the dissenters offered a more nuanced analysis of the balance between state action and inaction, and between positive and negative rights, than did their colleagues in the majority. In so doing, they developed an opinion that confirmed many of the arguments advanced by battered women's civil litigation over the previous decade. Acknowledging the validity of a negative rights reading of the due process clause, Brennan's dissent complicated that reading by noting that, in many cases, once a state chooses a particular course of action, it subjects itself to various obligations as a result. Given that "a State's actions . . . may impose upon the State certain positive duties," he concluded that "a State may be found complicit in an injury even if it did not create the situation that caused the harm."[168]

In particular, Brennan's dissent called attention to the fact that the state of Wisconsin had granted the DSS primary responsibility for addressing child abuse cases with an authority that superseded that of other state or private actors. In so doing, the state "relieved ordinary citizens and governmental bodies other than the [DSS] of any sense of obligation to do anything more than report their suspicions of child abuse to DSS."[169] The nature of this system dictated that ultimate responsibility for child abuse cases rested with DSS, and, should DSS fail to fulfill its duty toward a child, "no one will step in to fill the gap."[170] By creating a structure whereby other forms of recourse are displaced by the involvement of DSS, the state had created a system in which the failure of DSS places children in an ostensibly worse position than they would have occupied without the existence of the program.[171] For this reason, Brennan's dissent concluded that "inaction can be every bit as abusive of power as action" and that "oppression can result when a State undertakes a vital duty and then ignores it."[172] Criticizing the majority opinion for "constru[ing] the Due Process Clause to permit a State to displace private sources of protection and then, at the critical moment, to shrug its shoulders and turn away," Brennan concluded, "I cannot agree that our Constitution is indifferent to such indifference."[173] In this way, Brennan condemned the *DeShaney* majority for validating attitudes of noninterference in private violence at both the state and the community level.

THE IMPACT OF DESHANEY ON BATTERED WOMEN'S LITIGATION

Had Brennan's analysis been accepted by a majority of the justices, *DeShaney* would have been a powerful tool for battered women and their advocates in future litigation. By calling attention to the danger that results from reading ostensibly negative rights too simplistically, the dissenting opinion bolstered battered women's claims that in some cases, police or other state agents did owe them a duty of protection. Likewise, the dissent's willingness to accept state liability for inaction as well as action would reinforce battered women's damage claims against police who engaged in policies of non-arrest. Finally, Brennan's conclusion that state actors who bear the responsibility of protecting citizens from harm can and should be held liable for failing to execute that duty could have solidified the judicial foundation for battered women's future litigation against police. Ultimately, the *DeShaney* dissents had all the elements of a potentially landmark ruling for the future of battered women's civil litigation.

In reality, however, Justice Brennan was in the minority, and the majority opinion in *DeShaney* proved to be a significant blow to the battered women's movement in the civil courts. Lawyer-activists within the movement recognized the importance of *DeShaney* at once. Three months after the Court issued its opinion, the NCOWFL devoted the front-page article in its newsletter, *The Women's Advocate*, to explaining the opinion and assessing its impact on future litigation by battered women.[174] Subsequently, the NCOWFL issued an information packet on "The Implications of *DeShaney*" that included articles on the *DeShaney* opinion from a wide variety of sources, related cases, and memoranda.[175] Ultimately, lawyer-activist Joan Zorza wrote a lengthy article assessing the damage caused by the opinion and detailing several practical approaches to battered women's litigation in its aftermath. In particular, Zorza observed, battered women would do well in the future to avoid bringing cases on substantive due process grounds. Instead, she suggested (as other legal scholars have subsequently done) that cases based on equal protection grounds—that is, cases that asserted that battered women were not protected equally relative to men or to non-battered women—would have a much greater chance of success.[176]

Legal scholars responded to the opinion with equal gravity. To date, almost two hundred law review articles have addressed the case in some detail. Many of these have drawn explicit links between the *DeShaney* opinion and the future of battered women's litigation, with titles such as "Battered Women Suing Police for Failure to Intervene: Viable Legal Avenues After *DeShaney* v. *Winnebago County Department of Social Services*"[177] and "Battered Women's Substantive Due Process Claims: Can Orders of Protection Deflect *DeShaney*?" [178] These articles offered a variety of theories and suggestions on how battered women should proceed with civil litigation against police, from the most obvious courses of action (equal protection suits can still survive *DeShaney* and should be pursued)[179] to the most unusual approaches (the Thirteenth Amendment prohibition against slavery may provide new avenues of legal recourse for victims of domestic violence in the post-*DeShaney* context).[180] Despite the anxiety these articles generally expressed about the future of battered women's civil claims, the majority of them also suggested alternative avenues that, while potentially difficult, had not been entirely thwarted by the Court's holding in *DeShaney*.

Creative legal approaches notwithstanding, the results of battered women's lawsuits in the decade following the *DeShaney* ruling were fairly dismal. For those law enforcement agencies clearly uninterested in responding to domestic violence calls—a disdain perhaps rooted in misogyny as well as notions of privacy—*DeShaney* seemed to further justify their failure to respond. The most immediate and conspicuous example of *DeShaney*'s impact was in the 1990 case of *Balistreri* v. *Pacifica Police Department*.[181] The plaintiff, Jena Balistreri, was severely beaten by her husband in February 1982. While police did remove him from the home temporarily, they refused to arrest him; furthermore, one of the officers told Jena that she deserved the assault, and one pressured her into not pressing charges.[182] Subsequently, after repeated incidents of vandalism and harassment, Jena obtained a restraining order against her by-then ex-husband, who responded by crashing his car into her garage. Police responded to the scene but refused to arrest or even investigate.[183] Balistreri's subsequent reports to the police of harassment and vandalism were routinely ignored, as police officers denied the existence of the restraining order and even hung up on her.[184] After Balistreri's ex-husband firebombed her house in March 1983, police took 45 minutes to arrive at the scene, where they briefly questioned the ex-husband and promptly determined he was not responsible.[185] For the next two years, Balistreri was subjected to continuing telephone harassment and vandalism to which the police did not respond.[186]

Jena Balistreri brought a Section 1983 claim against the Pacifica Police Department based primarily on due process and equal protection grounds. When her case reached the Ninth Circuit, that court affirmed her due process claim based on its recognition of the special relationship that existed between the plaintiff and the Pacifica police. The court based its finding of a special relationship on the existence of the restraining order combined with the police's ongoing awareness of the violence (via the plaintiff's repeated requests for help).[187] The Ninth Circuit issued this opinion in March of 1988. In light of the 1989 *DeShaney* decision, however, the circuit court amended its opinion in 1990. Noting that, in *DeShaney*, "the Supreme Court limited the circumstances giving rise to a 'special relationship,'" the Ninth Circuit concluded that Jena had not in fact established such a relationship, and therefore dismissed her due process claim altogether.[188] This amended opinion provided the first and clearest indication of the kind of impact the *DeShaney* decision might have on future domestic violence civil litigation.

Unfortunately, *Balistreri* indeed proved to be the rule rather than the exception throughout the 1990s: courts in many subsequent cases declined to rule in favor of battered women plaintiffs as a result of *DeShaney*. Because the *DeShaney* opinion dealt most specifically with due process and special relationship issues, the cases that suffered, most predictably, in its aftermath were those brought on due process grounds. Courts assessing battered women's due process claims interpreted *DeShaney* broadly, using it as the basis for pronouncements such as "the state and its officials cannot be liable for simply failing, negligently or otherwise, to take affirmative measures to protect an individual,"[189] or, stated more simply, "there is no substantive due process clause right to protection from violence perpetrated by private actors."[190] One such case was brought by the surviving family of a woman killed by her husband directly outside the courtroom where they were about to undergo divorce proceedings.

Despite the existence of a restraining order at the time of the murder and the sheriff's agreement (and subsequent failure) to provide police protection to the plaintiff on the date of the hearing, the court in *Duong* v. *County of Arapahoe*[191] found the family's claims to be without merit. Relying almost exclusively on *DeShaney*, the court denied the existence of a special or custodial relationship, in spite of the fact that the state had required the plaintiff to be in the court- house at the time of her murder.[192] Cases like these effectively signaled that in the wake of *DeShaney*, battered women's due process claims would be all but impossible to prove.

   DeShaney's reach also extended beyond the realm of due process claims. Even cases brought on equal protection grounds—and therefore not necessarily subject to *DeShaney's* authority—were often stymied by judges' interpretation of that case. In the 1989 case of *McKee* v. *City of Rockwall*,[193] for example, the Fifth Circuit observed that while *DeShaney* did not "directly bar" plaintiff Mc- Kee's equal protection claim, it was "nonetheless relevant"[194]—and the court proceeded to rely on it heavily. The court's opinion noted that because of *De- Shaney*, police officers still enjoyed "some discretionary authority;"[195] this au- thority, in turn, helped to bolster the defendants' assertion that their arrest policies were not biased against women. Granting police wide discretion to implement policies and procedures, the court intoned, "This is the lesson of *DeShaney*: that law enforcement officers have authority to act does not imply that they have any constitutional duty to act."[196]

   Likewise, a 1994 equal protection case in the Eighth Circuit cited *DeShaney* as it voided a jury's award of $1.2 million to a battered woman and her family.[197] Courts' willingness to apply the spirit of *DeShaney*, even to those cases with very different doctrinal bases, indicated the extent of the setbacks that battered women's litigation had faced as a result of that ruling.

   Of course, not all courts dismissed battered women's claims after *DeShaney*. In fact, the ruling in the 1990 case of *Freeman* v. *Ferguson*[198] (in which a woman and her daughter were killed by the woman's estranged husband while she had a restraining order against him) even referenced *DeShaney* specifically when finding for the plaintiff. A due process case that could have easily been thwarted by *DeShaney*, *Freeman* instead offered a reading of *DeShaney* that was much less hostile to battered women. Specifically, the *Freeman* court found in *De- Shaney* "the possibility that a constitutional duty to protect an individual against private violence may exist in a non-custodial setting if the state has taken affir- mative action which increases the individual's danger of, or vulnerability to, such violence beyond the level it would have been absent state action."[199] While this approach was not adopted by the majority of courts, it suggested, at the very least, that *DeShaney* need not be the final word on battered women's civil suits. Likewise, battered women's post-*DeShaney* suits that *did* succeed provided hopeful indications that, while *DeShaney* may have effectively closed at least the substantive due process avenue, plaintiffs could still obtain civil relief on other grounds, primarily equal protection claims.[200]

CASTLE ROCK V. GONZALES

Ten years after the *DeShaney* decision came down, an escalating domestic violence situation in Colorado ended in tragedy. This incident and the events that preceded it—also resulting from a father's horrific violence against his own children—would eventually provide the basis for the Supreme Court's decision to re-examine *DeShaney*. On May 21, 1999, Jessica Gonzales obtained a temporary restraining order against her husband, Simon Gonzales, directing him to "not molest or disturb the peace of [Jessica Gonzales] or . . . any child."[201] The order stated that "the court . . . finds that physical or emotional harm would result if you [Simon Gonzales] are not excluded from the family home," and ordered him to stay at least one hundred yards away from the property at all times.[202] On June 4, 1999, the order was served and made permanent, and modified to outline specific "parenting time" that Simon Gonzales would be allowed to spend with the couple's three daughters: alternate weekends, two weeks during the summer, and, "upon reasonable notice . . . a mid-week dinner visit with the minor children [that] shall be arranged by the parties."[203]

Less than three weeks later, evening of Tuesday, June 22, 1999, Simon violated the order. Without any prior arrangement with Jessica to see the children, he came to the home and abducted all three girls, aged 10, 9, and 7, while they were playing outside. Upon learning of the girls' disappearance, Jessica contacted the Castle Rock Police Department, telling them she suspected the girls had been abducted by their father and asking them to enforce the restraining order against her husband. Two officers were dispatched to her home, where Jessica showed them a copy of the order and urged them to enforce it. The officers told Jessica that "there was nothing they could do" and suggested that she call the police department back if the children were not returned home by 10:00 that night.[204]

Approximately an hour later, Jessica reached Simon on his cell phone. He confirmed that the girls were with him at an amusement park in Denver. Jessica immediately called the Castle Rock Police Department again to relate this new information and to again urge the police to find and arrest Simon. The officer she spoke with refused, but suggested that she call back after 10 if the children were not returned home. At 10:10 p.m., she did just that, only to be told to wait for another two hours. At midnight, she called the police again, and then went to Simon's apartment complex. Finding no one home at Simon's apartment, she called the Castle Rock Police again. The dispatcher told her to wait there for a police officer to arrive. At 12:50 a.m., no officers had arrived, and she went to the police station. There, an officer took an incident report but took no further action. He then went to dinner.[205]

At 3:20 a.m., Simon arrived at the police station. Emerging from his truck, he began shooting at the police station with a semiautomatic handgun. He was quickly shot dead by the police. Searching the truck, police found the bodies of the three girls, Rebecca, Katheryn, and Leslie, whom Simon had murdered earlier that night.[206]

Jessica Gonzales brought a Section 1983 suit in federal court against the City of Castle Rock and the three individual officers for their failure to respond to her repeated requests for enforcement of her restraining order.[207] Her case alleged that she was denied both substantive and procedural due process rights by the Castle Rock Police Department in their failure to enforce the order. [208] She further claimed that the City of Castle Rock had a pattern and practice of failing to respond properly to violations of domestic violence restraining orders.[209]

The district court relied heavily on *DeShaney* in its analysis of Gonzales's substantive due process claims. Writing for the court, Judge Wiley Daniel claimed that "the starting point for analyzing the validity of Plaintiff [sic] substantive due process claim is *DeShaney* v. *Winnebago*," which he said, reveals that "[e]ven if the State knows of an individual's predicament or expresses intent to help an individual, its failure to protect does not violate substantive due process."[210] Judge Daniel conceded that, while "[t]he Tenth Circuit has recognized two exceptions to the general *DeShaney* rule: (1) the special-relationship doctrine, and (2) the danger-creation theory," Gonzales's case did not meet either of these criteria, because, "[c]onsistent with *DeShaney*, both exceptions apply *only where the State creates the danger*." [211] Specifically, Daniel concluded that the danger was a direct result of Simon Gonzales's action, not of police inaction, and that therefore, Jessica Gonzales had failed to state a claim of denial of her substantive due process rights.

Jessica's procedural due process claim, on the other hand, rested on a different foundation. To determine whether or not her procedural due process rights had been denied, the court had to consider whether or not she had been deprived of life, liberty, or property without "appropriate procedural safeguards."[212] In this case, Gonzales alleged that "the State, by failing to enforce the TRO [temporary restraining order] as required by [Colorado law], deprived her of the property interest created by the TRO without proper procedure such as notice and/or a hearing to vacate the TRO."[213] In other words, Gonzales argued that the state had deprived her of a property right without due process of law.

For the purposes of due process analysis, "property" has been described by the US Supreme Court as "a broad and majestic term."[214] The Court has noted that "property interests protected by procedural due process extend well beyond actual ownership of real estate, chattels, or money," and "may take many forms."[215] Specifically, "a property interest is created when a person has secured an interest in a specific benefit to which the individual has 'a legitimate claim of entitlement.'"[216] In the *Gonzales* case, the property interest at issue was Jessica Gonzales's expectation that her TRO would be enforced. For such a claim of entitlement to be legitimate, the statute or other objective measure creating the claim must contain "language [that] is so mandatory that it creates a right to rely on that language."[217] In short, the property interest cannot be based on an unfounded expectation; there must be explicit, *mandatory* language granting that benefit or service.

The district court's analysis of Jessica Gonzales's procedural due process claim, therefore, depended upon its opinion about whether or not she had been deprived of a property interest without appropriate procedural safeguards. Before answering that question, the court first wondered whether or not Jessica's expectation of the enforcement of her TRO constituted a property interest at all—and concluded that it did not. Judge Daniel observed that Colorado's mandatory arrest statute governing the enforcement of restraining orders required responding officers to make a determination of probable cause before making an arrest. Since police were required to use discretion in making that determination, he reasoned, they therefore were not obligated by any mandatory duty. He asserted, "No Colorado law . . . holds that a valid protective order creates a property interest that can only be removed through due process of law."[218] As such, he concluded, Gonzales had no "protectable property interest," and therefore no basis on which to claim that the state of Colorado had deprived her of that property interest without due process of law.[219] As a result, her procedural due process claim, in addition to her substantive due process claim, was dismissed.

Upon appeal in 2002, the Tenth Circuit agreed with the district court's analysis of Jessica's substantive due process claim. They disagreed, however, with regard to the procedural due process claim. The Tenth Circuit found that the restraining order, and the statute on which it was based—both of which explicitly command police to enforce the order—did create a property interest worthy of constitutional protection.[220] Subsequently, in a hearing en banc,[221] the circuit court went even further. The majority found not only that Gonzales had a property interest, but also that a particular process was indeed owed to her before she was deprived of that property.[222]

While the district court had claimed that police's ability to use discretion in determining probable cause meant that the statute did not mandate any particular police action, the circuit court strongly disagreed. Writing for the circuit court majority, Judge Stephanie Seymour stated that:

> [A]n officer's determination of probable cause is not so discretionary as to eliminate the protected interest asserted here in having the restraining order enforced according to its terms. . . . Moreover, once probable cause exists, any discretion the officer may have possessed in determining whether or how to enforce the restraining order is wholly extinguished. . . . [The responding officers] were not given carte blanche discretion to take no action whatsoever. The restraining order and its enforcement statute took away the officers' discretion to do nothing and instead mandated that they use every reasonable means, up to and including arrest, to enforce the order's terms.[223]

Judge Seymour's straightforward analysis of the police's duty to protect affirmed in many ways the claims made by anti-domestic-violence activists for years. Just because police had discretion in determining probable cause, she concluded, that discretion did not include the option of ignoring victims' requests for help, or of choosing not to make any probable cause determination at all.

When the city of Castle Rock appealed to the United States Supreme Court in 2005, the amicus briefs filed on behalf of Jessica Gonzales echoed similar sentiments. One such brief, submitted by the National Black Police Association, Women in Federal Law Enforcement, and others, flatly stated, "domestic violence can no longer hide behind soft language. It is not a 'quarrel,' 'spat,' or 'dispute.' It involves crimes that demand a law enforcement response, including arrest where probable cause and legal authority exist."[224] Another amicus brief, coauthored by the National Coalition Against Domestic Violence and the National Center for Victims of Crime, observed that "[u]ntil recently, law enforcement's under-enforcement of laws involving domestic violence was widespread," and noted the "archaic misconceptions and stereotypes" that have "contributed to law enforcement's failure to arrest men who were abusing their partners or violating protective orders."[225] Once again, anti-domestic-violence activists and their allies found themselves in the position of attempting to convince the court that the state—and specifically, law enforcement—had a duty to protect battered women from the violence in their homes.

Case Resources

Castle Rock v. Gonzales

Findlaw (http://laws.findlaw.com/us/000/04-278.html) (full text)

Oyez (http://www.oyez.org/cases/case?case=2000-2009/2004/2004_04_278) (oral arguments)

The United States Supreme Court, however, ultimately disagreed. In a 7-2 decision, the Court found that Jessica Gonzales's due process claim failed. Gonzales was not deprived of her due process rights, the Court concluded, because she did not have a property interest in police enforcement of her restraining order. Like the district court, the Supreme Court viewed the matter of police discretion as a barrier to this property interest. Writing for the majority, Justice Scalia was unconvinced that the language of Colorado's mandatory arrest statute truly required that such orders be enforced: "We do not believe that these provisions of Colorado law truly made enforcement of restraining orders *mandatory*. A well established tradition of police discretion has long coexisted with apparently mandatory arrest statutes." [226] Their stance on this issue—whether a statute could truly be considered mandatory given that it granted police the power of discretion in probable cause determinations—was central to the majority's reasoning in the *Gonzales* decision.[227]

The dissent, authored by Justices Stevens and Ginsburg, found this reasoning to be flawed. Like the amicus briefs filed for Gonzales, the dissent pointed out that domestic violence mandatory arrest statutes were a "unique case" to be considered, in light of the fact that "[s]tates passed a wave of these statutes in the 1980's and 1990's with the unmistakable goal of eliminating police discretion in this area."[228] This context and the well-documented history of police refusal to respond appropriately to domestic violence calls, the dissent claimed, were crucial to an understanding of the intent of mandatory arrest statutes, such as Colorado's, that targeted domestic violence.

Arguing for the importance of understanding this context, Justice Stevens made explicit reference to the problem of privacy, noting, "The crisis of underenforcement had various causes, not least of which was the perception by police departments and police officers that domestic violence was a private, 'family' matter and that arrest was to be used as a last resort."[229] This clear understanding and articulation of the links between the societal concept of privacy, the historical failure on the part of law enforcement to respond to domestic violence, and the resulting increased danger for victims of domestic violence was unprecedented on the United States Supreme Court. While Justices Stevens and Ginsburg were in the minority, their expression of this argument—advanced by anti-domestic-violence activists for decades—was a clear signal that at last this message had gotten through to at least some members of the Court.

Building on this concept and echoing Circuit Judge Seymour's earlier analysis, Justice Stevens took exception to the notion that police discretion could excuse a failure to act at all:

> the crucial point is that, under the statute, the police were *required* to provide enforcement; they *lacked the discretion to do nothing*. . . . Under the statute, if the police

have probable cause that a violation has occurred, enforcement consists of either making an immediate arrest or seeking a warrant and then executing an arrest—traditional, well-defined tasks that law enforcement officers perform every day.[230]

For these reasons, the dissent concluded, Jessica Gonzales had a property interest based on her legitimate expectation that her court-issued restraining order would be enforced. That property interest was worthy of constitutional due process protection, and that protection had been denied.

THE IMPLICATIONS OF GONZALES FOR FUTURE BATTERED WOMEN'S LITIGATION

Not surprisingly, anti-domestic-violence activists responded to the *Gonzales* decision with outrage and a profound sense of disappointment. Numerous publications of the battered women's movement featured articles explaining the decision and expressing their frustration with the Court's ruling. The lead article of the Family Violence Prevention Fund (FVPF) publication *Speaking Up*, for example, was devoted to the decision, which it denounced in harsh terms. Quoting FVPF's President, Esta Soler, the article stated,

> This damaging ruling may cause more family violence victims to live in terror, and more domestic violence injuries and deaths.

> Restraining orders aren't worth the paper they are written on when police do not enforce them. . . . This is a sad day and a giant step backward for a nation that had been making progress in stopping domestic violence and helping victims.[231]

Other movement publications expressed similar sentiments, while simultaneously seeking to answer the question: what legal remedies are still available to victims of domestic violence whom police fail to protect? Often, these articles sought to convey that despite the ruling, restraining orders could still be an important means of protection for battered women, in an attempt to counteract the media perception that *Gonzales* had rendered such orders essentially meaningless.[232] These authors also acknowledged, however, that when police failed to enforce the orders, legal recourse for victims had been severely limited by the *Gonzales* decision.

In *Gonzales*, the Supreme Court sent a clear message that the due process clause of the constitution was now effectively closed as an avenue through which battered women could pursue these "failure to protect" suits. While the *Gonzales* decision was limited to the procedural aspects of due process, it reinforced *De-Shaney* in further limiting the possibility of succeeding with such a suit on due process grounds. In fact, the *Gonzales* majority made this point rather explicitly, by linking the two decisions together to draw a general conclusion about the due process clause: "In light of today's decision and that in *DeShaney*, the benefit that a third party may receive from having someone else arrested for a crime generally does not trigger protections under the Due Process Clause, neither in its procedural nor in its 'substantive' manifestations."[233]

Given this reality, activist writings on still-existing remedies have focused primarily on state-level remedies for police failure to protect victims of domestic violence. These authors note that traditional avenues for enforcing orders still exist: civil and criminal contempt actions, for example, and state tort law. In some states, they note, state constitutional remedies may be available. They even note that federal equal protection arguments such as that used successfully in *Thurman* v. *Torrington* are still available. Likewise, substantive due process claims may still be available to a plaintiff who can prove that the state affirmatively created the danger she encountered. Both of these federal constitutional remedies, however, are noted with caution as to their limited likelihood of success, given the Court's tone in *DeShaney* and *Gonzales*.[234]

Last, activists writing in the wake of *Gonzales* urged others in the movement to work toward administrative and legislative ends: improving internal police accountability systems, and improving state tort laws. By continuing to educate law enforcement agencies and create standards of accountability at the local level, they suggest, advocates could help to create systems of "individualized oversight" that discipline officers who fail to comply with policies and laws.[235] Likewise, by improving state tort laws, advocates could create stronger mechanisms by which to motivate officers to comply, and hold them accountable for failure to do so.[236] In short, despite their disappointment with *Gonzales*, anti-domestic-violence advocates have continued to explore and promote a variety of legal and activist strategies for justice for battered women.

CONCLUSION

The decade of the 1980s was a crucial one for litigation by the battered women's movement. First, two early class-action lawsuits, *Bruno* v. *Codd* and *Scott* v. *Hart*, resulted in significant policy changes, both locally and in many other areas across the nation. Subsequently, battered women's civil litigation proliferated, as victims of domestic violence and their advocates brought cases on due process and equal protection grounds. Often challenged by the doctrines of special relationship and qualified immunity, many of these suits succeeded nonetheless, whether via judicial rulings, jury awards, or out-of-court settlements.

In 1989, the United States Supreme Court opinion in the child abuse case of *DeShaney* v. *Winnebago County* marked a significant turning point for battered women's civil litigation. Definitively proclaiming that the state has no obligation to protect individuals from private violence, the *DeShaney* opinion practically eliminated one of the most effective means of civil redress previously available to battered women—Section 1983 suits based on substantive due process claims. While most courts embraced *DeShaney* wholeheartedly, battered women plaintiffs continued to find some success in the civil arena with equal protection claims, suggesting that while *DeShaney* undeniably made such litigation more difficult, it did not render it impossible. In 2005, however, when the Court revisited this issue in the case of *Castle Rock* v. *Gonzales*, its decision closed off yet another avenue for battered women's claims, procedural due process suits. Perhaps just as important as its substantive holding, however, is the message the Court sent with the *Gonzales* decision. As the Court's second rejection of the Due Process clause as a basis for such suits, *Gonzales* strongly reinforces the overall tone of *DeShaney*, denying the state's obligation to protect citizens from private violence. Taken together, these two opinions seem to send this message so strongly that lower courts may even read the *Gonzales* opinion broadly to prohibit other constitutional arguments (such as equal protection claims), as happened in the wake of *DeShaney*. Whether that happens or not, it is clear that battered women can no longer rely on such suits for civil redress. Indeed, as options for a due-process-based remedy have all but vanished, the need for an affirmative right to privacy becomes even more urgent.

Overall, the civil lawsuits brought during this era were premised on the fact that battered women were not protected by police departments equally to victims of other crimes. Furthermore, this protection was being denied to them as a result of stereotypical ideas about gender roles and privacy, namely, the state's refusal to invade the sanctity of the private—often marital—home, no matter the injury to the woman inside. These suits deliberately attacked those conceptions of privacy, urging police and judges to make women's safety a higher priority than domestic privacy.

By insisting upon police protection for crimes of private as well as public violence, however, battered women and their advocates simultaneously implied that state intervention in the home was a desirable goal. Likewise, while this phase of the movement often succeeded in blurring the boundary between public and private spheres, plaintiffs in these suits were generally required to prove themselves worthy of this level of state protection, most often via the establishment of a "special relationship" with the local police. As such, these suits, which often achieved significant gains both for individual plaintiffs and for the movement as a whole, also reinforced a model of the state as protector. This model, while not necessarily negative, is nonetheless imbued with elements of paternalism that are problematic for the issue of domestic violence. Women's need for, desire for, and right to protection by the state thus creates an uneasy tension. On one hand, the civil suits of the 1980s represent battered women and their advocates demanding equal access to the protective power of the state to which they are constitutionally entitled. At the same time, they resist the ideo-logical constraints imposed by that power, having little need for a paternalistic state response that demands that women prove that they, or their relationships, deserve such protection. The paradox highlighted by battered women's demands for state protection echoes larger feminist debates about women's relationship to the state. These debates are at the core of the privacy issue for feminists who, while recognizing the need for police protection from abusive partners, question the extent to which state intervention should be pursued.

The history of battered women's civil litigation demonstrates the positive potential of state intervention in the home; namely, equal police protection for battered women. In the next chapter, however, I will explore the flip side of this issue; in particular, the dangers that exist for women (and men) in abusive same-sex relationships when the state enters the home. The historical develop-ment of the legal right to privacy outlined in chapter two reveals a clear privileg-ing of heterosexual, married relationships. The next chapter will examine the lasting implications of that legacy of privilege, further complicating the mean-ing of the "right to privacy" for battered women. Ultimately, given the inherent limitations of the state-as-protector model that chapter five will help to demon-strate, I will return to the assertion of an affirmative, *Liberta*-esque right to pri-vacy as a potential alternative to the privacy paradox.

NOTES

1. 64 N.Y.2d 152 (1984).

2. In *Monell* v. *Department of Social Services*, http://laws.findlaw.com/us/436/658 .html (full text), the Court reversed its previous ruling that municipalities could not be held liable under Section 1983, noting instead that municipalities should be con-sidered "persons" for such purposes and thus could now be held liable for damages under Section 1983. 436 U.S. 658, 1978: 700–701.

3. In addition to police departments, battered women's civil suits often named in-dividual police officers; prosecutors and/or other court personnel; and local govern-ing bodies with authority over these entities, such as city councils, as defendants.

4. 42 U.S.C. §1983, which will hereafter be referred to as "Section 1983," provides, "Every person who, under color of any statute, ordinance, regulation, custom, or usage, of any State or Territory or the District of Columbia, subjects, or causes to be subjected, any citizen of the United States or other person within the jurisdiction thereof to the deprivation of any rights, privileges, or immunities secured by the Constitution and laws, shall be liable to the party injured in an action at law, suit in equity, or other proper proceeding for redress."

5. 419 N.Y.S.2d 901 (1979).

6. No. C-76-2395 (N.D. Cal., filed Oct. 28, 1976).

7. 489 U.S. 189 (1989).

8. Ibid., 194.

9. Joan Zorza, "Suing the Police After *DeShaney*," n.d. Schlesinger Library, Radcliffe Institute for Advanced Study, Harvard University, National Center on Women and Family Law records, 96-M105, Box 36.

10. *Jessica Gonzales v. City of Castle Rock*, 307 F.3d 1258 (2002).

11. "Action Programs in Domestic Violence," 1978. Schlesinger Library, Radcliffe Institute for Advanced Study, Harvard University, National Organization for Women records, MC 496, Box 50, Folder 72.

12. Litigation Strategy Session Minutes, July 14, 1976. Schlesinger Library, Radcliffe Institute for Advanced Study, Harvard University, National Center on Women and Family Law records, 96-M105, Box 4.

13. See, for example, "Battered Women's Litigation Against Third Parties," n.d. NCOWFL Information Packet Item No. 24 (hereafter "Battered Women's Litigation"). Schlesinger Library, Radcliffe Institute for Advanced Study, Harvard University, National Center on Women and Family Law records, 96-M105, Box 36; "Recent Court Cases Concerning Battered Women," July 9, 1982, NCOWFL Information Packet (hereafter "Recent Court Cases"). Schlesinger Library, Radcliffe Institute for Advanced Study, Harvard University, National Center on Women and Family Law records, 96-M105, Box 36; and Laurie Woods, "Civil Litigation by Battered Women Against the Assailant and Against Government Officials," 1984 (hereafter "Civil Litigation"). Schlesinger Library, Radcliffe Institute for Advanced Study, Harvard University, National Center on Women and Family Law records, 96-M105, Box 24.

14. See, for example, *Nearing v. Weaver*, 295 Ore. 702 (1983).

15. See, for example, *Dudosh v. Allentown*, 629 F. Supp. 849 (1985), and *Bartalone v. County of Berrien*, 643 F. Supp. 574 (1986).

16. 595 F. Supp. 1521 (1984).

17. Ibid., 1527.

18. See, for example, *Doe v. Belleville*, No. 81-5256 (S.D. Ill. Sept. 9, 1983), and Earl Rinehart, "Judge Signs Decree on Handling of Domestic Cases," *Belleville [Illinois] News-Democrat* (September 11, 1983: 3A); and Earl Rinehart, "Police to End 'Cooling-Off Period' in Domestic Cases," *Belleville [Illinois] News-Democrat* (September 13, 1983: n. pg.).

19. "Recent Court Cases." Schlesinger Library, Radcliffe Institute for Advanced Study, Harvard University, National Center on Women and Family Law records, 96-M105, Box 36.

20. "Legal Advocacy for Battered Women," n.d., p. 1. Schlesinger Library, Radcliffe Institute for Advanced Study, Harvard University, National Center on Women and Family Law records, 96-M105, Box 22.

21. Laurie Woods, "Litigation on Behalf of Battered Women," *Women's Rights Law Reporter* 5 (1978): 31.

22. *Benway v. Watertown*, 1 A.D.2d 465 (1956).

23. *Morgan v. County of Yuba*, 230 Cal.App.2d 938 (1964).

24. *Jones v. Herkimer*, 51 Misc.2d 130 (1966).

25. *Zibbon v. Town of Cheektowaga*, 387 N.Y.S.2d 428 (1976).

26. *Canosa v. City of Mt. Vernon*, 327 N.Y.S.2d 843 (1971).

27. Pauline Gee, interview by author, May 24, 2002.

28. *Scott* Complaint, 3–7.

29. *Scott* Complaint, 6–7.

30. Ibid., 2.

31. Ibid., 7–8.

32. The OPD received funding from LEAA, the federal Law Enforcement Assistance Administration.

33. *Scott* Complaint, 8.

34. Unlike *Scott*, the *Bruno* complaint did not call attention to the race of its named plaintiffs, nor did it make any race-based discrimination claims (*Bruno* Complaint, 1–3).

35. Laurie Woods, "Litigation on Behalf of Battered Women," *Women's Rights Law Reporter* 5 (1978): 17.

36. *Bruno* Complaint, 77–81.

37. *Bruno v. Codd*, 1050.

38. Many victims of domestic violence obtain protective orders pro se or pro per, that is, "for themselves," or without the assistance of formal legal representation.

39. Laurie Woods, "Litigation on Behalf of Battered Women," *Women's Rights Law Reporter* 5 (1978): 17.

40. While plaintiffs recognized the federal claims available to them, such as the federal constitutional equal protection claim, they reserved those claims on the chance that, should they be granted class-action status yet lose on the merits, the resulting precedent would damage future federal actions on behalf of battered women. Laurie Woods, "Litigation on Behalf of Battered Women," *Women's Rights Law Reporter* 5 (1978): 21.

41. Ibid., 21.

42. Ibid., 24.

43. None of the official *Bruno* documents, nor the minutes from any of the litigation strategy sessions, mentions the issue of race, so neither the racial backgrounds of the named plaintiffs nor the reasons for the *Bruno* team's initial omission of a discussion about race from their suit is clear. During the appeals process, however, a coalition of groups representing the interests of women of color, including the Asian American Legal Defense and Education Fund and the National Conference of Black Lawyers, submitted an amicus brief on behalf of the *Bruno* plaintiffs. This brief ac-

knowledged that "the social and political issues affecting battered women cut across all class and racial lines" and that "[t]he denial of protection for battered women is part of the fabric of institutional malfeasance . . . which seriously affects the health or vitality of the poor and national racial communities" (*Bruno* Brief of Plaintiffs-Appellants, 13).

44. Gee, interview, 2002. Of course, New York City is no less racially diverse than Oakland, but the *Bruno* case did not directly address issues of race in its complaint (see previous footnote for further discussion).

45. *Scott* Complaint, 1–2, 7.

46. Gee, interview, 2002; *Scott* Complaint; *Scott* Amended Complaint.

47. Pauline Gee, "Class Action Challenges to the Criminal Justice System's Policy of Non-Intervention and Non-Arrest in Domestic Violence Cases," n.d., p. 4. Schlesinger Library, Radcliffe Institute for Advanced Study, Harvard University, National Center on Women and Family Law records, 96-M105, Box 24.

48. Ibid., 2.

49. Marjory Fields, interview by author, January 22, 2002.

50. Litigation Strategy Session Minutes, July 14, 1976. Schlesinger Library, Radcliffe Institute for Advanced Study, Harvard University, National Center on Women and Family Law records, 96-M105, Box 4.

51. Laurie Woods, "Litigation on Behalf of Battered Women," *Women's Rights Law Reporter* 5 (1978): 15–16.

52. Litigation Strategy Session Minutes, July 14, 1976; August 12, 1976; December 14, 1976; April 14, 1976. Schlesinger Library, Radcliffe Institute for Advanced Study, Harvard University, National Center on Women and Family Law records, 96-M105, Box 4.

53. J. C. Barden, "Wife Beaters: Few of them Even Appear Before a Court of Law," *New York Times*, October 21, 1974, n. pg.

54. "Batterers Beware! Oakland Police Department to Afford Better Police Protection to Battered Women." Schlesinger Library, Radcliffe Institute for Advanced Study, Harvard University, National Center on Women and Family Law records, 96-M105, Box 21.

55. In *Bruno*, the case against the probation and family court personnel was ultimately rejected by the court of appeals, which determined that those defendants either had already changed or were in the process of changing the challenged practices. For more information, see Laurie Woods, "Litigation on Behalf of Battered Women" (update), *Women's Rights Law Reporter* 7 (1981): fn 4.

56. The primary difference between these two types of agreements is that, unlike a consent judgment, a stipulation of settlement is not enforceable by judicial contempt proceedings (Laurie Woods, "Litigation on Behalf of Battered Women," *Women's Rights Law Reporter* 5 [1978]: 27). Nevertheless, both agreements provided significant measures of accountability and enforceability through a variety of mechanisms. Furthermore, while the differences between these two agreements are not insignificant, in the interest of simplicity, I use the terms "settlement" and "agreement" here generically and interchangeably to refer to both the settlement decree in *Scott* and the consent judgment in *Bruno*.

57. *Bruno* Consent Judgment, 32; *Scott* Settlement Decree, 2, 4.

58. *Bruno* Consent Judgment, 32–33; *Scott* Settlement Decree, 3–4.

59. *Bruno* Consent Judgment, 33; *Scott* Settlement Decree, 7.

60. *Bruno* Consent Judgment, 32; *Scott* Settlement Decree, 8; Pauline Gee, "Ensuring Police Protection for Battered Women: The *Scott* v. *Hart* Suit," *Signs: Journal of Women in Culture and Society* 8 (1983): 559.

61. While the language used in California is the more common "probable cause," the equivalent term in New York State is "reasonable cause."

62. Laurie Woods, "Litigation on Behalf of Battered Women," *Women's Rights Law Reporter* 5 (1978): 29.

63. *Scott* Complaint, 4; Gee, interview, 2002. Specifically, the *Scott* Complaint details a named plaintiff using this strategy in an attempt to obtain relief in a domestic assault, and notes, "Ms. Aubrey's past experience led her to conclude that the way to get the Oakland Police Department's assistance was not to identify the problem as involving a family dispute" (*Scott* Complaint, 4).

64. *Bruno* Consent Judgment, 32; *Scott* Settlement Decree, 5.

65. Of course, this problem represented a particularly insidious double-edged sword for battered women, who could certainly not get their partners arrested if they failed to call; yet, when they called frequently, were often designated pejoratively as "chronic callers," whose calls were subsequently ignored or not taken seriously (*Scott* Settlement Decree, 5).

66. *Bruno* Consent Judgment, 32; *Scott* Settlement Decree, 5.

67. *Bruno* Consent Judgment, 32.

68. *Scott* Settlement Decree, 5.

69. Gee, interview, 2002; *Scott* Settlement Decree, 10.

70. Gee, interview, 2002; *Scott* Settlement Decree, 10.

71. Gee, interview, 2002; *Scott* Settlement Decree, 10.

72. *Bruno* Consent Judgment, 33.

73. Ibid., 33.

74. Ibid., 33.

75. Gee, interview, 2002.

76. Fields, interview 2002; Gee, interview, 2002.

77. Gee, interview, 2002.

78. See, for example, "N.Y. Police Will Begin Arresting Wife Beaters," *Washington Post*, June 28, 1978, Wednesday, Final Edition, p. A10.

79. Laurie Woods, "Litigation on Behalf of Battered Women," *Women's Rights Law Reporter* 5 (1978): fn 154.

80. See *Thomas* v. *City of Los Angeles*, CA 00572/79 (Cal. Sup. Ct., filed Aug. 16, 1979, settled Nov. 4, 1985) and *Doe* v. *Belleville*, No. 81-5256 (S.D. Ill., filed Sept. 15, 1981; settled Sept. 9, 1983).

81. Pauline Gee, "Class Action Challenges to the Criminal Justice System's Policy of Non-Intervention and Non-Arrest in Domestic Violence Cases," n.d., p. 4. Schlesinger Library, Radcliffe Institute for Advanced Study, Harvard University, National Center on Women and Family Law records, 96-M105, Box 24.

82. See footnote 40, above.

83. For further information on this trend, see Douglas Martin, "The Rise and Fall of the Class Action Lawsuit," *New York Times*, January 8, 1988, p. B7; and Joel Seligman and Lindsey Hunter, "Rule 23: Class Actions at the Crossroads," *Arizona Law Review* 39 (1997): 407.

84. *Nearing v. Weaver*, 295 Ore. 702 (1983).

85. Ibid., 704.

86. *Huey v. Barloga*, 277 F. Supp. 864 (1967).

87. *Byrd v. Brishke*, 466 F.2d 6 (1972).

88. James T. R. Jones, "Battered Spouses' Section 1983 Damage Actions Against the Unresponsive Police After *DeShaney*," *West Virginia Law Review* 93 (1991): 264.

89. *Wright v. Ozark*, 715 F.2d 1513 (1983): 1516.

90. *Balistreri v. Pacifica*, 855 F.2d 1421 (1988): 1425.

91. Laura S. Harper, "Battered Women Suing Police for Failure to Intervene: Viable Legal Avenues After *DeShaney v. Winnebago County Department of Social Services*," *Cornell Law Review* 75 (1990): 1400–1402.

92. Ibid., 1400–1402.

93. *Harlow v. Fitzgerald*, 457 U.S. 800 (1982), 818, http://laws.findlaw.com/us/457/800.html (full text), http://www.oyez.org/cases/case?case=1980–1989/1981/1981_80_945 (audio).

94. See, for instance, *White v. Rochford*, 592 F.2d 381 (1979), *Jackson v. City of Joliet*, 715 F.2d 1200 (1983), *Lowers v. City of Streator*, 627 F.Supp. 244 (1985), *Escamilla v. City of Santa Ana*, 796 F.2d 266 (1986), *Sherrell v. City of Longview*, 683 F. Supp. 1108 (1987), and *Anderson v. Creighton*, 483 U.S. 635 (1987), http://laws.findlaw.com/us/483/635.html (full text), http://www.oyez.org/cases/case?case=1980–1989/1986/1986_85_1520 (audio).

95. *White v. Rochford*; *Jackson v. City of Joliet*.

96. *Lowers v. City of Streator*.

97. *Escamilla v. City of Santa Ana*.

98. Given the wide range of cases through which courts developed standards of immunity and liability at this time—including both domestic violence and nondomestic-violence cases—it appears that the standards did not discriminate, at least on the surface, between officers' responses to "public" violence (for instance, a bar fight) and "private" violence (such as domestic abuse). Nonetheless, as this book argues, state responses to these two kinds of violence have often differed dramatically.

99. *Anderson*, 641.

100. *Hynson v. City of Chester Legal Department*, 864 F.2d 1026 (1988).

101. See, for example, *Anderson*, *supra*, *Hynson*, *supra*, *Tarantino v. Baker*, 825 F.2d 772, 774 (1987), and *Turner v. Dammon*, 848 F.2d 440, 443 (1988).

102. *Nearing v. Weaver*, 295 Ore. 702 (1983).

103. Ibid., 741.

104. *Dudosh v. Allentown*, 629 F. Supp. 849 (1985).

105. Ibid., 855.

106. Ibid., 855.

107. It is important to note, however, that *Dudosh* was subsequently reconsidered by the district court, twice before and once after the *DeShaney* ruling. In each of these subsequent cases, the court accepted the Dudosh family's equal protection argument, but denied its substantive due process claim. *Dudosh v. Allentown*, 665 F. Supp. 381 (1987), *Dudosh v. Warg*, 668 F. Supp. 944 (1987), *Dudosh v. Allentown*, 722 F. Supp. 1233 (1989).

108. 643 F. Supp. 574.

109. Ibid., 575.

110. Ibid., 575.

111. Ibid., 577.

112. Ibid., 577.

113. 857 F.2d. 690 (1988).

114. Ibid., 691.

115. Ibid., 692. In this case, of course, the police's unwillingness to arrest one of their own undoubtedly contributed to their failure to intervene appropriately.

116. Ibid., 695.

117. Subsequently, on remand, the district court did grant qualified immunity in this case, but only to the individual officers. *Watson v. Kansas City*, Civil Action No. 84-2335-S (1989).

118. 595 F.Supp. 1521 (1984).

119. 65 N.Y.2d 461 (1985).

120. *Thurman*, 1525–26.

121. Ibid., 1526.

122. Ibid., 1528.

123. Ibid., 1528, 1529.

124. New York Family Court Act §168 states, in part, that "[t]he presentation of a copy of an order of protection or temporary order of protection or a warrant or a certificate of warrant to any peace officer, acting pursuant to his special duties, or police officer shall constitute authority for him to arrest a person charged with violating the terms of such order of protection or temporary order of protection and bring such person before the court and, otherwise, so far as lies within his power, to aid in securing the protection such order was intended to afford" (*Sorichetti*, 468).

125. Ibid., 465.

126. Ibid., 465.

127. Ibid., 465–66.

128. Ibid., 466–67.

129. Ibid., 467.

130. The jury originally awarded Dina three million dollars. The City, however, contested this amount, so, to avoid a new trial, plaintiffs agreed to a reduction of this verdict to two million dollars. Josephine's financial award was not affected by this development (*Sorichetti*, 461).

131. Ibid., 461.

132. Ibid., 471.

133. Ibid., 469.

134. Ibid., 469.

135. Ibid., 469.

136. See, for example, Greg Anderson, "*Sorichetti* v. *City of New York* Tells the Police that Liability Looms for Failure to Respond to Domestic Violence Situations," *University of Miami Law Review* 40 (1985): 333; Caitlin E. Borgmann, "Battered Women's Substantive Due Process Claims: Can Orders of Protection Deflect *DeShaney?*" *New York University Law Review* 65 (1990): 1280; Susanne M. Browne, "Due Process and Equal Protection Challenges to the Inadequate Response of the Police in Domestic Violence Situations," *Southern California Law Review* 68 (1995): 1295; Laura S. Harper, "Battered Women Suing Police for Failure to Intervene: Viable Legal Avenues After *DeShaney* v. *Winnebago County Department of Social Services,*" *Cornell Law Review* 75 (1990): 1393–1425; Carolyne R. Hathaway, "Gender Based Discrimination in Police Reluctance to Respond to Domestic Assault Complaints. *Thurman* v. *City of Torrington,*" *Georgetown Law Journal* 75 (1986): 667; Dirk Johnson, "Abused Women Get Leverage in Connecticut," *New York Times,* June 15, 1986: Section 4; Page 8; Lauren L. McFarlane, "Domestic Violence Victims v. Municipalities: Who Pays When the Police Will Not Respond?" *Case Western Reserve Law Review* 41 (1991): 929; Crystal Nix, "For Police, Domestic Violence is no Longer a Low Priority." *New York Times,* December 31, 1986: Section B; Page 1; Special to *New York Times,* "Court of Appeals Tells City to Pay $2 Million to Girl Father Stabbed," *New York Times.* July 10, 1985: Section B; p. 4; and Staff report, "Millions Awarded Beaten Wife Who Sued Connecticut Police," *Washington Post,* June 26, 1985: First Section; p. A7.

137. *A Cry for Help: The Tracey Thurman Story.* Dir. Robert Markowitz. Perf. Nancy McKeon, Bruce Weitz. Lifetime Original Movies, 1989.

138. *Collins* v. *Kings County,* 742 P.2d 185 (1987).

139. Ibid., 189.

140. Ibid., 189. As the *Collins* court noted, "the public policy that requires immunity for individual prosecutors also requires immunity for the county and the state. If it were otherwise, the objectives for granting immunity would be destroyed because the prosecutor would need to be concerned with potential tort litigation involving the county and state each time he made a prosecutorial decision. . . . This same public policy rationale applies to employees" (ibid., 270–71). This specific aspect of the *Collins* ruling, however, (extending this immunity to the county and the state) was overturned five years later in *Lutheran Day Care* v. *Snohomish County,* 829 P.2d 746 (1992).

141. 675 F. Supp. 314.

142. Ibid., 319.

143. Ibid., 317–18.

144. Ibid., 319.

145. 864 F.2d 1026.

146. Ibid., 1029.

147. Ibid., 1032.

148. See, for example, Justice Scalia's majority opinion in *Anderson* v. *Creighton,* noting that officers are protected by immunity *except* in those cases in which "a reasonable official would understand that what he is doing violates that right" (*Anderson,* 640).

149. Joan Zorza, "Suing the Police After *DeShaney*," n.d. Schlesinger Library, Radcliffe Institute for Advanced Study, Harvard University, National Center on Women and Family Law records, 96-M105, Box 36.

150. *DeShaney*, 192.

151. Ibid., 192.

152. Ibid., 193.

153. Ibid., 193.

154. Ibid., 193.

155. Ibid., 194.

156. The Court clearly acknowledged that the *DeShaney* case "invok[ed] the substantive rather than the procedural component of the Due Process Clause; petitioners do not claim that the State denied Joshua protection without according him appropriate procedural safeguards" (ibid., 195). Nonetheless, much of the majority opinion speaks generally about the due process clause without continuing to specify that it refers only to substantive, and not procedural, due process. This lack of specificity has invited some expansive interpretations of *DeShaney* in subsequent decisions by lower courts and the Supreme Court itself, as noted later in this chapter.

157. Ibid., 195.

158. Ibid., 196.

159. 448 U.S. 297.

160. *Harris* 1980, qtd. in *DeShaney*, 196.

161. *DeShaney*, 197.

162. See *Anderson v. Creighton* (1987).

163. *DeShaney*, 199–200.

164. Ibid., 200.

165. Ibid., 200.

166. I do not intend, here, to compare battered women's ability or inability to act on their own behalf to that of Joshua DeShaney. Much has been written debating the extent to which Battered Women's Syndrome does or does not render victims of domestic abuse helpless and unable to act for themselves, a conversation which is far outside the scope of this book. Instead, I am only calling attention here to the fact that the Court's insistence on a negative rights analysis obscured one of the most significant aspects of the case, thereby denying justice to the plaintiffs. The dangers inherent in this kind of analysis resonate strongly with those faced by battered women who are confronted with negative-rights interpretations of the right to privacy.

167. See, for example, *Bowen v. Kendrick*, 487 U.S. 589 (1988), http://laws.findlaw .com/us/487/589.html (full text), http://www.oyez.org/cases/case?case=1980–1989/19 87/1987_87_253 (audio); *Stanford v. Kentucky*, 492 U.S. 361 (1989), http://laws.findlaw .com/us/492/361.html (full text), http://www.oyez.org/cases/case?case=1980–1989/19 88/1988_87_5765 (audio); *Allegheny v. ACLU*, 492 U.S. 573 (1989), http://laws.findlaw .com/us/492/573.html (full text), http://www.oyez.org/cases/case?case=1980–1989/19 88/1988_87_2050 (audio); and *Webster v. Reproductive Health Services*, 492 U.S. 490 (1989), http://laws.findlaw.com/us/492/490.html (full text), http://www.oyez.org/ cases/case?case=1980–1989/1988/1988_88_605 (audio).

168. *DeShaney*, 207.

169. Ibid., 210.

170. Ibid., 210.

171. Ibid., 210.

172. Ibid., 212.

173. Ibid., 212.

174. "U.S. Supreme Court Ruling in DeShaney," *The Women's Advocate: Newsletter of the National Center on Women and Family Law* 10:2 (May, 1989): 1. Schlesinger Library, Radcliffe Institute for Advanced Study, Harvard University, National Center on Women and Family Law records, 96-M105, Box 24.

175. "The Implications of *DeShaney*," NCOWFL Information Packet. Item No. 40. Schlesinger Library, Radcliffe Institute for Advanced Study, Harvard University, National Center on Women and Family Law records, 96-M105, Box 24.

176. Joan Zorza, "Suing the Police After *DeShaney*," n.d. Schlesinger Library, Radcliffe Institute for Advanced Study, Harvard University, National Center on Women and Family Law records, 96-M105, Box 36. See also Laura Harper, "Battered Women Suing Police for Failure to Intervene: Viable Legal Avenues After *DeShaney* v. *Winnebago County Department of Social Services*," *Cornell Law Review* 75 (1990): 1393–1425.

177. Laura Harper, "Battered Women Suing Police for Failure to Intervene: Viable Legal Avenues After *DeShaney* v. *Winnebago County Department of Social Services*," *Cornell Law Review* 75 (1990): 1393–1425.

178. Caitlin E. Borgmann, "Battered Women's Substantive Due Process Claims: Can Orders of Protection Deflect *DeShaney*?" *New York University Law Review* 65 (1990): 1280.

179. Laura S. Harper, "Battered Women Suing Police for Failure to Intervene: Viable Legal Avenues After *DeShaney* v. *Winnebago County Department of Social Services*," *Cornell Law Review* 75 (1990): 1400–1402.

180. Akhil Reed Amar and Daniel Widawsky, "Child Abuse as Slavery: A Thirteenth Amendment Response to *DeShaney*," *Harvard Law Review* 105 (1992): 1359.

181. 901 F.2d 696 (1990).

182. Ibid., 698.

183. Ibid., 698.

184. Ibid., 698.

185. Ibid., 698.

186. Ibid., 698.

187. 855 F.2d 1421 (1988): 1426–27.

188. *Balistreri* 1990, 700.

189. *Brown* v. *City of Elba*, 754 F. Supp. 1551 (1990): 1555.

190. *Siddle* v. *City of Cambridge*, 761 F. Supp. 503 (1991): 508.

191. 837 P.2d 226 (1992).

192. Ibid., 229–30.

193. 877 F.2d. 409 (1989).

194. Ibid., 413.

195. Ibid., 414.

196. Ibid., 414.

197. *Ricketts v. City of Columbia*, 36 F.3d. 775 (1994), 778.

198. 911 F.2d. 52 (1990).

199. Ibid., 55.

200. See, for example, *Coffman v. Wilson*, 739 F. Supp. 257 (1990), *Raucci v. Rotterdam*, 902 F.2d 1050 (1990), *Hurlman v. Rice*, 927 F.2d 74 (1991), and *Roy v. City of Everett*, 738 P.2d 1090 (1992).

201. *Jessica Gonzales v. City of Castle Rock*, 366 F.3d 1093 (2004), 1096.

202. Ibid., 1096.

203. Ibid., 1097.

204. Ibid., 1097.

205. Ibid., 1098.

206. Ibid., 1098.

207. *Jessica Gonzales v. City of Castle Rock*, Civil Action No. 00-D-1285 (2001).

208. Gonzales's suit against the individual officers was later defeated at the Circuit Court level, where Judge Stephanie Seymour found that the individual officers—but not the city of Castle Rock—were entitled to the affirmative defense of qualified immunity. *Jessica Gonzales v. City of Castle Rock*, 366 F.3d 1093 (2004), 1118.

209. Ibid., 4.

210. Ibid., 8.

211. Ibid., 9; emphasis added.

212. Ibid., 12.

213. Ibid., 12.

214. *Board of Regents v. Roth*, 408 U.S. 564 (1972), 571, http://laws.findlaw.com/us/408/564.html (full text), cited in *Jessica Gonzales v. City of Castle Rock*, 366 F.3d 1093 (2004), 1101.

215. *Roth*, 571–72, 576, cited in *Jessica Gonzales v. City of Castle Rock*, 366 F.3d 1093 (2004), 1101.

216. *Roth*, 577, cited in *Jessica Gonzales v. City of Castle Rock*, 366 F.3d 1093 (2004), 1101.

217. *Cosco v. Uphoff*, 195 F. 3d. 1221 (1999), cited in *Jessica Gonzales v. City of Castle Rock*, 307 F.3d 1258 (2002), 1264.

218. *Jessica Gonzales v. City of Castle Rock*, Civil Action No. 00-D-1285 (2001), 13 (note 3).

219. Ibid., 14.

220. *Jessica Gonzales v. City of Castle Rock*, 307 F.3d 1258 (2002).

221. By the full court, as opposed to the smaller panel of judges that typically hears cases at this level.

222. *Jessica Gonzales v. City of Castle Rock*, 366 F.3d 1093 (2004).

223. *Jessica Gonzales v. City of Castle Rock*, 366 F.3d 1093 (2004), 1106.

224. Brief of National Black Police Association, National Association of Black Law Enforcement Officers, Women in Federal Law Enforcement, The National Center for Women & Policing, and Americans for Effective Law Enforcement, Inc., as Amici Curiae Supporting Respondent, p. 68 (February 10, 2005).

225. Brief of National Coalition Against Domestic Violence and National Center for Victims of Crime as Amici Curiae in Support of Respondent, p. 14 (February 10, 2005).

226. *Castle Rock* v. *Gonzales*, 125 S. Ct 2796 (2005), 2805; original emphasis.

227. Justice Scalia's disdain for the notion that enforcement of a restraining order could constitute a property interest was quite evident even at oral argument. He repeatedly referred to such a notion as "zany," as in the following: "[I]f Colorado chooses to nominate some utterly zany thing of property interest, it doesn't necessarily mean that it's a property interest for purposes of the Federal Constitution," and, "Do we have any cases involving a zany property interest having been found by a state? I don't think we have any." Oral Argument of *Castle Rock* v. *Gonzales*, Alderson Reporting Company, available at U.S. Supreme Court Online: http://www.supremecourtus.gov/oral_arguments/argument_transcripts/04-278.pdf, p. 14.

228. *Castle Rock* v. *Gonzales*, 125 S. Ct 2796 (2005), 2816.

229. Ibid., 2817.

230. Ibid., 2819–20; original.

231. "Gonzales Ruling a 'Serious Blow' to Victims of Violence Who Need Police Protection," *Speaking Up* [online publication of the Family Violence Prevention Fund]. June 27, 2005, vol. 11, issue 9, top story.

232. In an article entitled, "Law Enforcement Liability in the Wake of *Castle Rock* v. *Gonzales*," (*The Source, Newsletter of the Stalking Resource Center* 6 [Winter 2006]), Jim Ferguson notes,

> In the wake of the [*Gonzales* decision], it was widely reported that the Court had given law enforcement blanket immunity for failing to enforce protective orders. See, for example, *Cold Law at Castle Rock*, CLEV. PLAIN DEALER, July 5, 2005, at B8 ("The 7-2 court majority made clear, as the court had ruled before, that police have no responsibility to protect any individual citizen."); Sarah M. Buel, Commentary, *Battered Women Betrayed*, L.A. TIMES, July 4, 2005, at B13 ("Last week, the Supreme Court ruled that police are not required to enforce restraining orders, even if state law mandates that they do so."); *High Court Deals Out a Low Blow*, KAN. CITY STAR, June 29, 2005, at B1 ("The Supreme Court ruled in Castle Rock v. Gonzales that the cops are under no real obligation to protect you and yours-even when it's a matter of a court order."); *High Court Shields Police Who Fail to Enforce Restraining Orders*, L.A. TIMES, June 28, 2005, at A19 ("The Supreme Court ruled Monday that police departments can't be sued for failing to enforce restraining orders . . . .")

233. *Castle Rock* v. *Gonzales*, 125 S. Ct 2796 (2005), 2810.

234. See, for example, Emily J. Martin and Caroline Bettinger-Lopez, "*Castle Rock* v. *Gonzales* and the Future of Police Protection for Victims of Domestic Violence," *Domestic Violence Report*, October/November 2005, vol. 11, no. 1; Julie Hilden, "Must the Government Protect Its Citizens If It Learns They Are in Danger? The Supreme Court Considers How Far Responsibility Reaches" (Findlaw.com, Mar. 29, 2005): http://writ.news.findlaw.com/hilden/20050329.html, and Joan Zorza, "Things

We Still Can Do After the *Castle Rock* v. *Gonzales* Decision, *Domestic Violence Report*, October/November 2005, vol. 11, no. 1.

235. Martin and Bettinger-Lopez, 15.

236. Emily J. Martin and Caroline Bettinger-Lopez, "*Castle Rock* v. *Gonzales* and the Future of Police Protection for Victims of Domestic Violence," *Domestic Violence Report*, October/November 2005, vol. 11, no. 1, and Joan Zorza, "Things We Still Can Do After the *Castle Rock* v. *Gonzales* Decision, *Domestic Violence Report*, October/November 2005, vol. 11, no. 1.

5. PRIVACY AND DOMESTIC VIOLENCE
IN SAME-SEX RELATIONSHIPS

INTRODUCTION

The history of battered women's civil litigation, explored in the previous chapter, demonstrates the extent to which women's safety has been linked to the state's willingness—or refusal—to intervene in the violent home. Those civil suits of the 1980s underscored the fact that the characterization of the domestic sphere as inherently private—and therefore impermeable by the state—often results in danger or death for victims of domestic violence. Yet these cases, like many of the criminal cases that preceded them, dealt almost exclusively with heterosexual relationships. Even when an alternative vision of privacy was articulated in the courts with regard to domestic violence—for instance, in the *Liberta*[1] case—it too emerged from within the context of a marital relationship, and reflected that heterosexual model. As a result, both the positive and negative conceptions of domestic privacy that have emerged thus far have related primarily to married couples, and almost exclusively to heterosexual relationships.

Yet the problem of domestic violence is not confined to marriage or to heterosexual relationships. In fact, available statistics[2] suggest that rates of intimate partner violence in same-sex relationships parallel those within "straight" relationships.[3] Likewise, as numerous scholars have demonstrated, battered gay men and lesbians experience the same types of domestic violence as those that emerge in heterosexual relationships (including physical, verbal, sexual, emotional, and economic abuse).[4] At the same time, however, victims of same-sex battering are often subject to additional dimensions of abuse not encountered by their heterosexual peers, such as threats of "outing" by their batterer, the stress of revealing their sexual orientation when seeking services, social stigma from within as well as outside of LGBT communities, and, frequently, a lack of social services and/or legal recourse should they decide to report the abuse.[5] For these reasons, the analysis presented in this chapter takes as its starting point the recognition that same-sex violence, despite sharing some important similarities with heterosexual battering, is not its equivalent, and requires different analytical frameworks.

The paucity of legal options is a particularly significant factor compounding the problem of same-sex domestic violence. As of 2005, six states still explicitly exclude victims of same-sex domestic violence from civil legal protection, while another 14 states refuse this protection unless the couple has cohabitated.[6] As Pam Elliott suggests, "All battering victims perceive isolation, but gays and lesbians who have no hope of asking for help because of a lack of civil rights protection, and because of having no access to the legal system by definition, are the most isolated victims in society."[7] While this lack of legal recourse is certainly complicated by other categories of identity such as class and race, Elliot highlights the general isolation and invisibility that victims of same-sex violence experience within the judicial system.

Furthermore, the issue of legal privacy has always proven particularly problematic when applied to intimate same-sex relationships. As each of the previous chapters have demonstrated, concepts of privacy, both judicial and popular, have been critical to American society's understandings of and responses to domestic violence. At the most immediate level, notions of privacy and the sanctity of the home often determine whether and to what extent police provide protection to victims. Inside the courtroom, judicial formulations of privacy establish whether or not grievances are addressed, victims are compensated, and perpetrators are punished. For heterosexual relationships, as chapters one through four have demonstrated, this model has been well established. When violence occurs between intimate partners of the same sex, however, the role of privacy becomes more complicated, for privacy has particular and unique implications for lesbians and gay men.

In direct contrast to the state's ongoing reluctance to intervene in the heterosexual home, gay and lesbian relationships have historically been subject to intense levels of state interference and scrutiny. Criminal sodomy laws, in particular, have codified a government view of same-sex intimate relationships as deviant and even felonious. State criminal codes from the nineteenth century that prohibited sodomy[8] and other "crimes against nature"[9] generally excluded married couples from their reach, whether officially or in practice.

When confronting the problem of same-sex domestic violence, all of these issues converge: the existence of domestic violence within homosexual relationships, the overall lack of legal recourse for its victims, and the tension between the LGBT community and legal notions of privacy. In fact, the confluence of these issues only serves to highlight the ways in which the state's construction of privacy rights has played such a critical role in the reinforcing of patriarchal family forms, its reverence for the "traditional," nuclear family home only matched by its disregard for families and people outside of that model. The implications of this situation for gay and lesbian victims of domestic violence have been profound. As this chapter demonstrates, the legal response to same-sex domestic violence has been particularly shaped by the concept of privacy. An examination of the problem of same-sex domestic violence (and the legal response to it) thus provides additional insight into the limitations of the existing privacy model. In particular, this analysis reveals the exclusionary nature of the right to privacy as currently understood and, as such, highlights the need for a new model of privacy.

I begin this chapter, therefore, by discussing and building upon two theoretical concepts that are particularly relevant to the problem of same-sex domestic violence: Kendall Thomas's analysis of privacy as secrecy,[10] and Ruthann Robson's concept of hetero-relationizing.[11] I then trace the implications of the historical relationship between judicial privacy and sodomy laws for lesbians and gay men. This section, which culminates in a critical case analysis of the two US Supreme Court cases that have addressed this issue, *Bowers* v. *Hardwick*[12] and *Lawrence* v. *Texas*,[13] explores criminal sodomy laws as a locus for judicial homophobia. It is this judicial homophobia that has served as the basis for denying a right of privacy to homosexuals.

After tracing the unique history and implications of privacy for homosexuals, I then examine the issue of same-sex domestic violence. I first discuss the activism that has been undertaken to address this problem, including the factors that have inhibited these efforts. Next, I trace the outcomes of same-sex domestic violence cases in state courts; my analysis focuses on published, appellate-level opinions.[14] These cases not only illustrate the limitations of the current model of privacy for same-sex victims of domestic violence, but also highlight the need for a new vision of privacy more broadly. The chapter concludes with an analysis of the implications of privacy for the issue of same-sex domestic violence, and an exploration of the potential for an alternative model of privacy.

PRIVACY AS SECRECY AND THE PROBLEM OF HETERO-RELATIONIZING

For gay men, lesbians, transgendered people, and others whose sexual relationships are not represented within the dominant heterosexual paradigm, privacy has traditionally been a double-edged sword. Instead of invoking the sanctity of the marital home, privacy in this context often invokes both the safety and the restriction of the closet. The privacy of not revealing one's sexual orientation to a hostile public can signify a survival strategy in light of the hegemonic structures that enforce compulsory heterosexuality. As Kendall Thomas has observed,

> for [gay men and lesbians], the claim of privacy always also structurally implies a claim to secrecy. Under the existing legal and political regime, gay men and lesbians are aware that the chief value of the language of privacy is that it can be used not so much to provide a space for self-discovery, but to provide against the dangers of disclosure.[15]

Those "dangers of disclosure" are all too real in a society in which homosexual relationships are rendered invisible by the state or even criminalized. Indeed, laws such as the Defense of Marriage Act[16] and criminal sodomy statutes codify this invisibility and criminality. Furthermore, as Janet Halley has observed, the secrecy of the closet also results in a social and political invisibility that renders gay men and lesbians unable to assert their political claims. Within this paradigm, when members of the LGBT community do become visible, it is often in the most unusual (and negative) circumstances—thus reinforcing homophobic stereotypes within the dominant culture.[17]

Thus, from the perspective of a community where secrecy is, by necessity, employed strategically, privacy is quite a loaded concept. This idea has two important implications for privacy as it relates to the problem of domestic violence. First, any study of same-sex domestic violence must recognize that the state's reverence for the privacy of the marital home does not generally apply to homosexual relationships. Indeed, when the concept of privacy is applied by the state to these relationships, it is to render them invisible and disempowered. Instead, privacy in this context often refers to individual efforts to shield personal relationships from state scrutiny. Second, the mainstream battered women's movement's urgent call for increased state intervention in the home during violent incidents carries significantly increased danger for gay men and lesbians, whose desire or need for secrecy (or at least, greater control over their exposure to public scrutiny), particularly from the state, is often paramount. It is critical, therefore, to understand the nuanced ways in which privacy shapes the problem of same-sex domestic violence, often operating quite differently than it does in the context of violent heterosexual relationships.

A related problem occurs when researchers, activists, advocates, judges, or juries attempt to apply heterosexual models of domestic violence to homosexual relationships. Ruthann Robson has coined the term "hetero-relationizing" to describe these attempts to force problems that occur across a wide range of intimate relationships into a strictly heterosexual mold.[18] The inclination to do so may arise because both types of violent relationships share some similarities, including similar types and rates of violence, as noted above. Nevertheless, as several scholars have argued, the unique issues faced by victims of same-sex violence merit more specific analytical approaches.[19] Robson has observed that judges and juries seeking to understand and assess a case of lesbian domestic violence will often attempt to designate one partner as the "male" of the relationship, and the other as the "female."[20] This assignation of binary gender roles in order to determine the aggressor often obscures and oversimplifies the reality of the violence that occurs between partners of the same sex.

In the same way that such hetero-relationizing can seriously distort a trial, it can also impede scholarly research into same-sex domestic violence. As Mary Eaton has suggested, theorizing that attempts to equate intra-lesbian violence with heterosexual violence can be offensive, inaccurate, and unproductive:

> [F]eminist theory of this sort feeds general heterosexist stereotypes about lesbians in which fulfilling sexual connection is deemed impossible in the absence of gender alterity, at best a bad copy and unfulfillable attempt to simulate the "real thing." This imposition of a heteronormative framework upon lesbian relationships is not only insulting, it is especially dangerous as a cognitive device for understanding lesbian battering, because it feeds the common myth about abusive lesbian relationships that "butches" are batterers and "femmes" their victims.[21]

In addition to reinforcing misconceptions about same-sex relationships, research that imposes heterosexual models on all domestic violence also renders invisible the particular challenges confronted by lesbian and gay male victims and the skills they have developed for confronting these challenges.

Responding to the falsely universalizing tendency of heteronormative research models, Eaton further contends that such attempts are inherently inadequate. While such models have done much to increase our understanding of intimate violence within heterosexual relationships, they cannot claim to be— nor should they attempt to be—all-encompassing. Instead, she suggests that research on heterosexual battering simply clarify its parameters and acknowledge its applicability only to heterosexual relationships—thereby narrowing its focus and increasing its utility. Likewise, she suggests that new theories and research must be developed that focus exclusively and specifically on intra-lesbian violence in order to begin to understand its nuances. While I concur with Eaton's caution about the dangers of universalizing, as well as her call for new scholarship that specifically addresses same-sex violence, I would go one step further. I believe that examining the problem of same-sex domestic violence, particularly given its unique relationship to the issue of privacy, sheds important light on the issues of domestic violence and privacy more broadly, and helps us to understand some of the deficiencies within the existing frameworks for understanding heterosexual domestic violence, as well. Thus, my research yields two critical results: first, it helps to illuminate the still vastly understudied problem of same-sex domestic violence. At the same time, applying the lens of sexual orientation to the problem of intimate partner violence provides significant insights about the complexity of the interaction between domestic violence and privacy in general. Ultimately, my approach seeks to initiate the articulation of an alternative, affirmative vision of privacy that is both inclusive and proactive in its protection of all victims of intimate partner violence.

PRIVACY AND SODOMY

INTRODUCTION

Courts and legislatures have considered issues of homosexuality in many aspects of life, from employment to military service to freedom of speech to immigration.[22] These issues generally pertain to civil law and have specific applications (subject to military or immigration status, for example). Sodomy statutes, by contrast, exist in the criminal arena, and could potentially apply to almost all lesbians and gay men at some point in their lives. While some criminal sodomy statutes have been directly aimed at homosexuals, or have specifically exempted married couples,[23] many have simply addressed the act of sodomy itself and not the sexual orientation of those committing the "crime against nature."[24] In practice, however, regardless of whether the language of the statute is neutral with regard to sexual orientation, sodomy laws over the last century have been enforced primarily against lesbians and gay men.[25] As a result, these statutes have created an inherent tension between the LGBT community and the law, a dynamic that has significant implications for the issue of same-sex domestic violence.

Like other criminal laws, sodomy laws might be presumed to target a particular behavior or action. Since the late nineteenth century, however, while people of all sexual orientations have engaged in sodomy, heterosexuals—particularly married couples—have been exempt from state punishment for the behavior, whether as a matter of law, or in practice, or both. This exemption has occurred because, in its effort to protect and exalt heterosexual marriage, the state has often conflated homosexual identity with the act of sodomy. Seeking to circumscribe the limits of acceptable intimate relationships, courts and legislatures have sought to penalize those who do not conform to the heterosexual model. In so doing, they have, as Janet Halley has observed, "treat[ed] sodomy as a metonym for homosexual personhood,"[26] thereby attempting to criminalize homosexuality itself. By conflating the action of sodomy with the identity of homosexuality, sodomy laws in recent memory have seemed uniquely targeted at a category of people rather than at a specific form of conduct.

Yet this emphasis on identity instead of behavior as the locus of punishment did not occur until the turn of the twentieth century, according to William Eskridge. Prior to that time, he notes, sodomy laws—also known as buggery, carnal knowledge, or crime-against-nature laws—focused on behavior rather than identity, and prohibited "unnatural" sexual relations between men and women, as well as between two men. Often deliberately vague, such laws were nonetheless generally understood to refer to anal intercourse, and did not apply to sexual acts between two women.[27] Eskridge cites late-nineteenth-century American society's preoccupation with the enforcement of strict gender roles as the basis for the increasing societal focus on the moral implications of homosexuality. In particular, the rise of urbanization and the visibility of prostitution—along with the corresponding social purity movement and emphasis on true womanhood— led to the usage of sodomy laws as an instrument of social control.[28] During this era, both courts and legislatures added the crime of oral sex to sodomy statutes. This addition, according to Eskridge, served several purposes. First, the more widespread practice of oral sex by both women and men allowed for more arrests. In addition, the fact that oral sex was committed by female couples allowed for the criminalization of lesbian relationships.[29]

After the amendment of many state sodomy laws to include oral sex, arrests for sodomy—particularly homosexual sodomy—rose dramatically. This wave of arrests continued, with various ebbs and flows, throughout the first half of the twentieth century.[30] After the beginning of the gay rights movement in the late 1960s,[31] activists increasingly turned their attention toward repealing sodomy laws. In fact, by the mid-1980s, 37 states had either legislatively repealed or judicially nullified their sodomy laws pertaining to consenting adults, or reduced the offense of consensual sodomy from a felony to a misdemeanor.[32] Concurrently, however, a backlash trend was occurring that specifically targeted gay men and lesbians. Some state legislatures, while relaxing their proscriptions of heterosexual sodomy, simultaneously enacted new laws criminalizing same-sex sodomy.[33] Similarly, courts in two states found sodomy statutes written in gender-neutral language to be inapplicable to consensual heterosexual sodomy — and therefore applicable only to homosexual sodomy.[34]

Case Resources
Griswold v. *Connecticut*
Findlaw (http://laws.findlaw.com/us/381/479.html) (full text)
Oyez (http://www.oyez.org/cases/case/?case=1960-1969/1964/1964_496) (oral arguments)

From within this complex political climate emerged a landmark case regarding consensual homosexual sodomy, entitled *Doe v. Commonwealth's Attorney for Richmond*.[35] In this 1975 case, two gay men challenged Virginia's criminal sodomy statute in federal district court, seeking a declaratory judgment that the statute was unconstitutional and injunctive relief against its enforcement. (The statute made consensual sodomy a felony; the gender-neutral wording included both oral and anal sex.) Their claim was rooted in numerous constitutional bases, including the due process clauses of the Fifth and Fourteenth Amendments, the First Amendment right of freedom of expression, the right to privacy (which they located in the First and Ninth Amendments), and the prohibition of cruel and unusual punishment in the Eighth amendment.[36] Primarily, the plaintiffs relied on the construction of the fundamental right to privacy, as articulated in *Griswold v. Connecticut*,[37] as the source of their assertion that the statute was unconstitutional.

Case Resources
Poe v. *Ullman*
Findlaw (http://laws.findlaw.com/us/367/497.html) (full text)
Oyez (http://www.oyez.org/cases/case/?case=1960-1969/1960/1960_60) (oral arguments)

The district court hearing the case disagreed, emphasizing instead the fact that *Griswold* bestowed the right to privacy on married couples specifically. The opinion then recalled Justice Harlan's dissent in the contraception case prior to *Griswold*, *Poe v. Ullman*.[38] In that opinion, Harlan had articulated a right to privacy that was defined, in part, by its limitations; he stated clearly that only marital relationships deserved this right to privacy, while all other sexual relationships simply did not. In addition, he noted, "[L]aws forbidding adultery, fornication and homosexual practices . . . , [and] confining sexuality to lawful marriage, form a pattern so deeply pressed into the substance of our social life that any Constitutional doctrine in this area must build upon that basis."[39] Relying heavily on this construction of the privacy right, the *Doe* court concluded that state proscription of sodomy was a perfectly legitimate enterprise. Here again, however, the court conflated homosexuality and sodomy, asserting that "homosexuality . . . is obviously no portion of marriage, home or family life—the next question is whether there is any ground for barring Virginia from branding it as criminal."[40] The "it" in the latter half of the sentence clearly refers to homosexuality, not to sodomy. As with other state formulations of sodomy, this court substituted the identity of homosexuality for the practice of sodomy, disregarding the fact that the statute could also be applied to heterosexual sodomy. By singling out for punishment only one class of people engaging in an activity, the *Doe* court, in effect, affirmed Virginia's right to penalize its citizens based on their identity rather than their actions. When, upon appeal, the US Supreme Court summarily affirmed the district court's decision, the *Doe* opinion gained significant judicial weight and remained the last word on the subject for more than a decade. Yet, as the next section will demonstrate, judicial homophobia and its implications for the right of privacy reached even greater proportions in the case of *Bowers* v. *Hardwick*.

THE CASE OF BOWERS V. HARDWICK

The US Supreme Court had the opportunity to consider the issues of privacy, sodomy, and homosexuality again eleven years later in the landmark case of *Bowers* v. *Hardwick*.[41] While the facts of the *Bowers* case differed greatly from those in *Doe*, the outcome was very similar. Ultimately, in *Bowers*, as in *Doe*, the court's disapproval of homosexuality and desire to condemn homosexual relationships overrode its concern for privacy rights. In a plurality opinion characterized primarily by its homophobia and roundly criticized by legal scholars for both its erroneous representation of history and its faulty reasoning,[42] the Supreme Court flatly refused to consider the case as a matter of privacy. Instead, the Court chose to reflect on whether or not the US Constitution confers a fundamental right to engage in homosexual sodomy. Formulated this way, the question was easily answered by the Court in the negative, and the privacy rights of homosexuals remained unrecognized.

As a challenge to a state sodomy law, the facts of *Bowers* could not have made for a more promising test case. In August 1982 in Atlanta, Michael Hardwick, a 29-year-old employee of a gay bar, was holding a beer as he left work and was subsequently arrested under a recently enacted city ordinance prohibiting the possession of open containers of alcohol in public places. Having been issued a citation, Hardwick initially failed to appear for his court date, but went to the courthouse the following day and paid the fine. Hardwick's failure to appear had nonetheless triggered an arrest warrant and, days later, a police officer arrived at Hardwick's house to serve the warrant. Hardwick's roommate allowed the officer to enter the house. The officer found Hardwick's bedroom door ajar and witnessed the young man engaging in consensual oral sex with another man. The officer subsequently arrested Hardwick for violation of Georgia's criminal sodomy statute.[43]

At the time, local gay rights activists had been looking for a test case with which to challenge the sodomy statute. After hearing of Hardwick's arrest, several of these activists—in addition to Hardwick's mother, who was in town visiting him at the time—convinced him to allow the case to go forward, although the authorities did not seem to be pursuing it vigorously.[44]

While the Georgia chapter of the American Civil Liberties Union (ACLU) was not immediately willing to become directly involved in the case, one of its board members, John Sweet, was. He asked one of his staff members, attorney Kathleen Wilde, to take the case.[45] At the time, the case hung in a kind of legal limbo: the district attorney's office, which had not dropped the charges, had also decided not to present the case to a grand jury "unless further evidence develop[ed]."[46] Because an employee in the DA's office suspected that to pursue a prosecution might open the door for a test case, Hardwick was not prosecuted on the sodomy charge. With no criminal indictment to appeal, Wilde instead brought a civil suit under Section 1983 against Michael Bowers, the Attorney General of Georgia.[47] Because the sodomy statute was written using gender-neutral language, a married couple (known in the suit as Jane and John Doe) also joined the suit as plaintiffs.

Despite the fact that, as Wilde observed, "We had the best facts anyone could hope for,"[48] the district court dismissed the suit immediately. The court concluded that the married couple failed to present a justiciable controversy, for they had not demonstrated that they or any other married couples were in danger of prosecution under the existing statute. Next, they rejected all of Hardwick's constitutional arguments by relying exclusively on *Doe* v. *Commonwealth's Attorney.*[49]

Case Resources

Carey v. *Population Services International*

Findlaw (http://laws.findlaw.com/us/431/678.html) (full text)

Oyez (http://www.oyez.org/cases/1970-1979/1976/1976_75_443/) (opinion announcement)

New York v. *Uplinger*

Findlaw (http://laws.findlaw.com/us/467/246.html) (full text)

Oyez (http://www.oyez.org/cases/case?case=1980-1989/1983/1983_82_1724) (oral arguments)

Wilde began the appeals process at once, and *Hardwick* v. *Bowers*[50] received a much warmer reception in the Eleventh Circuit appellate court. Considering two recent actions taken by the US Supreme Court, the circuit court concluded that *Doe* was no longer controlling. In particular, the circuit court noted the Supreme Court's assertion, in *Carey* v. *Population Services*,[51] that "the Court has not definitively answered the difficult question whether and to what extent the Constitution prohibits state statutes regulating [private consensual sexual] behavior among adults . . . and we do not purport to answer that question now."[52] In addition, the *Hardwick* court observed that the US Supreme Court had granted, although subsequently dismissed, a writ of certiorari to hear the case of *New York* v. *Uplinger*,[53] which urged review of that state's consensual sodomy statute. In light of these developments, the circuit court concluded that the constitutional issues presented by *Hardwick* had not been resolved, and *Doe* could no longer be seen as controlling in this area.

Case Resources

Roe v. *Wade*

Findlaw (http://laws.findlaw.com/us/410/113.html) (full text)

Oyez (http://www.oyez.org/cases/case/?case=1970-1979/1971/1971_70_18) (oral arguments)

Eisenstadt v. *Baird*

Findlaw (http://laws.findlaw.com/us/405/438.html) (full text)

Oyez (http://www.oyez.org/cases/case/?case=1970-1979/1971/1971_70_17) (oral arguments)

The circuit court thus viewed Hardwick's constitutional claims more favorably than the district court had, and considered the statute a violation of his right to privacy. This opinion, written by Judge Johnson, adopted a view of privacy that privileged neither the home itself nor the marital relationship. Instead, Johnson's articulation of the privacy right emphasized personal autonomy and decision making, particularly with regard to intimate relations. Relying heavily on reproductive rights cases such as *Roe* v. *Wade*[54] and *Eisenstadt* v. *Baird*,[55] he wrote:

> The Constitution prevents the States from unduly interfering in certain individual decisions critical to personal autonomy because those decisions are essentially private and beyond the legitimate reach of a civilized society. . . .
>
> While the constitutional source of these limitations of the power of the State has been termed the "right to privacy," it is not limited to conduct that takes place strictly in private. Some personal decisions affect an individual's life so keenly that the right

to privacy prohibits state interference even though the decisions could have significant public consequences. . . .

> The Supreme Court has indicated in *Griswold* . . . and *Eisenstadt* . . . that the
> intimate associations protected by the Constitution are not limited to those with a
> procreative purpose. . . . The intimate association protected against state interfer-
> ence does not exist in the marriage relationship alone. . . . For some, the sexual activ-
> ity in question here serves the same purpose as the intimacy of marriage.[56]

Thus, the Circuit Court found the Georgia statute unconstitutionally violative of the Ninth Amendment (echoing *Griswold*) and the Fourteenth Amendment right to due process.

While this decision was a solid victory for the Hardwick team, they knew the
battle was far from over; Wilde notes that "it was pretty clear from the beginning
that the case was going all the way up [to the United States Supreme Court]."[57]
Indeed, Bowers quickly appealed the circuit court's ruling to the US Supreme
Court. By this time, a groundswell of support for the case had developed among
activists and attorneys both locally and nationally. An ad hoc group devoted to
working on legal issues for the gay community met regularly to discuss the direction of the case. The Lambda Legal Defense Fund, the Georgia ACLU, the New
York ACLU, and many prominent attorneys endorsed Hardwick's position and
provided support for the case. Renowned attorney Laurence Tribe offered to serve
as counsel at the Supreme Court level; Wilde and another attorney, Kathleen Sullivan, served as co-counsel. Assessing the composition of the Court at that time,
the coalition of lawyers and activists supporting Hardwick were cautiously opti-
mistic, figuring that "this was the best court we'd have for the next ten years."[58]

At the Supreme Court level, the Hardwick camp continued to highlight the
privacy argument that had served them well in the circuit court. The language
they adopted echoed that of the circuit court's opinion, as they referred to Hardwick's "fundamental constitutional right to personal autonomy and privacy."[59]
In so doing, Hardwick's attorneys made two significant rhetorical moves. First,
they framed the issue as being primarily about the right to privacy, rather than
about sexual orientation or particular sexual practices. Second, the assertion
of a fundamental right to "personal autonomy and privacy"—rather than just
"privacy"—drove a wedge between the association of privacy with the marital
relationship, replacing it instead with notions of individual autonomy and independence.

These two rhetorical strategies were essential in the Hardwick team's effort
to portray the case as primarily a matter of privacy. In fact, while the amicus
briefs that were written for Hardwick came from a wide range of groups, they all

adopted these two strategies, to varying degrees. Citing many of the contraceptive and family privacy cases from earlier in the twentieth century,[60] several of the amicus groups observed that the Supreme Court had previously recognized a right of privacy related both to location (i.e., the home itself) and to the realm of personal decision making. This case, they noted, implicated both of those types of privacy.[61] These briefs deliberately echo the Court's own language in earlier privacy cases, while broadening it to include all citizens, not just married couples. Thus, the briefs refer to "[t]he fundamental sanctity of a *person's* home,"[62] and "private consensual sexual conduct,"[63] rather than to the marital home and marital intimacy.

The amicus groups accomplished this move toward inclusion by first invoking Douglas's impassioned conclusion to the *Griswold* opinion, a fitting reference given the facts of *Bowers*: "Would we allow the police to search the sacred precincts of marital bedrooms for telltale signs of the use of contraceptives? The very idea is repulsive to the notions of privacy . . ."[64] They then applied the logic of *Eisenstadt* to this scenario: "If the right of privacy means anything, it is the right of the *individual, married or single,* to be free from unwarranted governmental intrusion into matters so fundamentally affecting a person as the decision whether to bear or beget a child."[65] In this way, amici suggested that the unequal application of the privacy right would contradict the Court's previous rulings.

Several amicus groups took this argument one step further, pointedly observing that *Bowers* had as much to do with discrimination as with privacy. Noting the trend of disproportionate enforcement of sodomy laws against gay men and lesbians and the fact that "Hardwick represents an oft-despised and heavily stereotyped sexual minority,"[66] these briefs contended that the sodomy law in question denied privacy rights to homosexuals as a matter of discrimination.[67] Indeed, several amici linked this discrimination explicitly to the history of judicial bias against women and people of color.[68] Together with the briefs that demonstrated scientific, religious, and public support for homosexual lifestyles,[69] these briefs powerfully declared the right of privacy to be the defining issue in the *Bowers* case, and the unequal application of that right to be a severe injustice.

The oral argument that Tribe presented to the Court on behalf of Hardwick echoed this reasoning. Tribe framed the case as a privacy issue from the outset, beginning his argument with the simple assertion that "this case is about the limits of governmental power."[70] Describing the contours of the fundamental right to privacy invoked on behalf of Hardwick, Tribe stated that "with respect to the intimacy decision, we rely heavily on *Griswold* and on *Eisenstadt* to show that *Griswold* cannot be limited to married couples."[71] Furthermore, Tribe's concept of privacy reflected the dual approach adopted in the amicus briefs: the privacy of the home, and the privacy of intimate (adult, consensual, and non-commercial) relationships. Grounding the fundamental right to privacy in these two areas, Tribe characterized it as a negative right—a freedom from state interference—but one that is no longer based on marital status.

The attorneys for Bowers, on the other hand, rejected the notion that the case—or the sodomy statute itself—involved a right to privacy. The contrast between their framing of the case and Tribe's is clear in Attorney Michael Hobbs's opening statement during oral argument: "This case presents the question of whether or not there is a fundamental right under the Constitution of the United States to engage in consensual private homosexual sodomy."[72] Sidestepping the privacy issues almost completely, Hobbs instead focused on homosexual sodomy, characterizing it as a societal danger akin to "polygamy; . . . consensual incest; prostitution; fornication; adultery; and . . . [possession of] illegal drugs."[73] When questioned by the Court, Hobbs conceded that the Georgia statute would be unconstitutional if applied to a married couple, because of "the right of marital intimacy" and "[t]he right of marital privacy."[74] For the Bowers attorneys, then, the case involved Hardwick's search for a constitutional right to engage in homosexual sodomy. Furthermore, from this perspective, the privacy right was irrelevant, for the intimacy it protected applied only to marital relationships.

The amicus briefs for Bowers elaborated on this stance, claiming that the constitutional right to privacy was grounded in a "fidelity to family interests"—and homosexual relationships most certainly fall far outside this definition of family. Likewise, each of these briefs suggested, as Hobbs did at oral argument, that Hardwick had claimed a fundamental right to engage in homosexual sodomy;[75] the brief submitted by the Catholic League for Religious and Civil Rights keenly observed that there was no judicial precedent to support "a privacy right for totally unrelated people to engage in homosexual sodomy."[76] Thus, by linking this activity with other "private consensual activities—including incest, polygamy, bestiality, etc.,"—and, in effect, criminalizing the identity of homosexuality itself—these amicus groups were able to rationalize the exclusion of gay men and lesbians from a right to privacy.[77]

Case Resources

Bowers v. Hardwick

Findlaw (http://laws.findlaw.com/us/478/186.html) (full text)

Oyez (http://www.oyez.org/cases/case/?case=1980-1989/1985/1985_85_140) (oral arguments)

The majority of Supreme Court justices deciding the *Bowers* case agreed with this perspective. In an opinion authored by Justice White, the Court wrote

that "The issue presented is whether the Federal Constitution confers a fundamental right upon homosexuals to engage in sodomy."[78] Having accepted Bowers's formulation of the case as presenting a "right-to-sodomy" question, White's
opinion concluded, not surprisingly, that the Constitution guarantees no such
right. The Court's opinion, like the briefs submitted on behalf of Bowers, invoked notions of traditional morality in order to justify its logic, claiming that
"Proscriptions against [homosexual sodomy] have ancient roots"[79] and referring
to "the many States that still make such conduct illegal and have done so for a
very long time."[80] This disapproval of homosexual sodomy translated quickly, in
White's opinion, into a rejection of homosexuality itself. Discussing the "presumed belief" of a majority of Georgia voters, the Court conflated the act of
sodomy with the identity of homosexuality and concluded that "majority sentiments about the morality of homosexuality" were an adequate basis for upholding the sodomy statute.[81] Furthermore, the opinion vilified homosexual relationships by casting them in direct contrast to traditional family forms: "No
connection between family, marriage, or procreation on the one hand and homosexual activity on the other has been demonstrated."[82] In so doing, the Court
reinforced the notion of homosexual relationships as unnatural and unacceptable family forms.

In a dissenting opinion, Justice Blackmun—joined by three other justices—
rejected the idea that the case implicated a right to sodomy, claiming instead
that the right to privacy was the central issue, and that "the majority has dis-
torted the question this case presents."[83] Harshly critiquing the majority's "almost obsessive focus on homosexual activity," Blackmun's dissent agreed with
the proposition advanced by Hardwick's attorneys that this case implicated
"both the decisional and the spatial" aspects of the fundamental right to privacy.[84] The dissent also dismissed the majority's characterization of homosexual
relationships as deviant, instead asserting their legitimacy as a type of family:

> The fact that individuals define themselves in a significant way through their inti-
> mate sexual relationships with others suggests, in a Nation as diverse as ours, that
> there may be many "right" ways of conducting those relationships, and that much of
> the richness of a relationship will come from the freedom an individual has to *choose*
> the form and nature of these intensely personal bonds.[85]

Conceding that the privacy right had developed primarily in cases pertaining to traditional families and childrearing, Blackmun contended that "we protect the family because it contributes so powerfully to the happiness of individuals, not because of a preference for stereotypical households."[86] Ultimately, by
addressing the privacy issues at stake in *Bowers,* and by viewing homosexual people and relationships as deserving of privacy rights equal to those of heterosexuals,

Blackmun envisioned an inclusive right to privacy that is not contingent upon marital status or sexual orientation.

The *Bowers* majority, however, was unable to conceive of privacy in this way, because their view of privacy was predicated upon notions of exclusion. In other words, privacy as perceived by the majority Court was defined by its privileging of "family, marriage, or procreation," all construed narrowly to exclude non-heterosexual relationships. Thus, despite the expansion of the privacy right in cases such as *Roe* and *Eisenstadt* to encompass nonmarital relationships, the *Bowers* majority remained unable to apprehend an inclusive form of privacy that they could apply to same-sex relationships. The Court's reliance on a model of privacy that privileges marital status (or, the potential for marriage and procreation in heterosexual couples) suggested that it still understood the right of privacy to be fundamentally exclusionary. Furthermore, the majority's insistence upon this model indicated that the right of privacy would continue to be enforced in ways that support that ideology.

In addition to the Court's "willful blindness" regarding the possibility of an inclusive right of privacy,[87] the sheer force of its homophobia overrode the central concern of the *Bowers* case. As Kathleen Sullivan observed,

> The majority rewrote the case as if it was just about homosexual sodomy . . . And yet the law itself referred to any oral- or anal-genital contact, so we litigated it as if it were a prohibition on the privacy of any consenting adults. . . . Certainly if it were a married couple that were [involved in the case], the court would've been in a real bind trying to say that there's no right to practice the sexual intimacy of one's choice, and so I thought that what the court did was in a sense rewrite the statute to make it politically easier for it to rule the way it did. So that was the surprise and disappointment of the case.[88]

Indeed, the majority's insistence on reinforcing traditional family forms (to the neglect of other, critical issues within a case) is a problem that also plagues gay men and lesbians seeking justice in cases of same-sex domestic violence. Likewise, the Court's justification for discrimination against homosexual relationships—in particular, its reliance on religion and supposedly traditional morality—is echoed in cases of same-sex domestic violence. As such, *Bowers*, which had such liberatory potential for the rights of the LGBT community, became a vehicle for their continued discrimination instead.

For the next fourteen years, *Bowers* stood as the definitive word on the issue—a fairly brief shelf life for a Supreme Court opinion. In June of 2003, the Court issued an opinion in *Lawrence* v. *Texas*[89] that overruled *Bowers* quite emphatically. It was a sea change for same-sex privacy rights.

THE CASE OF LAWRENCE V. TEXAS

The facts of *Lawrence* bore some resemblance to those that initiated the *Bowers* case. Just as in *Bowers*, *Lawrence* involved police entry into a private residence on a different matter, where police witnessed a consensual sex act taking place between adults. Specifically, in the *Lawrence* case, police in Houston, Texas responded to a call from a neighbor who claimed that "a black male was going crazy in the apartment and he was armed with a gun."[90] Upon arriving at the scene to investigate the alleged weapons disturbance, the neighbor directed officers to the apartment in question, where they "observed the defendant engaged in deviate sexual conduct[,] namely, anal sex, with another man."[91] John Geddes Lawrence, a 55-year-old white male, and Tyron Garner, a 31-year-old black male, were both arrested and convicted of violating Texas Penal Code Ann. §21.06(a), which prohibits "deviate sexual intercourse with another individual of the same sex," and defines deviate sexual intercourse as "(A) any contact between any part of the genitals of one person and the mouth or anus of another person; or (B) the penetration of the genitals or the anus of another person with an object," §21.01(1).[92]

At trial, Lawrence and Garner challenged the statute on equal protection grounds, citing both the Fourteenth Amendment and the Texas Constitution. When their arguments were rejected, they pled nolo contendere and were fined two hundred dollars and court costs.[93] They appealed to the Court of Appeals for the Texas Fourteenth District, where they again raised their equal protection arguments. In a 7-2 decision, the appellate court rejected those claims and affirmed the judgment of the trial court.[94] In so doing, the majority applied a rational basis standard of review and relied heavily on *Bowers*, noting that "homosexual conduct has historically been repudiated by many religious faiths. Moreover, Western civilization has a long history of repressing homosexual behavior by state action."[95] Focusing on homosexual conduct and claiming a historical basis for discrimination against homosexuals, the appellate court echoed the spirit as well as the reasoning of *Bowers*.

The two dissenting justices criticized "the majority's Herculean effort to justify the discriminatory classification" represented by the Texas statute,[96] and argued for a heightened standard of judicial scrutiny of the law in question. Heightened or intermediate scrutiny would be appropriate, they reasoned, given that the statute in question was based on a gender-based classification. The dissent claimed that the statute failed the intermediate scrutiny test, and concluded that "[t]he Legislature's removal of the prohibition on heterosexual sodomy while retaining it for homosexual sodomy cannot . . . be explained by anything but animus toward the persons it affects."[97] The dissent further addresses the issue of "private morality" versus "public morality," noting that the majority opinion fails to explain

> how government interference with the practice of adult only, consensual personal choice in matters of intimate sexual behavior out of view of the public and with no commercial component will serve to advance the cause of "public morality" or do anything other than restrict individual conduct and impose a concept of private morality chosen by the State.[98]

In posing the question of public versus private morality, the dissenting justices here expose the privacy paradox as it pertains to same-sex couples: the imposition of a state-sponsored "private morality" enforces the privacy of the closet by marking homosexual conduct as immoral, while simultaneously denying them the right of privacy that would protect their relationships from state intrusion.

Having lost their appeal, Lawrence and Garner appealed their case again, this time to the United States Supreme Court. Once the case was accepted by the Supreme Court, the amicus briefs submitted in support of both sides bore a strong resemblance to those advanced on behalf of Bowers and Hardwick over a decade before. The briefs for the petitioners, Lawrence and Garner, focused primarily on the issues of equal protection, liberty, and privacy. A brief submitted on behalf of multiple organizations, including the Human Rights Campaign and the National Gay and Lesbian Task Force, argued that the Texas statute in question violated both the Due Process and Equal Protection clauses of the Fourteenth Amendment. Furthermore, amici noted, "Sodomy laws today serve no function other than to reinforce the vestiges of a noxious history of discrimination."[99] While the brief mentioned the right to privacy, it argued that the case should turn on the more pressing issues of due process and equal protection as viewed within the context of the historical pattern of discrimination against homosexuals.

Other briefs, such as that submitted by the National Gay and Lesbian Law Association and other legal organizations, echoed this focus on the history of discrimination. Like the Texas appellate court dissent, their brief suggested that this history required the application of heightened scrutiny to the equal protection analysis. The brief also focused on homosexuality as an immutable characteristic as further justification for proposing that the law be subjected to heightened scrutiny.[100] Adopting a slightly different approach to equal protection analysis, the brief for the Republican Unity Coalition claimed that while the statute should properly be considered under the rational basis standard, it would not survive even that review. Citing the many indications of "a pervading animus toward gays as a class," this brief concluded that Texas failed to offer a legitimate justification for its discriminatory law. [101]

The most influential of the amicus briefs submitted on behalf of petitioners, however, was that of the Cato Institute, which, according to its mission statement, "seeks to broaden the parameters of public policy debate to allow consideration of the traditional American principles of limited government, individual liberty, free markets and peace."[102] Like the others, this brief found the Texas statute to be a clear violation of the Equal Protection clause. But, it declared, "There is a deeper problem with the . . . law." This deeper problem, according to the Cato Institute, had everything to do with privacy. In their brief, privacy is construed broadly, and described as both a positive and a negative right:

> America's founding generation established our government to protect rather than invade fundamental liberties, including personal security, the sanctity of the home, and interpersonal relations. So long as people are not harming others, they can presumptively engage in the pursuit of their own happiness.[103]

Here, the government's affirmative duty to "protect . . . fundamental liberties" stands side-by-side with the traditional notion of "the sanctity of the home."

The Cato Institute brief further alleged that the *Bowers* ruling, upon which the lower court had relied so heavily, demonstrated both an "incomplete reading of history" (with its reference to the "ancient roots" of proscriptions against homosexual sodomy) and an "inconsistency with . . . this Court's privacy precedents." Specifically, the brief noted, the *Bowers* opinion incorrectly read the Court's previous privacy rulings as limited to decisions regarding pregnancy, thereby ignoring those cases that "assur[ed] a right of bodily integrity outside of pregnancy."[104] Furthermore, the *Bowers* opinion provided only a partial understanding of "American traditions of liberty," because it failed to see that "[t]he fundamental freedoms Americans enjoy have included choices involving the deployment of the body, intimate relationships, and the home."[105] As a result, the brief concluded, the *Bowers* decision should be overruled. In addition, while detailing the failures of *Bowers* and arguing for its overruling, the Cato Institute brief provided a compelling roadmap for the Court of what an affirmative privacy right, based on notions of liberty and bodily integrity, might look like.

The amicus briefs for the State of Texas had a very different tone. When Justice Blackmun criticized the majority's opinion in *Bowers* for its "almost obsessive focus on homosexual activity," he could not have predicted that it would pale in comparison with the same obsession in the briefs submitted on behalf of Texas in the *Lawrence* case. Several of these briefs lingered much longer on specific sexual acts, or the particular circumstances surrounded the sex act at issue in the case, than on the arguments surrounding equal protection, due process, or privacy. The brief submitted by the American Center for Law and Justice, for example, suggested that the petitioners were asking the court "[t]o recognize extramarital sex acts as 'fundamental rights,'" but insisted that "the Constitution . . . neither does nor ought to enshrine the Sexual Revolution."[106] After expressing some frustration with the lack of detail in the arrest records, the authors speculated about many different scenarios surrounding the act in question:

> The record does not reflect whether the sodomy was coerced or consensual, performed for pay or not, displayed to members of the public (e.g., done in full view of others in the room or in front of an unobstructed picture window) or not, incestuous or not, part of a long-standing practice or simply a one-time anonymous tryst in response to an internet solicitation.[107]

The brief provides no basis for these queries or suppositions, and virtually no explanation regarding why their answers would be significant. As a result, these musings appear as little more than voyeuristic imaginings, far removed from the constitutional issues in question. When the brief does take up the constitutional questions, it strays from them rather quickly, with declarations such as, "A crucial unspoken premise of petitioners' argument is that the election of anal sodomy, as opposed to vaginal intercourse, is merely a matter of 'preference,' like selecting what wine to have with dinner. . . . This completely ignores human anatomy and biology,"[108] and "Anal sodomy is an abusive act, i.e., a misuse of the organs involved."[109]

A brief submitted by the Pro-Family Law Center, the Traditional Values Coalition, and others, took these musings much further. Also noting the lack of some detail in the record, they wondered "whether Petitioners engage in what might be characterized by them as 'safe' sodomy," and focused the issue of HIV/AIDS.[110] After suggesting that the petitioners were asking the Court to "sanctify[y] sodomy as a jewel in the crown of Constitutional liberty,"[111] they asserted, "In assessing obligations to the Constitution, it does not matter that Petitioners have the strongest of desires, whether genetic or intentional, to place each other at the risk of contracting deadly diseases, in the Petitioners' ill-defined interest in 'privacy.'"[112] Quoting liberally from Web sites devoted to HIV-positive men who engage in unprotected anal sex, they find that a subset of homosexuals includes "persons who wantonly act towards spreading and receiving AIDS."[113] By focusing on the furthest fringes of homosexual behavior, the authors sought to pathologize all same-sex couples as potentially dangerous. The existence of these websites therefore provided the basis for their conclusion that the statute passes the equal protection test: the state has a legitimate interest in promoting public health, and criminalizing same-sex sodomy is rationally related to that goal.

The briefs for the respondent also claimed that to invalidate the statute and overrule *Bowers* would be a threat to marriage itself. The Center for Marriage Law filed a brief to this effect, claiming that such a ruling would undermine existing state laws regulating marriage.[114] The American Center for Law and Justice avowed that "the distinction between heterosexual and homosexual unions is the hallmark of marriage law"[115] and that if the Court ruled in favor of the petitioners, it should be "prepared to announce the unconstitutionality of marriage."[116] Echoing the public policy debates over same-sex marriage, these and other briefs for Texas suggested that to end discrimination against same-sex couples would dismantle the foundations of the institution of marriage itself.

This focus on marriage was closely linked with the way that the amici for respondents conceptualized the right to privacy. A brief submitted on behalf of Texas legislators stated flatly that "the right of privacy is not absolute," and perceived that right to be circumscribed quite clearly by subject matter. Citing the line of reproductive rights cases from *Griswold* to *Casey*, the brief concluded, "Decisions regarding marriage and procreation receive special protection from this Court. Other individual choices among consenting adults do not."[117] By focusing narrowly on the subject matter of these cases, the brief deliberately set aside the recognition of decisional autonomy and bodily integrity as components of that right that these opinions developed. In the brief of the Pro-Family Law Center, the concept of privacy itself is repeatedly vilified, as when the brief claims that "Health consequences are not an easily perceived concern of Petitioners, or their supporters, as privacy and fulfillment of Dionysian self-interest are the ultimate moral ends by which they live, and expect all others to live,"[118] or disparagingly references, as noted above, "the Petitioners' ill-defined interest in 'privacy.'"[119]

Case Resources

Lawrence v. Texas

Findlaw (http://laws.findlaw.com/us/000/02-102.html) (full text)

Oyez (http://www.oyez.org/cases/case/?case=2000-2009/2002/2002_02_102) (oral arguments)

The *Lawrence* court, however, perceived and applied the right of privacy quite differently. The Court's opinion, authored by Justice Kennedy and joined by four other justices, situated the right to privacy clearly within a liberty framework and used it as the foundation for the opinion. The very first paragraph of the opinion establishes the Court's vision of the privacy right unequivocally; the closing lines of that paragraph read as follows: "Liberty presumes an autonomy of self that includes freedom of thought, belief, expression, and certain intimate conduct. The instant case involves liberty of the person both in its spatial and more transcendent dimensions."[120] Framing the case in terms of liberty and privacy, Justice Kennedy takes *Griswold* as his starting point. He notes that in *Griswold*, the Court "described the protected interest as a right to privacy," and that "After *Griswold* it was established that the right to make certain decisions regarding sexual conduct extends beyond the marital relationship."[121] Moving on to *Eisenstadt, Roe,* and *Carey,* he notes that the Court in those cases confirmed that *Griswold's* reasoning was not confined solely to the rights of married adults.[122]

The state of Texas in this case argued for a right of privacy demarcated by a "line at the bedroom door of the heterosexual married couple."[123] Given the development of the privacy right through the reproductive rights cases, the Court rejected that assessment, instead describing a right of privacy that extends beyond the bounds of marriage, and that protects not only spatial but decisional freedom. Applying the privacy right in this way to the facts of the case, Kennedy declared that

> The petitioners are entitled to respect for their private lives. The State cannot demean their existence or control their destiny by making their private sexual conduct a crime. Their right to liberty under the Due Process Clause gives them the full right to engage in their conduct without intervention of the government.[124]

With this statement, the Court not only provided significant clarity regarding the scope of the right to privacy, but also made a powerful statement about the rights of those who engage in same-sex sexual conduct.

In fact, the *Lawrence* opinion is unabashedly clear regarding the rights of homosexuals. Justice Kennedy describes homosexual relationships as being "within the liberty of persons to choose without being punished as criminals."[125] His opinion demonstrates an understanding of the role of the state in perpetuating discrimination against homosexuals, and the complicated relationship between privacy and shame for this population: "When homosexual conduct is made criminal by the law of the State, that declaration in and of itself is an invitation to subject homosexual persons to discrimination both in the public and in the private spheres. . . . The stigma this criminal statute imposes, moreover, is not trivial."[126] Noting the important role that sexuality plays in forming intimate relationships, he makes a sweeping yet pointed statement: "When sexuality finds overt expression in intimate conduct with another person, the conduct can be but one element in a personal bond that is more enduring. *The liberty protected by the Constitution allows homosexual persons the right to make this choice."*[127] Instead of claiming, as Justice White did in the *Bowers* opinion, that this case was asking the Court to consider a constitutional right to engage in sodomy, Kennedy presents a more nuanced analysis of the links between sexuality and liberty. And by framing expressions of sexuality in terms of decisional autonomy, Kennedy establishes a logical platform from which to argue that homosexuals clearly have the right to engage in this decision-making.

Much of the *Lawrence* opinion, not surprisingly, responds quite directly to the *Bowers* opinion. Kennedy's extensive critique of *Bowers* notes that the opinion revealed a flawed (or at best, incomplete) understanding of the history of sodomy laws. Relying heavily on the amicus brief submitted by the Cato Institute, he concludes that the extensive history of proscriptions against homosexual sodomy upon which the *Bowers* opinion rested is actually much more complex than that Court acknowledged. Noting that the central holding of Bowers "demeans the lives of homosexual persons," he states unequivocally that "*Bowers* was not correct when it was decided, and it is not correct today. It ought not to remain binding precedent. *Bowers* v. *Hardwick* should be and now is overruled."[128] With that statement, the already much-maligned *Bowers* opinion ended its short-lived reign as judicial precedent in matters of same-sex privacy rights.

It is worth noting that, in overruling *Bowers*, the Court does not stop at the formulation of same-sex rights. Instead, by referring to the European Court of Human Rights, the majority invokes the notion of human rights. Specifically, Kennedy cites a 1981 decision by that court that laws proscribing homosexual conduct violated the European Convention on Human Rights. In so doing, he refutes the claim in *Bowers* that Western civilization has roundly decried such conduct.[129] He also cites several of that court's decisions after *Bowers* that continued to protect, rather than deny, the rights of homosexuals to engage in such conduct. Citing the line of cases developed in the European Court of Human Rights, as well as several from other nations, he observes, "The right the petitioners seek in this case has been accepted as an integral part of human freedom in many other countries."[130] By employing this language, and citing the line of human rights cases, the Court establishes the framework for understanding these rights as human rights. As we continue to consider the possibility of an alternative vision of the right to privacy—an affirmative right that emphasizes personal autonomy and bodily integrity—this formulation may provide quite a useful framework. The particular way in which the right to privacy has been constructed for and denied to LGBT individuals has had a significant impact on the issue of same-sex domestic violence, as the next section will demonstrate.

SAME-SEX DOMESTIC VIOLENCE

ACTIVISM AGAINST SAME-SEX DOMESTIC VIOLENCE

To understand the problem of same-sex domestic violence, it is helpful to consider its treatment both within the courtroom and outside of it; namely, by activists. Primarily, activism directed at eliminating same-sex domestic violence has come from the battered women's movement and the LGBT community. These efforts, however, have been somewhat slow to start and have not achieved nearly the visibility as those efforts targeting heterosexual domestic violence. Activism confronting the problem of battering in lesbian and gay male relationships has been hampered by a variety of ideological and practical constraints. Specifically, both the gay rights and the mainstream battered women's movements have been hesitant to address this problem, each for very different reasons.

From the perspective of the gay rights movement, raising the issue of same-sex battering poses significant hazards. As the movement seeks to gain rights and opportunities for lesbians and gay men that equal those afforded to heterosexuals in this society, it has combated various forms of homophobia—including the pernicious myth, discussed throughout this chapter, that homosexuality itself is a pathological and deviant condition. In so doing, the movement has also worked to demonstrate that same-sex relationships are not pathological, but rather expressions of mutual love and affection that are at least as healthy and natural as heterosexual relationships are perceived to be. Within this context, the movement has been reluctant to publicize the problem of intimate partner violence, fearing the homophobic culture that would exploit this problem as evidence of the inherent deviance of same-sex relationships. As Elliott observes,

> The gay and lesbian community shares responsibility for keeping same-sex domestic violence in the "closet." Though well-known as a significant problem for years, the community sought to keep this issue quiet due to shame and the reluctance to provide ammunition for the homophobic majority who would use such problems to demonstrate supposed inferiority. Gays and lesbians, even as they themselves were beaten, maintained the illusion that they were more enlightened than heterosexual society and, therefore, not subject to the same uncivilized behaviors.[131]

The battered women's movement has also failed to confront the problem of homosexual domestic violence with the same vigor it has applied to violence in straight relationships. This can be attributed, in part, to homophobia within the movement itself.[132] Additionally, the problem of same-sex domestic abuse complicates the analysis, central to the movement, of domestic violence as primarily a manifestation of gender inequality. As such, the movement's limitations in addressing same-sex domestic violence probably also stem at least in part from its reluctance to disrupt this powerful yet heterocentric analytical framework.[133] Ironically, as Barbara Hart has observed, lesbians have constituted much of the movement's leadership since its earliest days. Nonetheless, the problem of same-sex battering took a long time to surface within the movement, as some lesbians within the movement found the problem difficult to believe or to confront. In an interview, Hart recalled that

Much of the leadership of any number of these [early] organizations [was held by lesbians] . . . There were many lesbians that were very powerful . . . [S]o . . . we had that first sort of national meeting on battering in lesbian relationships at NCADV [National Coalition Against Domestic Violence]. It was an incredibly difficult meeting, because some people didn't want to believe that it was happening, that women could assault other women. But this was almost ten years after we started NCADV. The reason that lesbians came to the work was not because they wanted to deal with lesbian battering. They came to the work because they were seeking justice [for women more broadly], and because they were able, as lesbians, even if they were closeted, to understand I think in profound ways that justice-seeking requires organizing.[134]

Finally, the battered women's movement, like the gay rights movement, has sought legitimacy within mainstream culture. Particularly when attempting to secure funding for shelters and other programs, the movement has often sought to reassure the public that it is not—despite some suggestion to the contrary from conservative quarters—seeking to dismantle the family unit. In its efforts to appear nonthreatening to traditional families, the mainstream battered women's movement has sometimes distanced itself from homosexuals, and lesbians in particular, often in response to overtly homophobic rhetoric from funders and others. In 1985, for example, the NCADV applied for grant money from the Justice Department. When conservative activist Patrick McGuigan learned that the group was scheduled to receive $625,000 to fund battered women's shelters, he appealed to then-Attorney General Edwin Meese, as well as to conservative congressional representatives, to block the grant. In his letter to Meese, Republican House Representative Mark Siljander implored Meese not to award the money to "pro-abortion, pro-lesbian, anti-Reagan radical feminists."[135] Sharon Parker, then-Executive Director of the NCADV, noted that Siljander's letter "had unfairly tagged her group with 'a boilerplate label,' radical lesbians."[136] Assistant Attorney General Lois Herrington, who had originally approved the grant, characterized the NCADV as "pro-family," noting, "I certainly don't see that the percentage of lesbians [in NCADV] is any greater than the national norm."[137] In this case, while the mainstream movement did not disown its lesbian members altogether, it certainly distanced itself from them and their interests for the sake of political expediency.[138]

The activism that has occurred on behalf of battered lesbians and gay men, therefore, has happened in spite of all of these constraints—a fact which perhaps speaks to the prevalence and the urgency of the problem of same-sex domestic violence. Indeed, efforts to combat the problem of same-sex domestic violence have been undertaken in increasing numbers, especially in recent years. This work has mirrored the efforts to combat heterosexual domestic abuse, but goes further, including attention to issues particularly germane to LGBT communities. For example, programs serving LGBT victims often explore the problem of domestic violence in relationship to HIV/AIDS—examining how public perception of the disease affects cultural attitudes toward same-sex domestic violence and the implications for activists working on both problems simultaneously.[139] In addition, LGBT domestic violence programs also focus on peer support, shelter, crisis lines, provision of basic services, and legal and legislative advocacy.[140] The expansion of services available to lesbian and gay male victims of battering provides a hopeful indication that, while such services are still far from plentiful, awareness of this problem is continuing to grow.

PRIVACY AND SAME-SEX DOMESTIC VIOLENCE IN THE COURTS

The brief of the Lesbian Rights Project, et al., submitted in support of Hardwick in the *Bowers* case, has proven to be quite prescient with regard to the issue of domestic violence.

> [T]he denial of any right of privacy to gay and lesbian persons represents an approval, however tacit and sublimated, of . . . related forms of discrimination. . . . Criminalization translates readily into permission to discriminate, to malign, to stigmatize and to multiply the harms already suffered by gay and lesbian persons in this culture, society, and legal system. . . . [A] determination by this Court that states are free to criminalize gay/lesbian sexual activities *per se* would reinforce the homophobic elements of . . . the anti-gay legal decisions that are proliferating at the present time.[141]

Indeed, this excerpt alludes to several critical aspects of the right to privacy as it relates to same-sex relationships. First, the acknowledgment of the stigma surrounding these relationships recalls the link between privacy and the shame of the closet for LGBT people as described by Kendall Thomas. In addition, the excerpt calls attention to the negative power the *Bowers* opinion held to serve as a kind of judicial endorsement for other homophobic rulings. As this section's analysis of state appellate domestic violence cases will show, the courtroom homophobia exhibited by judges, attorneys, jurors, and litigants has often served as a significant barrier to justice for victims and their families.

The types of abuse experienced by victims of same-sex domestic violence are much the same as those experienced within heterosexual relationships, as noted at the beginning of this chapter. Likewise, victims of same-sex domestic violence face many of the same challenges to addressing the problem as do their heterosexual counterparts. Often, however, those challenges are exacerbated for LGBT victims as a result of their sexual orientation. For example, the failure of law enforcement officers to respond appropriately to domestic violence calls in straight relationships was pervasive enough to warrant the civil cases of the 1980s discussed in the previous chapter. In the context of lesbian and gay male partner violence, however, the problem of nonresponse can be complicated by police amusement, contempt, or failure to recognize the relationship as one of intimate partners. These negative attitudes, lack of awareness, and subsequent failure to act on the part of police officers can result in extreme danger for battered lesbians and gay men.

In addition, like many victims of domestic violence, gay and lesbian victims often find that their problem is not taken seriously by the courts. Continuing to view domestic violence as a private matter, some courts send the message that such matters are trivial and a waste of their time. When the victim is the same sex as the batterer, however, courts may be even more dismissive, expressing anything from disgust to amusement that such a problem is even possible. Last, just as some courts have suggested that domestic violence is more expected or acceptable within some relationships than others (based on the race or socio-economic status of the people involved), they may also minimize the severity of same-sex domestic violence by implying that these victims are only experiencing the natural outcome of an inherently deviant relationship.

The following study of same-sex domestic violence cases at the appellate level reveals that homophobia often operates on several levels in the courtroom. First, the problem of hetero-relationizing may occur in these cases, as courts insist on identifying who served in the "male" or "female" role in the relationship, as a means of resolving the case. In addition, in some cases, lawyers, judges, or juries become overly preoccupied with the homosexual nature of the relationship itself, often to the point of obscuring or diminishing the violence at issue. Furthermore, the homosexual nature of the relationship may be submitted or viewed in some courts as an indication of the deviance or bad character of one or both parties. In any and all of these scenarios, victims of domestic violence are denied fair treatment by the justice system as a result of their sexual orientation.

The tendency of courts to hetero-relationize can manifest in several ways in same-sex domestic violence cases. The Oklahoma case of *Allen v. State*,[142] for example, was an appeal from a lesbian who had been convicted of murdering her girlfriend. One of the bases for her appeal was her contention that "the trial court erred in allowing in evidence Appellant was the 'man' in her homosexual relationship with the decedent . . ." which "was used to show Appellant was the aggressive person in the relationship, while the decedent was more passive."[143] The appellate court rejected this claim, concluding instead that "[t]he evidence would help the jury understand why each party acted the way she did both during events leading up to the shooting and the shooting itself."[144] By rejecting this claim, the court implicitly accepted this hetero-relationizing, despite its inherent inaccuracy as a means of understanding same-sex relationships.

Hetero-relationizing can also result when judges have difficulty envisioning intimate violence outside of the context of heterosexual relationships. As a result, they often blame both parties equally for the violence, even when the evidence suggests otherwise. In *Annette F. v. Sharon S.*,[145] a California case relating to libel and custody, the court's own description of the facts noted two separate incidents of violence in which only Sharon suffered injuries, one in which Annette admitted to provoking the physical contact. The court also noted that, when Sharon sought a protective order against Annette, a lower court made a finding that Annette had perpetrated domestic violence against Sharon.[146] Still, the court did not identify either party as victim or perpetrator, noting only in its initial characterization of the relationship that "[t]heir relationship was volatile, and each ultimately accused the other of engaging in physical and verbal abuse."[147] With no evidence whatsoever to suggest that Sharon was the primary aggressor, it is noteworthy that the court described the relationship in such neutral terms. That they did so indicates an interesting reluctance to recognize this as an abusive relationship with only one perpetrator.

In other cases, the judicial system's preoccupation with same-sex relationships takes precedence over the other aspects of the case. A court's view of same-sex relationships as illegitimate, combined with its insistence on pathologizing homosexual litigants, often serves to justify the violence in question. The homophobia of the judge, jury or attorneys frequently plays a central role in the case, at the expense of the facts.

In the 1973 case of *Perez v. State*,[148] for example, a Texas appeals court rejected Maria Perez's appeal from her conviction for the murder of her ex-girlfriend. Despite the serious nature of the issue before the court, the proceedings focused primarily on the sexual nature of the relationship between the two women. In fact, well over half of the text of the court's three-page opinion was devoted to establishing that Perez is indeed a lesbian, citing testimony from a witness who claimed that Perez "always dressed like a man; kept her hair cut like a man; wore men's clothing, including men's shoes; had never [had] a date with a man; and '. . . always takes a man's place.'"[149] This witness's testimony was further corroborated by "State's Exhibit No. 2, a photograph of [Perez], showing her with a short haircut. He stated it depicted the way appellant looked during the twenty years he had known her."[150] The court only briefly mentioned previous incidents of violence between Perez and her ex-girlfriend and the facts surrounding the murder in question, but devoted most of its efforts to identifying Perez as a lesbian. Here, the gravity of the act that occurred and the significance of the charges against Perez were both overshadowed by the court's homophobic insistence on establishing Perez as a lesbian first and a murderer second.

Similar instances of inappropriate and often demeaning emphasis on the sexual orientation of defendants in lesbian domestic violence cases are also revealing. In *Wiley v. Florida*,[151] Queen Wiley appealed her murder conviction in part on the basis that the prosecution inappropriately attacked her character by describing her as "a 'bull dagger'—a lesbian that assumes the male role during sexual intercourse."[152] The court dismissed this assertion, arguing that Wiley herself had used the epithet in her testimony (when quoting a threat her girlfriend had made to her), and then commenting snidely that "the State's only crime here was to try to explain to the jury exactly what a 'bull dagger' is."[153] Likewise, Ruthann Robson recounts an unpublished case of lesbian murder in Florida, in which two potential jurors discussed a desire to be chosen for the jury "in order to 'hang that lesbian bitch.'"[154] While focusing on, commenting on, or trying to prove the parties' sexual orientation, courtroom participants in these cases did a serious disservice to those seeking justice.

Evidence of homosexuality itself is often presented or seen in courts as proof of the deviance of one or both parties or of their relationship. In the case of domestic violence, this line of thinking can be particularly dangerous. In the California case of *People v. Beasley*,[155] for example, a man appealed his conviction for murder partly on the grounds that the prosecution had unfairly introduced evidence of his homosexuality. In particular, he observed that the prosecutor said, in his closing argument,

> We, who are in law enforcement work, . . . see homosexuals, sex perverts and criminals . . . sometimes we don't understand why an average, normal citizen, who doesn't come in contact with them the way we do, is at a loss to understand the motives or reasons that cause them to act the way they do. . . . Passions and jealousies between homosexuals are even more exaggerated than they are in normal people.[156]

The appellant claimed that the prosecution's attempt to show him as a homosexual was intended solely to prejudice the jury. The court, noting that the prosecution never did prove Beasley's homosexual relationship with the deceased, agreed, noting that, "[h]omosexuality is a subject upon which the public generally looks with disfavor. It is a disgusting subject to some and a distasteful subject to others."[157] To introduce it, therefore, particularly without proving it, was an error the court could not allow.

Because the *Beasley* case took place in 1958, some might be tempted to attribute this overt homophobia to that particular era. Yet the case of *Tennessee v. Herron*,[158] decided over thirty years later, finds these prejudices still solidly in place, providing further evidence that courts and juries often do see homosexuality itself as evidence of bad character. In this same-sex murder case, the court noted that there was "an unusual relationship"[159] between the victim and the perpetrator of the murder (i.e., a homosexual one). The court also noted that for the trial court to have allowed evidence of the victim's homosexuality would have been, in effect, to "assassinate the victim's character."[160] Likewise, in the Texas case of *Rotondo* v. *State*,[161] the defendant admitted to the crime of murder, but objected to the admission of evidence that he had engaged in homosexual conduct. The appellate court disagreed, stating that it was relevant as one of the facts surrounding the murder he committed. Yet the fact that Rotondo confessed to murder but did not want the jury to know he had engaged in homosexual activity says much about the way in which homosexuality has been received by the justice system.

In other same-sex domestic violence cases, defendants have objected to the introduction of evidence regarding their homosexuality, and courts have properly found such information admissible only for a specific reason related to that case.[162] In particular, *Gilpin* v. *State*,[163] a 1991 Texas case, helpfully clarified the particular uses to which evidence of sexual orientation could be put in a same-sex domestic violence case. In this case, the appellant had objected to the introduction of photos of himself and the deceased engaged in sadomasochistic activities. The court conceded that there was the potential for such photos to be used solely to inflame the jury, but that given the particular circumstances of this case (including some allegedly consensual violence in the relationship), they provided important evidence related to motive. Explaining its reasoning, the court noted:

> The sexual orientation and fetishes of the accused in a murder prosecution are not *per se* relevant, and such information cannot be admitted solely to prejudice and inflame the minds of the jurors. However, where evidence regarding a sexual relationship between the accused and the deceased is relevant, it will not be excluded merely because the relationship in question was homosexual in nature.[164]

Given the history of courtroom homophobia against which these cases are set, the notion that sexual orientation should only be used for specific evidentiary purposes, rather than inflammatory ones, is a refreshing departure.

In each of these cases of same-sex domestic violence, the sexual orientation of the parties involved played some role in the progression of the case. Regardless of the ultimate disposition of the case, the sexual orientation of the defendant/appellant at the very least preoccupied the court, and, at worst, influenced or determined the outcome. Thus, while cases of heterosexual domestic violence are often mishandled by courts' unwillingness to interfere in the domestic sphere, the opposite is true for their LGBT counterparts. Too often, in cases involving same-sex domestic violence, courts are all too eager to invade the private lives of the parties, even when the details sought are entirely irrelevant to the case itself. In this way, courts have, in effect, denied lesbians and gay men the right of privacy that they readily bestow upon heterosexual couples in the context of domestic violence.

Privacy thus takes on an entirely different meaning within the context of same-sex domestic violence. As a result, lesbian and gay male victims are compelled to use different strategies than those of straight battered women when seeking legal refuge from violence. The civil litigation brought by the battered women's movement in the 1980s, for example, encouraged increased state intervention in the home at particular moments. By contrast, gay and lesbian victims must, in the course of seeking legal redress, also attempt to keep the court out of their bedrooms, for the purposes of keeping the trial focused on the issues at hand. Not surprisingly, therefore, the kinds of civil cases brought by battered straight women that proliferated during the 1980s (such as *Bruno* or *Thurman*) have been quite rare in the realm of same-sex domestic violence.

Nevertheless, a few courts have successfully rejected homophobic attitudes in cases of same-sex domestic violence and, in so doing, have pioneered new frameworks for other courts to follow. In some cases, this has meant taking the somewhat unusual step of treating these cases just like other cases, without focusing unnecessarily on the details of the sexual relationship, or concluding that both parties must be depraved in order to engage in a homosexual relationship at all.[165] In other cases, courts have deliberately chosen to extend to lesbians and gay men the same protection from domestic violence as their heterosexual counterparts receive. Just as the *Liberta* court had, in 1984, moved dramatically away from contemporary judicial treatments of marital rape laws, the 1991 case of *Ohio* v. *Hadinger*[166] was the first to explicitly grant legal protection to gay and lesbian victims of domestic violence. The *Hadinger* opinion was brief and simple, yet powerful. In this case, the Court of Appeals of Ohio reviewed a case of lesbian domestic violence in which a lower court had dismissed the criminal charges simply because both the victim and the perpetrator were women. The lower court had determined that because two women could not be legally married in Ohio, the victim could not be considered to be "living as a spouse" with the defendant, as was required in order to be protected by the state's domestic violence statute.

The appeals court disagreed with this construction, noting the gender-neutral language of the statute and concluding that "to read the . . . statute otherwise would eviscerate the efforts of the legislature to safeguard, regardless of gender, the rights of victims of domestic violence. We decline to adopt such a restrictive position and therefore conclude that [the statute] . . . does not in and of itself exclude two persons of the same sex."[167] With this simple conclusion, the court granted legal protection to victims of same-sex domestic violence, while simultaneously providing judicial recognition of the problem itself.[168] Since that time, several other state courts have clarified that their domestic violence statutes apply to same-sex couples as well as heterosexual couples.[169]

Five years later, another Ohio court relied on *Hadinger* as the basis for an even stronger and more forceful assertion of the rights of gay men and lesbians to state protection from domestic violence. Citing *Hadinger*, the court deciding *State v. Linner*[170] went on to assert that "assaults between homosexuals are just as worthy of protection as assaults between heterosexuals."[171] In a remarkable display of judicial sensitivity, the opinion, written by Judge Timothy Black, also evinced an awareness of one of the problems unique to lesbian and gay victims of domestic violence; namely, the additional threat of public "outing" for the victim who presses criminal charges against his or her batterer. As a result of this additional peril, Black suggested, homosexual victims may have an even greater need for the protection of domestic violence laws than do heterosexuals.[172] Expressing a clear desire to achieve "the twin goals of ensuring the victim's safety and holding the batterer accountable,"[173] the opinion also relies heavily on an equal protection analysis. Declaring that the statute would be unconstitutional if applied only to heterosexuals, the court even cites the 1984 case of *People v. Liberta* to bolster its equal protection argument.

This equal protection argument was echoed two years later in a Kentucky appellate court addressing the same issue—that is, whether that state's domestic violence statute should apply to same-sex couples. Like the *Hadinger* court, the judges deciding *Ireland v. Davis*[174] also relied on the statute's broad, gender-neutral language to conclude that it should cover gay men and lesbians as well as heterosexuals. In addition, while the *Ireland* court did not ultimately decide their case on equal protection grounds, they referenced its applicability, noting that "to exclude same-sex couples [from the scope of the statute] would be to deny them the same protection that other couples are afforded."[175] Thus, while *Hadinger* had taken the formidable, initial step of including gay men and lesbians in a state domestic violence statute, *Linner* and *Ireland* strengthened that position by undergirding such decisions with the logic and weight of the equal protection clause. In so doing, they sent a message to courts and legislatures that to exclude victims of same-sex domestic violence from the protection of such laws would be not only unconscionable, but unconstitutional.

Furthermore, by including members of homosexual couples within the scope of a state's domestic violence statutes, courts implicitly acknowledge these couples as legitimate family forms. Cases such as *Hadinger* and *Linner* grapple with the meaning of such phrases as "person living as a spouse"[176] and respond by constructing new and inclusive definitions of family. The *Linner* court, for example, found the heterosexual model to be only one possible family form, noting that, for the purpose of the statute, "cohabitation as a spouse" could include consideration of such factors as shared expenses, jointly owned property, joint socializing, and shared parenting responsibilities.[177] Applying this analysis to the couple involved in the case before them, the court found the two women to be indeed "cohabiting as spouses"—as the opinion explained, "living as lovers in an intimate relationship, sharing in the support of children and of each other."[178] By allowing for the decentering of the heterosexual model, these cases promoted a broader view of family, one that provides gay men and lesbians full access to the protection of the law in this area.

In cases such as *Hadinger, Linner,* and *Ireland,* judicial recognition of same-sex families provides the critical step in securing the equal protection of domestic violence laws. Conversely, it is the censuring of gay and lesbian relationships that often provides a barrier to legal relief for victims of same-sex domestic violence. The role of privacy is also significant here, for it has failed, in very different ways, both straight and gay victims of domestic violence. The state's reverence for the domestic sphere inhabited by heterosexual couples has meant, in practice, a reluctance to intervene in it—at the expense of battered women's safety. This attitude found judicial expression in the early contraceptive cases such as *Poe* and *Griswold,* which extolled "the sacred precincts of marital bedrooms."[179] Even in those early cases, this exalting of marital relationships was predicated upon the devaluing of other relationships—most notably, homosexual ones. As Justice Harlan observed in *Poe,* "The right of privacy most manifestly is not an absolute. Thus, I would not suggest that adultery, homosexuality, fornication and incest are immune from criminal enquiry, however privately practiced."[180] The right to privacy promised in those cases, therefore, was not accorded to same-sex couples in the same measure.

In fact, just the opposite has been the case. As a result, the state's eagerness to invade the private lives of homosexual couples has often meant that instead of legal protection, victims of same-sex domestic violence receive only condemnation from the state about the nature of their relationship. A new model of privacy is needed; one that, like *Hadinger, Linner,* and *Ireland,* neither exalts nor demeans particular family forms based on sexual orientation. Furthermore, this new model must reject principles of secrecy, which, while sometimes useful as a survival strategy in a homophobic culture, nonetheless encourage the invisibility of lesbians and gay men. Instead of being exclusionary, an alternative model of privacy should be inclusive and empowering for victims of domestic abuse, regardless of sexual orientation. In the next chapter, I will propose a model that incorporates each of these elements.

CONCLUSION

Intimate violence within same-sex relationships is a problem requiring particular solutions. While this chapter has begun to examine the treatment of this issue in the judicial and activist arenas, the subject merits further study. As is the case with heterosexual domestic violence, privacy is a central component of legal and societal formulations of this problem. The role that privacy plays, however, differs significantly in each context. While courts have consistently granted married and other heterosexual couples a right of privacy that often prevents state intervention into a violent home, they have denied that kind of privacy to homosexual couples. Instead, courts and other state actors have freely intruded into the private activities of gay men and lesbians—most often for the purpose of condemning them. The stigma imposed upon these relationships, by courts and by the larger society, has significantly complicated the meaning of privacy in this context. Instead of an implicit right recognized by the state in heterosexual relationships, privacy within homosexual relationships often represents either a mechanism of legal invisibility or a strategy used to shield individuals from the disapproval of the state—and often, from criminal sanctions.

In fact, criminal sodomy laws have often served to codify homophobic attitudes and legitimize discrimination against gay men and lesbians. The history of the 1986 Supreme Court case of *Bowers* v. *Hardwick*, "an exemplar of legal homophobia,"[181] reveals the extent to which such judicial homophobia can determine the outcome of a case. The majority opinion in *Bowers* denied a right of privacy to gay men and lesbians by characterizing homosexual relationships as illegitimate family forms. While the implications of *Bowers* were profound, the homophobic tone of the opinion was not unique. By casting homosexuals and their intimate relationships outside of the boundaries of acceptable families, *Bowers* echoed decades of judicial opinions that had employed similar biases. This judicial bias against same-sex relationships—combined with the not-uncommon courtroom practice of using homosexuality as a proxy for bad character—has served as a justification for denying lesbians and gay men access to a wide range of legal protections. The implications of the recent *Lawrence* opinion, which definitively overruled *Bowers*, remain to be seen. As a watershed case for same-sex privacy rights, it laid the foundation for a more expansive understanding of the right to privacy as well as equal treatment for same-sex couples in other arenas as well.

The traditionally unequal application of the laws has been particularly pronounced for homosexuals in the arena of family law, especially in cases of same-sex domestic violence. In these cases, judges, jurors, and attorneys have persistently focused on the sexuality of the parties involved to the detriment of the other aspects of the case. Likewise, courtroom homophobia has, until recently, generally resulted in the exclusion of gay men and lesbians from the protection of state domestic violence laws. While a few courts (and more legislatures) have extended such laws to protect same-sex relationships, it is nevertheless clear that with regard to domestic violence, gay men and lesbians are still not receiving equal treatment under the law.

Furthermore, while being treated equally to victims of heterosexual violence would arguably be an improvement for victims of same-sex violence, such a response would hardly bring them justice. As the previous chapters have demonstrated, battered straight women often remain in danger even after seeking protection from the state, because the right to privacy has proven to be a consistent barrier to their safety. At the root of this privacy right—interpreted by courts as the right to freedom from state intervention—is a reverence for the heterosexual domestic sphere. At the same time, this privileging of heterosexual relationships has provided the justification for the state's failure to extend such a right to homosexual relationships. Predicated on a premise of exclusion, therefore, this model of privacy has been applied unevenly and has proved dangerous to victims of domestic violence.

An affirmative model of privacy, on the other hand, based on notions of bodily integrity, would apply to individuals regardless of race, sexual orientation, ability, or other categories of identity or relationship status, and would prove empowering to victims of domestic violence. In the concluding chapter, I will outline what such a model might look like, and how it could be fruitfully applied to assisting all victims of domestic violence.

NOTES

1. *People v. Liberta*, 64 N.Y.2d 152 (1984).

2. As several scholars have observed, studies attempting to discern the prevalence of violence within same-sex intimate relationships have yielded widely varying results (Claire M. Renzetti, *Violent Betrayal: Partner Abuse in Lesbian Relationships* [Newbury Park, CA: Sage, 1992]: 17–19; Pam Elliott, "Shattering Illusions: Same-Sex Domestic Violence," in *Violence in Gay and Lesbian Domestic Partnerships*, ed. Claire M. Renzetti and Charles Harvey Miley, 1–8 [New York: Haworth Press, 1996]: 2–3; Paula B. Poorman, "Forging Community Links to Address Abuse in Lesbian Relationships," in *Intimate Betrayal: Domestic Violence in Lesbian Relationships*, ed. Ellyn Kaschak, 7–24 [New York: Haworth Press, 2001]: 8–11). Discrepancies among findings result from numerous factors, including varying definitions of violence

(which may include any combination of physical, sexual, verbal, and emotional abuse); varying forms of measurement (diverse survey instruments, surveys versus interviews, etc.); and the necessity of using self-selected and therefore nonrandom samples. Despite these obstacles, however, such studies tend to agree that domestic violence is a very real problem for same-sex couples as well as their heterosexual counterparts, often at similar rates (see, for instance, P. A. Brand and A. H. Kidd, "Frequency of Physical Aggression in Heterosexual and Female Homosexual Dyads," *Psychological Reports* 59 [1986]: 1307–13, which found roughly equivalent rates of physical abuse and rape among their sample of lesbian and heterosexual couples).

3. The terminology I use in this chapter reflects the language adopted by courts as well as the language employed by gay rights activists. As such, I use the words "heterosexual" and "straight" to refer to people who are involved in intimate relationships with members of the opposite sex. Those terms, as well as "different-sex," are also used to characterize the relationships themselves. I use the words "gay" and "homosexual" to refer to people who are involved in intimate relationships with members of the same sex. Those terms, as well as "same-sex," are also used to characterize the relationships themselves. When referring specifically to homosexual men and their intimate relationships, I specify "gay men" or "gay male," and I refer to homosexual women and their intimate relationships as "lesbian." When referring to gay men and lesbians collectively as a social group, I often employ the phrase "LGBT community," which refers to lesbian, gay male, bisexual, and transgender individuals. While this chapter does not address concerns specific to bisexual and transgender individuals, the discrimination they experience under the law often parallels that of lesbians and gay men. Finally, usage of these terms and categories is not in any way meant to refute or disregard the insight provided by feminist theorists that gender and sexual orientation are not fixed categories, but are instead fluid and shifting modes of identity (see, for instance Judith Butler, *Gender Trouble: Feminism and the Subversion of Identity* [London: Routledge, 1990/1999]). Instead, this chapter by necessity addresses human relationships as perceived by the state, which generally leaves little room for fluidity and proceeds according to categories of identity that are perceived to be static.

4. See, for example, Kerry Lobel, ed., *Naming the Violence: Speaking Out About Lesbian Battering* (Seattle: Seal Press, 1986); Beth Leventhal and Sandra E. Lundy, eds., *Same-Sex Domestic Violence: Strategies for Change* (Thousand Oaks, CA: Sage, 1999); Claire M. Renzetti, *Violent Betrayal: Partner Abuse in Lesbian Relationships* (Newbury Park, CA: Sage, 1992); Pam Elliott, "Shattering Illusions: Same-Sex Domestic Violence," in *Violence in Gay and Lesbian Domestic Partnerships*, ed. Claire M. Renzetti and Charles Harvey Miley, 1-8 (New York: Haworth Press, 1996); Paula B. Poorman, "Forging Community Links to Address Abuse in Lesbian Relationships," in *Intimate Betrayal: Domestic Violence in Lesbian Relationships*, ed. Ellyn Kaschak, 7–24 (New York: Haworth Press, 2001).

5. See, for example, Charlene Allen and Beth Leventhal, "History, Culture, and Identity: What Makes GLBT Battering Different," in *Same-Sex Domestic Violence: Strategies for Change*, ed. Beth Leventhal and Sandra E. Lundy, 73–82 (Thousand Oaks, CA: Sage, 1999); Claire M. Renzetti, *Violent Betrayal: Partner Abuse in Les-*

bian Relationships (Newbury Park, CA: Sage, 1992); Pam Elliott, "Shattering Illusions: Same-Sex Domestic Violence," in Violence in Gay and Lesbian Domestic Partnerships, ed. Claire M. Renzetti and Charles Harvey Miley, 1–8 (New York: Haworth, 1996).

6. National Gay and Lesbian Task Force, "Domestic Violence Laws in the U.S." http://www.thetaskforce.org/downloads/reports/issue_maps/domesticviolencelaws map.pdf

7. Pam Elliott, "Shattering Illusions: Same-Sex Domestic Violence," in Violence in Gay and Lesbian Domestic Partnerships, ed. Claire M. Renzetti and Charles Harvey Miley, 1–8 (New York: Haworth, 1996): 5.

8. Throughout this chapter, I refer only to consensual sodomy between adults, generally defined as anal and/or oral sex. "Sodomy" in this chapter does not refer to behavior involving minors or any type of sexual assault or commercial practice, and laws proscribing those behaviors are not at issue here.

9. This wording comes from William Blackstone, Commentaries on the Laws of England v.1 (Oxford: Clarendon Press, 1765): 215.

10. Kendall Thomas, "Beyond the Privacy Principle," Columbia Law Review 92 (1992): 1431.

11. Ruthann Robson, "Lavender Bruises: Intra-Lesbian Violence, Law and Lesbian Legal Theory," Golden Gate University Law Review 20 (1990): 567–91.

12. 478 U.S. 186 (1986).

13. 539 U.S. 558 (2003).

14. For a more detailed description of the case selection method for each chapter, see the appendix.

15. Kendall Thomas, "Beyond the Privacy Principle," Columbia Law Review 92 (1992): 1455.

16. The Defense of Marriage Act (DOMA), enacted in 1996, defines the term "marriage" for federal purposes as "a legal union between one man and one woman as husband and wife" (104 P.L. 199). The DOMA was created for the purpose of refusing legal legitimacy to same-sex unions. Specifically, the act was generated in response to the emerging possibility that Hawaii, through its judicial system, might be on the verge of granting legal recognition to same-sex marriages. By the time the Hawaii court ruled against legalizing gay marriage (Baehr v. Miike, 994 P.2d 566 [1999]), the DOMA was already in place to ensure that no other state would be obligated to recognize such a union.

17. Janet E. Halley, "Reasoning About Sodomy: Act and Identity in and After Bowers v. Hardwick," Virginia Law Review 79 (1993): 1721.

18. Ruthann Robson, "Lavender Bruises: Intra-Lesbian Violence, Law and Lesbian Legal Theory," Golden Gate University Law Review 20 (1990): 572. Of course, the problem of hetero-relationizing is not unique to the arena of domestic violence. Courts, scholars, and the general public often apply heterosexual models to many aspects of same-sex relationships—as, for example, in the custody decisions discussed later in this chapter.

19. See, for example, Kerry Lobel, ed., Naming the Violence: Speaking Out About Lesbian Battering (Seattle: Seal Press, 1986); Ruthann Robson, "Lavender Bruises:

Intra-Lesbian Violence, Law and Lesbian Legal Theory," *Golden Gate University Law Review* 20 (1990): 567–91; Beth Leventhal and Sandra E. Lundy, eds., *Same-Sex Domestic Violence: Strategies for Change* (Thousand Oaks, CA: Sage, 1999); Claire M. Renzetti, *Violent Betrayal: Partner Abuse in Lesbian Relationships* (Newbury Park, CA: Sage, 1992); Mary Eaton, "Abuse by Any Other Name: Feminism, Difference, and Intralesbian Violence," in *The Public Nature of Private Violence: The Discovery of Domestic Abuse*, ed. Martha Albertson Fineman and Roxanne Mykitiuk (New York: Routledge, 1994): 195–223; Pam Elliott, "Shattering Illusions: Same-Sex Domestic Violence," in *Violence in Gay and Lesbian Domestic Partnerships*, ed. Claire M. Renzetti and Charles Harvey Miley (New York: Haworth Press, 1996): 1–8; Paula B. Poorman, "Forging Community Links to Address Abuse in Lesbian Relationships," in *Intimate Betrayal: Domestic Violence in Lesbian Relationships*, ed. Ellyn Kaschak (New York: Haworth Press, 2001): 7–24.

20. Ruthann Robson, "Lavender Bruises: Intra-Lesbian Violence, Law and Lesbian Legal Theory," *Golden Gate University Law Review* 20 (1990): 571–74.

21. Mary Eaton, "Abuse by Any Other Name: Feminism, Difference, and Intralesbian Violence," in *The Public Nature of Private Violence: The Discovery of Domestic Abuse*, ed. Martha Albertson Fineman and Roxanne Mykitiuk (New York: Routledge, 1994): 195–223; see esp. p. 207.

22. For a more thorough discussion of these issues, see Rhonda R. Rivera, "Our Straight-Laced Judges: The Legal Position of Homosexual Persons in the United States," *Hastings Law Journal* 30 (1979): 799–955.

23. For further information on consensual sodomy statutes targeting homosexuals specifically and/or exempting married or heterosexual couples from their reach, see William N. Eskridge Jr., *Gaylaw: Challenging the Apartheid of the Closet* (Cambridge, MA: Harvard University Press, 1999): 328–37.

24. Ibid.

25. For further information on the enforcement of sodomy laws against homosexuals, see ibid., 63–66.

26. Janet E. Halley, "Reasoning About Sodomy: Act and Identity in and After *Bowers v. Hardwick*," *Virginia Law Review* 79 (1993): 1747.

27. William N. Eskridge Jr., *Gaylaw: Challenging the Apartheid of the Closet* (Cambridge, MA: Harvard University Press, 1999): 157–58.

28. Ibid., 19–20.

29. Ibid., 158–59.

30. Ibid., 159–60.

31. As with most social movements, the gay rights movement cannot be said to have an exact starting date, but many scholars have identified the Stonewall riot of 1969 as one major signal of its inception. (See, for instance, ibid., 99.)

32. Ibid., 160.

33. These states were Arkansas, Kansas, Kentucky, Missouri, Montana, Nevada, and Texas (for more information, see ibid., 150, fn a.).

34. These states were Oklahoma and Maryland (for more information, see ibid., 150, fn a.).

35. 403 F. Supp. 1199 (1975).

36. Ibid., 1200.

37. 381 U.S. 479 (1965).

38. 367 U.S. 497 (1961).

39. Ibid., 546.

40. *Doe*, 1202.

41. 478 U.S. 186 (1986).

42. See, for example, Anne Goldstein, "History, Homosexuality, and Political Values: Searching for the Hidden Determinants of *Bowers* v. *Hardwick*," *Yale Law Journal* 97 (1988): 1073; Janet E. Halley, "Reasoning About Sodomy: Act and Identity in and After *Bowers* v. *Hardwick*," *Virginia Law Review* 79 (1993): 1721; Kendall Thomas, "Beyond the Privacy Principle," *Columbia Law Review* 92 (1992): 1431.

43. George Brenning, interview by author, November 3, 2002; Peter Irons, *The Courage of Their Convictions* (New York: Free Press, 1988).

44. Brenning, interview, 2002.

45. Kathleen Wilde, interview by author, October 30, 2002; Brenning, interview, 2002.

46. Letter from District Attorney Lewis Slaton, January 7, 1983.

47. Brenning, interview, 2002.

48. Wilde, interview, 2002.

49. Order of District Court, April 18, 1985.

50. 760 F.2d 1202 (1985).

51. 431 U.S. 678 (1977).

52. Ibid., fn. 17, qtd. in *Hardwick* v. *Bowers*, 1209.

53. 464 U.S. 812 (1983).

54. 410 U.S. 113 (1973).

55. 405 U.S. 438 (1972).

56. *Hardwick*, 1211–12.

57. Wilde, interview, 2002.

58. Ibid.

59. Brief of Respondents in Opposition to Petition for Writ of Certiorari, September 12, 1985.

60. The list of cases cited in the briefs is extensive, but some examples of often-cited cases include *Pierce* v. *Society of Sisters*, 268 U.S. 510 (1925), http://laws.findlaw.com/us/268/510.html (full text), *Skinner* v. *Oklahoma*, 316 U.S. 535 (1942), http://laws.findlaw.com/us/316/535.html (full text), *Stanley* v. *Georgia*, 394 U.S. 557 (1969), http://laws.findlaw.com/us/394/557.html (full text), http://www.oyez.org/cases/case/?case=1960-1969/1968/1968_293 (audio), *Poe*, *Griswold*, *Eisenstadt*, *Roe*, and *Carey*.

61. Brief for Respondent, January 31, 1986; Brief of the New York City Bar Association, January 27, 1986.

62. Brief of the New York City Bar Association, January 27, 1986; emphasis added.

63. Brief of Attorneys General of New York and California, January 31, 1986.

64. *Griswold*, 485–86; cited in Brief of the New York City Bar Association, January 27, 1986.

65. *Eisenstadt,* 453; cited in Brief of Attorneys General of New York and California, January 31, 1986; emphasis in original.

66. Brief of Lesbian Rights Project, et al., January 29, 1986.

67. Brief of National Gay Rights Advocates et al., January 31, 1986; Brief of Lambda Legal Defense and Education Fund et al., January 31, 1986; Brief of Lesbian Rights Project, et al., January 29, 1986.

68. Brief of Lesbian Rights Project, et al., January 29, 1986; Brief of the National Organization for Women, January 31, 1986.

69. See Brief of the American Psychological Association and American Public Health Association, January 31, 1986; Brief of the Presbyterian Church et al., January 31, 1986; and the Brief of the American Jewish Congress, January 31, 1986.

70. Oral Argument of *Bowers v. Hardwick, Landmark Briefs and Arguments of the Supreme Court of the United States* vol. 164 (Washington: University Publications of America): 642.

71. Ibid., 652.

72. Ibid., 633.

73. Ibid., 641.

74. Ibid., 636.

75. See Brief of the Rutherford Institute et al, Amicus Curiae, December 19, 1985; Brief of Concerned Women of America, Amicus Curiae, December 19, 1985; Brief of the Catholic League for Religious and Civil Rights, Amicus Curiae, December 13, 1985.

76. Brief of the Catholic League for Religious and Civil Rights, Amicus Curiae, December 13, 1985.

77. Brief of the Rutherford Institute et al., December 19, 1985.

78. *Bowers v. Hardwick,* 190.

79. Ibid., 192.

80. Ibid., 190.

81. Ibid., 196.

82. Ibid., 191.

83. Ibid., 200.

84. Ibid., 204.

85. Ibid., 205; original emphasis.

86. Ibid., 205.

87. Ibid., 205.

88. Kathleen Sullivan, interview by author, November 19, 2002.

89. 539 U.S. 558 (2003).

90. Probable cause affidavits authored by Officer Quinn, qtd. in Brief of Amici Curiae Texas Legislators, February 18, 2003.

91. Ibid.

92. *Lawrence v. Texas,* 539 U.S. 558 (2003), 563.

93. Ibid., 563.

94. *Lawrence v. Texas,* 41 S.W.3d 349 (2001).

95. Ibid., 361.

96. Ibid., 366.

97. Ibid., 375.

98. Ibid., 375.

99. Amicus Brief of Human Rights Campaign; National Gay and Lesbian Task Force; Parents, Families and Friends of Lesbians and Gays; National Center for Lesbian Rights; Gay and Lesbian Advocates and Defenders; Gay and Lesbian Alliance Against Defamation; Pride at Work, et al., January 16, 2003, p. 2.

100. Brief of the National Lesbian and Gay Law Association, the Asian American Legal Defense and Education Fund, Action Wisconsin, the Bay Area Lawyers for Individual Freedom, the Bay Area Transgender Lawyers' Association, et al. as Amici Curiae, January 16, 2003.

101. In its brief, the Republican Unity Coalition describes itself as "a national organization of conservative Republicans committed to making sexual orientation a 'non-issue' within the Republican Party and throughout the Nation." Brief of Amici Curiae Republican Unity Coalition and the Honorable Alan K. Simpson, January 16, 2003, p. 1.

102. http://www.cato.org/about/about.html

103. Brief of the Cato Institute as Amicus Curiae, January 16, 2003, p. 2

104. Ibid., 23

105. Ibid., 24.

106. Amicus Brief of the American Center for Law and Justice, February 18, 2003, p. 1.

107. Ibid., 4.

108. Ibid., 9.

109. Ibid., 19.

110. Brief of Amici Curiae, Pro-Family Law Center, Traditional Values Coalition, Traditional Values Education and Legal Institute and James Hartline, February 18, 2003, p. 4.

111. Ibid., 5.

112. Ibid. 6.

113. Ibid., 4, 11.

114. Brief Amici Curiae of the Center for Marriage Law, February 18, 2003, p. 3.

115. Brief of the Center for Law and Justice International as Amicus Curiae, February 18, 2003, p. 3.

116. Ibid., 13.

117. Brief of Amici Curiae Texas Legislators, Representative Warren Chisum, et al., February 18, 2003, p. 8.

118. Brief of Amici Curiae, Pro-Family Law Center, Traditional Values Coalition, Traditional Values Education and Legal Institute and James Hartline, February 18, 2003, p. 3.

119. Ibid., 6.

120. *Lawrence v. Texas*, 539 U.S. 558 (2003), 562.

121. Ibid., 565.

122. Ibid., 565–66.

123. Oral Argument of *Lawrence v. Texas*, Alderson Reporting Company, available at U.S. Supreme Court Online: http://www.supremecourtus.gov/oral_arguments/argument_transcripts/02-102.pdf, p. 35.

124. *Lawrence v. Texas*, 539 U.S. 558 (2003), 578.

125. Ibid., 567.

126. Ibid., 575.

127. Ibid., 567; emphasis added.

128. Ibid., 578.

129. Ibid., 573.

130. Ibid., 576.

131. Pam Elliott, "Shattering Illusions: Same-Sex Domestic Violence," in *Violence in Gay and Lesbian Domestic Partnerships*, ed. Claire M. Renzetti and Charles Harvey Miley (New York: Haworth Press, 1996): 1–8; see esp. pp. 6–7. See also L. Kevin Hamberger, "Intervention in Gay Male Intimate Violence Requires Coordinated Efforts on Multiple Levels," in *Violence in Gay and Lesbian Domestic Partnerships*, ed. Claire M. Renzetti and Charles Harvey Miley (New York: Haworth Press, 1996): 83–92; see esp. pp. 86–87.

132. See Pam Elliott, "Shattering Illusions: Same-Sex Domestic Violence," in *Violence in Gay and Lesbian Domestic Partnerships*, ed. Claire M. Renzetti and Charles Harvey Miley (New York: Haworth Press, 1996): 1–8; see esp. p. 6.

133. Ibid., 6.

134. Barbara Hart, interview by author, May 1, 2002. See also Barbara Hart, preface, in Kerry Lobel, ed., *Naming the Violence: Speaking Out About Lesbian Battering* (Seattle: Seal Press, 1986): 9–16; see esp. p. 12.

135. Howard Kurtz, "Meese Delayed Grant When Conservatives Balked; Decision on Coalition Against Domestic Violence Indicates Split in Ranks," *Washington Post*, August 9, 1985, p. A8.

136. Ibid.

137. Howard Kurtz, "Meese Clears Disputed Grant for Aid to Battered Women; Group is 'Pro-Family,' Conservative Critics Told," *Washington Post*, August 10, 1985: p. A2.

138. This tendency within the battered-women's movement unfortunately mirrors several points within the mainstream feminist movement in which women from marginalized communities (whether lesbians, women of color, or poor women) were disowned in some way for similarly political reasons.

139. See Curt Rogers, "Six Steps: Organizing Support Services and Safe-Home Networks for Battered Gay Men," in *Same-Sex Domestic Violence: Strategies for Change*, ed. Beth Leventhal and Sandra E. Lundy (Thousand Oaks, CA: Sage, 1999): 111–23.

140. Ibid., 113. See also Beth Crane et al., "Lesbians and Bisexual Women Working Cooperatively to End Domestic Violence," in *Same-Sex Domestic Violence: Strategies for Change*, ed. Beth Leventhal and Sandra E. Lundy (Thousand Oaks, CA: Sage, 1999): 125–34; Jennifer Grant, "An Argument for Separate Services," in *Same-Sex Domestic Violence: Strategies for Change*, ed. Beth Leventhal and Sandra E. Lundy

(Thousand Oaks, CA: Sage, 1999): 183–91; L. Kevin Hamberger, "Intervention in Gay Male Intimate Violence Requires Coordinated Efforts on Multiple Levels," in *Violence in Gay and Lesbian Domestic Partnerships,* ed. Claire M. Renzetti and Charles Harvey Miley (New York: Haworth Press, 1996): 83–92; and Robb Johnson, "Groups for Gay and Bisexual Male Survivors of Domestic Violence," in *Same-Sex Domestic Violence: Strategies for Change,* ed. Beth Leventhal and Sandra E. Lundy (Thousand Oaks, CA: Sage, 1999): 111–23.

141. Brief of Lesbian Rights Project, et al., January 29, 1986.

142. 871 P.2d 79 (1994).

143. Ibid., 95.

144. Ibid., 95.

145. 119 Cal. App. 4th 1146 (2004).

146. Ibid., 1155–56.

147. Ibid., 1154.

148. 491 S.W.2d 672.

149. Ibid., 673.

150. Ibid., 673–74.

151. 427 So.2d 283 (1983).

152. Ibid., 285.

153. Ibid., 285.

154. Ruthann Robson, "Lavender Bruises: Intra-Lesbian Violence, Law and Lesbian Legal Theory," *Golden Gate University Law Review* 20 (1990): 575.

155. 328 P.2d 834 (1958).

156. Ibid., 839.

157. Ibid., 839.

158. 1985 Tenn. Crim. App. LEXIS 3087

159. Ibid., 2.

160. Ibid., 12–13.

161. 860 S.W.2d 575 (1993).

162. See, for example, *Bailey v. Texas,* 1993 Tex. App. LEXIS 1253, in which the court allowed evidence of a prior abusive same-sex relationship as a means of establishing motive for the murder.

163. 1991 Tex. App. LEXIS 1396.

164. Ibid., 3–4.

165. See, for instance, *In Interest of Jones,* 429 A.2d 671 (1981), *People v. Woodhull,* 481 N.Y.S.2d 749 (1984), *People v. Newbern,* 579 N.E.2d 583 (1991), and *In re Lowe,* 130 Cal. App. 4th 1405 (2005).

166. 573 N.E.2d 1191 (1991).

167. Ibid., 1193.

168. The long-term effects of this case remain to be seen, given a development in that state's constitutional history. In 2004, Ohio voters agreed to amend their state constitution to deny the right of marriage and other related benefits to same-sex couples. In particular, the constitution now requires that the state deny any legal recognition "that intends to approximate the design, significance or effect of marriage" to

relationships between unmarried individuals. One consequence of this development has been the defense—raised by those accused of domestic violence—that the state domestic violence statute does not apply to them if they are not married to their accuser. This development has sweeping implications for both straight and LGBT victims of domestic violence. Trial and appellate courts in Ohio have produced conflicting rulings, and the issue is currently under consideration by the Ohio Supreme Court.

169. See, for example, *Bryant v. Burnett*, 624 A.2d 584 (1993), *Cusseaux v. Pickett*, 652 A.2d 789 (1994), and *Peterman v. Meeker*, 855 So. 2d 690 (2003).

170. 665 N.E.2d 1180 (1996).

171. Ibid., 1184.

172. Ibid., 1184.

173. Ibid., 1185.

174. 957 S.W.2d 310 (1997).

175. Ibid., 312.

176. *Hadinger*, 1192.

177. Ibid., 1184.

178. Ibid., 1184.

179. *Griswold*, 485.

180. *Poe*, 553.

181. William N. Eskridge Jr, *Gaylaw: Challenging the Apartheid of the Closet* (Cambridge, MA: Harvard University Press, 1999): 150.

6. CONCLUSION

Toward a New Model of Privacy

THE HISTORICAL DEVELOPMENT OF PRIVACY
AND DOMESTIC VIOLENCE

The problem of domestic violence in the United States has been inextricably linked with cultural and judicial constructions of privacy. The history of privacy in this country—as it has been recognized, understood, and continually reinterpreted by both state actors and the general public—has had significant and lasting implications for the issue of domestic violence. Specifically, the various ways in which courts, police, and battered women's advocates have understood privacy have determined the extent of civil and criminal protection afforded to victims of intimate partner violence—and, concurrently, the extent of punishment meted out to batterers. An understanding of the historical development and application of the privacy right is therefore crucial to understanding the history of domestic violence in this country. The preceding chapters have examined the many ways that shifting meanings of privacy have shaped responses to the issue of domestic abuse, from condoning the problem to ignoring or minimizing it to recognizing it as an infringement on women's rights.

Rooted in liberal individualism, privacy has most often been construed as a negative right: the freedom of individuals from state intervention in the home. Historically, however, this right has been imbued with two powerful assumptions, both of which have significantly affected the application of the right to privacy. First, the home has generally been presumed to be the haven of a traditional, nuclear (and often white, middle-class) family. Second, this family is presumably headed by a man who can do as he pleases—the "king of his castle." As a result of these underlying assumptions, the privacy right has primarily served the interests of such men and privileged the patriarchal and heterosexual family form.

The judicial implications of these assumptions for battered women became clear in the late nineteenth century. When state appellate courts began to hear domestic violence cases at this time, they considered the privacy implications of these cases first, and the violence second. Thus, even when courts did condemn the abusive acts, they often refused to punish the perpetrators out of respect for the privacy of the domestic sphere. Interestingly, when judges finally, unequivocally repudiated the right of chastisement—and punished batterers— they often did so in cases involving batterers whose claim to a right of privacy was diminished as a result of their racial identity and/or class status.[1] In this way, courts were able to condemn domestic violence without fundamentally altering the hierarchical implications of the right to privacy.

The uneasy relationship between privacy and domestic violence continued throughout the twentieth century and into the twenty-first. After several decades of relative silence from courts and activists around this issue, domestic violence garnered public attention in the early 1970s via the consciousness-raising efforts of the second-wave women's movement. The battered women's movement emerged just as another goal of the women's rights movement was nearing fruition: the securing of reproductive rights. Judicial and activist debates about the legality of contraception and abortion helped shape the evolution of the privacy right from the 1950s through the 1970s, and the resulting judicial construction of privacy proved significant for battered women and their advocates as well. The privacy right established in this line of reproductive rights cases continued to follow the rhetoric of liberal individualism, prohibiting state interference in the domestic sphere (and, by extension, in a woman's right to choose). This construction of the privacy right, however, had potentially dangerous implications for battered women, whose safety often depended upon state intervention in the home. Nonetheless, one case initiated during this era suggested another, very different version of privacy. Perhaps because the unusual circumstances of the case necessitated a creative approach, the lawyer-activists working on *People* v. *Liberta*[2] developed an innovative model of privacy that the court then accepted. The *Liberta* briefs acknowledged and relied on the reproductive rights cases, but simultaneously transformed that concept of privacy into a positive right for battered women. By focusing on issues of personal autonomy and bodily integrity in their articulation of the privacy right, these lawyer-activists provided the first key component to an alternative model of privacy.

Case Resources

DeShaney v. *Winnebago County*

Findlaw (http://laws.findlaw.com/us/489/189.html) (full text)

Oyez (http://www.oyez.org/cases/case?case=1980-1989/1988/1988_87_154) (oral arguments)

Castle Rock v. *Gonzales*

Findlaw (http://laws.findlaw.com/us/000/04-278.html) (full text)

Oyez (http://www.oyez.org/cases/case?case=2000-2009/2004/2004_04_278) (oral arguments)

The type of privacy advocated in *Liberta,* however, did not become the prevailing model. Despite tremendous legislative advances made by the battered women's movement, police and judicial attitudes towards domestic violence continued to support notions of privacy that enshrined even an abusive man as the unchallenged head of the patriarchal household. In practice, such attitudes resulted in police ignoring or mishandling domestic violence calls, and judges and other state entitities often supporting such inaction by further minimizing the seriousness of the abuse. During the 1980s, many battered women and their advocates brought civil lawsuits against police and other government bodies for their often willful failure to respond appropriately—or at all—to reports of domestic abuse. These civil suits achieved increasing success throughout the early 1980s, culminating in several significant and highly publicized financial awards to plaintiffs in the cases of *Thurman* v. *Torrington*[3] and *Sorichetti* v. *New York.*[4] As the decade progressed, however, similar suits faced increasing judicial resistance, until the notorious 1989 case of *DeShaney* v. *Winnebago County*[5] rendered future such litigation nearly impossible. Holding that the state has no affirmative duty to protect private citizens from violence, the *DeShaney* court effectively closed this era of battered women's litigation and reinforced the notion of privacy as a negative right. Sixteen years later, the case of *Castle Rock* v. *Gonzales*[6] provided further confirmation that the era of successful civil suits was indeed long over.

Case Resources

Bowers v. *Hardwick*

Findlaw (http://laws.findlaw.com/us/478/186.html) (full text)

Oyez (http://www.oyez.org/cases/case?case=1980-1989/1985/1985_85_140) (oral arguments)

Lawrence v. *Texas*

Findlaw (http://laws.findlaw.com/us/000/02-102.html) (full text)

Oyez (http://www.oyez.org/cases/case/?case=2000-2009/2002/2002_02_102) (oral arguments)

While most domestic violence court cases have focused primarily on heterosexual relationships, some activists within the battered women's movement have observed for years that domestic abuse occurs between same-sex couples as well. Victims of homosexual partner violence have faced additional obstacles in the pursuit of safety and justice. The challenges that gay and lesbian victims continue to face in the courtroom often result from the troubled relationship that has historically existed between homosexuals and the legal right to privacy. Specifically, as part of their refusal to acknowledge the legitimacy of same-sex relationships, courts have often been unwilling to extend the right of privacy to them. While it was eventually overturned in 2005, the 1986 Supreme Court case of *Bowers* v. *Hardwick*[7] exemplified this disregard for the privacy of same-sex partnerships. Likewise, in cases of same-sex domestic violence, courts have accorded these relationships neither privacy nor justice, but an excessive and inappropriate focus on the homosexual nature of the union. Judges, juries, and lawyers have often used these cases to promulgate the view of homosexual relationships as inherently pathological, therefore minimizing the violence at issue and denying justice to victims. As a result, the right of privacy has, in very different ways, served as a barrier to effective legal protection for victims of intimate partner violence, both homosexual and heterosexual.

A NEW MODEL OF PRIVACY

Considering this historical development of the right to privacy, its influence on state responses to domestic violence, and its role in reinforcing heterosexist norms, the influence of privacy on American judicial discourse in this arena is clear. Privacy's roots in liberal individualism and its continued evolution throughout the nineteenth, twentieth, and twenty-first centuries have secured it a place in our nation's judicial lexicon. In addition, two recent developments have ensured that the right to privacy remains the focus of ongoing concern. First, the proliferation of internet usage has generated substantial debate about the extent to which private lives and personal information may be shielded from unwanted scrutiny. Second, the ever-increasing power of the federal government to monitor the lives of its citizens in the name of "homeland security" has engendered concern about the limits of state power in relation to individual privacy rights. The pervasiveness and immediacy of both of these issues have thus placed the right of privacy at the center of much current debate.

Given that privacy remains so thoroughly ingrained in our national consciousness, ignoring or downplaying its relevance is not an option. Alternatively, some feminist scholars, such as Catharine MacKinnon, have suggested that feminists reject privacy altogether as too detrimental to women, and focus instead on issues of nondiscrimination.[8] This suggestion, however, is an equally unfeasible response, given the prevalence of notions of privacy in American culture. For those seeking to end domestic violence, such an approach would be particularly dangerous, for several reasons. First, privacy has continued to play such a crucial role in defining the state's response to the problem of domestic violence that it cannot be rejected outright. In addition, the concept of privacy is so deeply embedded in our culture that it carries legitimacy and power that, constructed differently, could benefit victims of domestic violence. Finally, to reject privacy altogether would be to ignore its implications for gay men and lesbians, for whom privacy poses ongoing challenges.

Instead of refusing to engage with issues of privacy, therefore, addressing the problem of intimate partner violence requires confronting privacy directly. Understanding its origins and historical development, as well as its ongoing impact on domestic violence, are critical steps in this process. Having fully apprehended the dangers inherent in prevailing models of privacy, one may then begin to articulate an alternative vision of privacy. Feminist scholars such as Patricia Boling, [9] Dorothy Roberts,[10] and Elizabeth Schneider[11] have called for the development of just such a model. In particular, Boling has called for a critical reevaluation of privacy that resists jettisoning the concept altogether. Instead, Boling urges feminist scholars to assess the negative aspects of existing models of privacy, but also to consider the potential utility of privacy as a "political tool" for women.[12] She further suggests that feminists consider "how issues rooted in private life can be made politically recognizable and actionable."[13] Roberts critiques the formulation of privacy as a purely negative right, advocating instead the development of a model that provides an "affirmative guarantee of personhood and autonomy."[14] Roberts's ideal model promotes the needs of the individual as well as the needs of the community, paying particular attention to issues of race and class. Such a model, she suggests, could conceivably "forge a finer legal tool for dismantling institutions of domination."[15]

Similarly, Schneider also promotes a critique and revisioning of privacy, and she applies her argument specifically to the issue of domestic violence. Like Roberts, Schneider advocates a revisioning of privacy as an affirmative right, one that holds "radical potential" for battered women. Schneider suggests that feminists continue to critique the public/private dichotomy, and develop a new form of privacy that is not "synonymous with the right to state noninterference with actions within the family."[16] Like Boling and Roberts, Schneider sees the positive potential of a new form of privacy, but she does not specifically articulate what it might look like.

Case Resources
Doe v. *Bolton*
Findlaw (http://laws.findlaw.com/us/410/179.html) (full text)
Oyez (http://www.oyez.org/cases/case?case=1970-1979/1971/1971_70_40) (oral arguments)

I begin the process of outlining a new model of privacy here by synthesizing and expanding upon some preliminary formulations already advanced by both scholars and judges. For example, Schneider has suggested that Justice Douglas's concurrence in the 1973 case of *Doe* v. *Bolton* (the companion case to *Roe* v. *Wade*)[17] provides an exemplar for a new model of privacy. In that opinion, Douglas elaborated on three aspects of liberty closely related to the privacy right, each of which provides rich potential for an alternative form of privacy: first, "the autonomous control over the development and expression of one's intellect, interests, tastes, and personality;" second, the "freedom of choice in the basic decisions of one's life respecting marriage, divorce, procreation, contraception, and the education and upbringing of children;" and third, "the freedom to care for one's health and person, freedom from bodily restraint or compulsion, freedom to walk, stroll, or loaf."[18] Each of these three components centers on affirmative notions of privacy and autonomy that include decision-making but also involve bodily integrity. Instead of focusing on protecting individuals from the state, these principles focus on allowing people to fulfill their potential. As such, they contain significant possibilities for the empowerment of battered women.

Case Resources
Olmstead v. *United States*
Findlaw (http://laws.findlaw.com/us/277/438.html) (full text)
Oyez (http://www.oyez.org/cases/case?case=1901-1939/1927/1927_493) (oral arguments)

Interestingly, a similar precedent for this model of privacy comes from none other than the often-cited *Olmstead* dissent of 1928.[19] Justice Brandeis's characterization of privacy as "the right to be let alone" has been quoted frequently by judges and legal scholars writing about the right to privacy as a negative right.[20] Despite the popularity of this phrase, however, the context in which he wrote it has been significantly overlooked. In fact, the right of privacy that Brandeis envisioned was much more comprehensive than the well-known phrase would suggest. Specifically, Brandeis wrote:

> The protection guaranteed by the Amendments is much broader in scope. The makers of our Constitution undertook to secure conditions favorable to the pursuit of happiness. They recognized the significance of man's spiritual nature, of his feelings and of his intellect. They knew that only a part of the pain, pleasure and satisfactions of life are to be found in material things. They sought to protect Americans in their beliefs, their thoughts, their emotions and their sensations. They conferred, as against the Government, the right to be let alone—the most comprehensive of rights and the right most valued by civilized men. To protect that right, every unjustifiable intrusion by the Government upon the privacy of the individual, whatever the means employed, must be deemed a violation of the Fourth Amendment.[21]

The ideal that Brandeis asserted in *Olmstead*, therefore, was not simply as one-dimensional as "the right to be let alone." Certainly, Brandeis did position privacy as the right to be free from government intrusion. Yet he valued this right primarily as a means of asserting affirmative principles of self-fulfillment and the pursuit of happiness. Far more than simply a protection from state intrusion, Brandeis delineated a right that supported the development and expression of citizens' "spiritual nature, . . . feelings, . . . intellect" as well as "beliefs, . . . thoughts, . . . emotions and . . . sensations." Thus, while privacy was framed here as a negative right—protection from government interference—the context of the familiar quote reveals this protection to be primarily a means of safeguarding the more significant, affirmative rights: to pursue fulfillment and happiness in a variety of areas. When Brandeis spoke of privacy in this context, it was those aspects of human life that he was seeking to elevate and protect.

Drawing on the ideals articulated by these jurists, as well as those suggested by feminist scholars, my conclusions here outline some key elements that I believe are essential to a successful, alternative model of privacy. In particular, a version of privacy that could empower victims of domestic violence must contain the following components. First, it must be an affirmative right articulated within the context of a liberty interest. Second, it must be premised on notions of equality and reflect an awareness of gender, race and ethnicity, class, sexuality, and physical ability. Third, it must promote autonomy and bodily integrity, and the related ideals of self-expression and self-determination. And finally, it must accrue to all individuals equally and not be dependent upon marital, familial, or relationship status.

For privacy to become a tool of empowerment for battered women—rather than an instrument of their continued oppression, as it has so often served in the past—several fundamental changes must occur in the ways that courts, activists, and all of us think about privacy. Writing about privacy in the context of domestic violence, Schneider asserts that "[t]he challenge is to develop a right to privacy which is not synonymous with the right to state noninterference with actions within the family . . . but which recognizes the affirmative role that privacy can play for battered women."[22] In taking up this challenge, I believe that the first and most critical step in this process is to re-examine our understanding of privacy as freedom. The traditional model of privacy construes it as a *negative* freedom—the freedom *from* state intervention in the home. An alternative model would also view privacy as a freedom, but not in a negative sense. Instead, the model I propose here constructs privacy as an *affirmative* right and a critical aspect of personal liberty: the freedom to control one's own life. This freedom encompasses the freedom to choose what happens to one's own body and the freedom to decide how to conduct intimate relationships. Thus drawn, the right of privacy inherently engages individual autonomy, bodily integrity, self-expression, and self-determination, while not entirely excluding the concept of freedom from state interference. These principles are already well-entrenched within American constitutional and judicial discourse; what is new here is their application to a new understanding of the right to privacy. In fact, as this discussion will show, kernels of these ideas already exist within our judicial tradition, and a revisioning of privacy would only require recalling and further advancing these ideas.

The notion of privacy as an affirmative right—a freedom *to* rather than a freedom *from*—contains substantial possibilities. Justice Stevens, registering his dissent in the *Bowers* case, highlighted this important distinction in his discussion of privacy. Recalling words he had written in an earlier case, he noted that many cases involving privacy "do not deal with the individual's interest in protection from unwarranted public attention, comment, or exploitation," but rather "the individual's right to make certain unusually important decisions."[23] The first type of privacy described by Stevens—the negative formulation, the "protection from"—lends itself quite readily to protecting batterers and preserving the immunity of the patriarchal home from state intervention. The second type of privacy he cites—the "right to"—sharply contrasts the negative model, however, and suggests a right that battered women themselves might easily invoke.

Expanding upon this latter model, Stevens further appeals to "the American heritage of freedom—the abiding interest in individual liberty."[24] The invocation of liberty is significant here, for liberty is a critical element in the formulation of an affirmative right to privacy. From its earliest expression in the nation's founding documents,[25] liberty has connoted both individual and collective empowerment, reinforcing the affirmative aspects of freedom. As Rebecca Brown has observed,

> [T]he emphasis on liberty in the founding period was not accidental. To a generation of revolutionaries who wished to rouse a population to rebellion in the name of

clear and passionately held visions of a better life, a clamor for liberty sounded a stir-
ring call to action. . . . [T]he very feature that made liberty a . . . rousing revolution-
ary cause [was] its powerful promise of better lives for citizens. . . . [L]iberty constraints seem to tell legislatures that there are certain important human interests that
they cannot impair . . . [26]

Ultimately, these associations of independence and the "right to" implied by
the rhetoric of liberty provide a solid foundation for an alternative model of
privacy as an affirmative right.

An alternative model of privacy that would empower battered women must
also be informed by an awareness of and sensitivity to gender inequality. According to Schneider, Douglas's innovative interpretation of the privacy right in
his *Roe* concurrence was influenced by the women's rights activism that surrounded that case.[27] Clearly informed by the amicus briefs submitted by feminist organizations, Douglas's concurrence described the far-reaching effects of
unwanted pregnancy on women's well-being:

[Women denied abortion] are required to endure the discomforts of pregnancy; to
incur the pain, higher mortality rate, and aftereffects of childbirth; to abandon educational plans; to sustain loss of income; to forgo the satisfactions of careers; to tax
futher mental and physical health in providing child care . . . [28]

I agree with Schneider's implication that Douglas's sensitivity to gender
issues was critical to his formulation of an affirmative privacy right, and I
would add that this awareness should be further expanded to include issues of
race and ethnicity, class, sexuality, and physical ability. In her discussion of
the prosecution of crack-addicted mothers, Dorothy Roberts suggests that a
form of privacy informed by such awareness would entail affirmative governmental responsibilities; for example, "Under this post-liberal doctrine, the
government is not only prohibited from punishing crack-addicted women for
choosing to bear children; it is also required to provide drug-treatment and
pre-natal care."[29]

Similarly, the same-sex domestic violence case of *State* v. *Linner*[30] suggests
another manifestation of such a right. The *Linner* court, recognizing the particular hardships faced by lesbian and gay male victims of domestic abuse, concluded that these challenges rendered homosexuals all the more deserving of
access to and protection by domestic violence laws. As these examples suggest,
a right to privacy conceived within an affirmative liberty context promotes equality among citizens, ensuring that *all* citizens have the right to control their own
lives. An awareness of social identity categories such as gender, race, and sexuality only enhances this drive toward equality. Furthermore, sensitivity toward
identity issues directly contradicts the traditional model of privacy as the freedom

from state intervention, which historically has protected only those already privileged by their gender, race, class, or sexuality.

Case Resources

Griswold v. *Connecticut*

Findlaw (http://laws.findlaw.com/us/381/479.html) (full text)

Oyez (http://www.oyez.org/cases/case/?case=1960-1969/1964/1964_496) (oral arguments)

Eisenstadt v. *Baird*

Findlaw (http://laws.findlaw.com/us/405/438.html) (full text)

Oyez (http://www.oyez.org/cases/case/?case=1970-1979/1971/1971_70_17) (oral arguments)

Roe v. *Wade*

Findlaw (http://laws.findlaw.com/us/410/113.html) (full text)

Oyez (http://www.oyez.org/cases/case/?case=1970-1979/1971/1971_70_18) (oral arguments)

Conceived as an affirmative right with a sensitivity toward identity issues, an alternative model of privacy would also emphasize autonomy and bodily integrity. As the right of privacy evolved through the line of reproductive rights cases that led up to *Roe*, it leaned increasingly toward this formulation. While *Griswold*[31] had focused explicitly on locational privacy—specifically, that of the home, and particularly of the marital bedroom—the *Eisenstadt*[32] opinion spoke of decisional privacy, regarding "matters . . . fundamentally affecting a person."[33] Blackmun's majority opinion in *Roe* advanced this notion further, asserting "a right of personal privacy" that "is broad enough to encompass a woman's decision whether or not to terminate her pregnancy."[34] As the privacy right thus progressed from the strictly locational formulation to include decisional aspects as well, it became increasingly associated with notions of individual autonomy. Likewise, Douglas's emphasis on privacy as autonomy in his *Roe* concurrence, articulated in part as "the freedom to care for one's health and person, freedom from bodily restraint or compulsion," further strengthens the links between privacy, autonomy, and bodily integrity.

Applied to the domestic violence context, the privacy right thus construed could become a tool for the empowerment of battered women. In contrast to the traditional formulation of privacy that has served to protect batterers from state censure, this alternative model centered on personal autonomy could serve to protect the victims of intimate partner violence themselves. The assertion of a privacy right on behalf of battered women, rather than on behalf of their abusive partners, also finds support in the *Liberta* opinion. No doubt influenced by the amicus briefs submitted by the feminist lawyer-activists working on the case, the court's opinion specifically referenced "the bodily integrity of the victim" and relied upon several reproductive rights cases to affirm a woman's "right to control her own body."[35] Furthermore, *Liberta* emphasized that the presumed right of "marital privacy" asserted on behalf of the abuser could not, in fact, protect him; instead, the court contended, "this right of privacy protects [only] consensual acts."[36] This inversion of the traditional privacy paradigm, citing the primacy of autonomy and bodily integrity, creates a rhetorical tool that enables the right of privacy to serve as a vehicle for battered women's justice.

Related to the ideals of autonomy and bodily integrity are self-expression and self-determination, which recall the first two components of Douglas's description of liberty: freedom to control the development of one's own personality, and freedom to make the most basic and important life decisions. These two related values also suggest the freedom to choose the nature and character of intimate relationships, a critical component of the alternative model of privacy. Justice Blackmun's dissent in *Bowers* emphasized self-definition as a central characteristic of the right to privacy and invoked "the fundamental interest all individuals have in controlling the nature of their intimate associations with others."[37] This freedom to determine the nature and direction of one's life—and, particularly, one's intimate relationships—could prove a significant source of protection for battered women. By focusing on privacy as the affirmative ability to control one's life, such a right would expand to protect battered women's liberty, rather than protecting their abusers from punishment.

An emphasis on privacy as an *egalitarian* right is also central to the alternative model. The traditional construction of privacy, which often translated into a protection of the presumed "head of the household," created implicit hierarchies based upon familial and marital status. An alternative model of privacy, by contrast, would respect a diversity of intimate partnerships—as demonstrated by the *Linner* opinion—but it would not require such relationships as a condition of access to the right. Such a right would not depend upon marital or heterosexual relationships, nor would it privilege traditional, patriarchal family forms. Instead, this version of the privacy right would emphasize self-fulfillment, whereby individual interests are valued equally and not subordinated to the perceived interests of the marital or familial relationship.

This emphasis on self-fulfillment and autonomy would not, however, assert the primacy of the individual at the expense of the community. As Julie Mertus has observed,

> The liberal recognition of individual worth does not negate the importance of communal life. Individuals are not free floating entities; they exist and gain meaning through social relationships and communal responsibilities and duties. . . . Thus, a

liberal feminist agenda may very well incorporate a communal orientation along with recognition of the rights of individuals within communities.[38]

This type of privacy would thus subvert the presumed hierarchy of the marital or familial relationship by championing the rights of individuals equally, regardless of their roles in intimate relationships. This emphasis on the consistent application of individual rights is crucial for a new understanding of privacy, for it undermines one of the most damaging facets of the traditional right to privacy: the notion that a victim's rights are contingent upon her relationship to her abuser.

The model I have proposed raises the questions: How would this understanding of the privacy right operate? How might it affect the lives of victims of intimate partner violence? To understand the potential of this type of privacy, we have only to look at the ways in which domestic violence cases have been affected by the traditional model of privacy. The late-nineteenth-century cases discussed in chapter two would have been resolved far more fairly with the application of an alternative model of privacy. Instead of a privacy right that protects batterers even in the commission of an acknowledged crime of violence, this alternative model could have been invoked on behalf of the victims, whose right to bodily integrity and autonomy has been violated. The same would have applied to the civil cases of the 1980s, when battered women brought numerous lawsuits against police and other government bodies for privileging the sanctity of the home over women's physical safety. In each of these cases (ranging from *Bruno*[39] and *Scott*,[40] to *Torrington* and *Sorichetti*, up to *DeShaney* and *Gonzales*), an alternative model of privacy would have relieved plaintiffs from the burden of having to prove themselves worthy of state protection. Rather than having to establish a "special relationship" with the state in order to merit that protection, plaintiffs instead could have claimed that the harm they suffered violated their *own* rights to privacy by diminishing their control over their own bodies and intimate relationships.

Finally, an alternative model of privacy would go a long way toward protecting victims of same-sex domestic violence. With its emphasis on autonomy and equality and its attendant sensitivity toward issues of gender and sexual orientation, the new model of privacy could be invoked by victims of same-sex domestic violence as readily as by their heterosexual counterparts. While such a model would not rid this culture of homophobia, it would serve as a tool for ensuring that the problem of same-sex domestic violence is not exacerbated within the courtroom, as it so often is currently. In particular, courts would be unable to refuse to extend a right of privacy to gay men and lesbians based on the perceived illegitimacy of their relationships under this new model, which specifically claims a right of privacy for *all* citizens as individuals, regardless of the nature of their intimate relationships or family forms.

While this proposed model represents a departure from the privacy right as it is most often construed by courts today, the seeds of this vision have already been sown—not just by feminist scholars seeking to protect battered women, but also by jurists, addressing subjects from abortion (the *Roe* concurrence) to wiretapping (the *Olmstead* dissent) to sexuality (the *Bowers* dissents, the *Lawrence* majority, and the *Linner* majority) to marital rape (the *Liberta* majority opinion). Such judicial precedents point the way toward the revisioning of the right to privacy as it is currently understood. Indeed, given the proliferation of debates within contemporary media about the nature and extent of the privacy right, such a project may be a necessary undertaking in the near future. The relationship of privacy to the problem of domestic violence is open to much future work, both scholarly and activist. Feminist scholars such as Schneider and Boling began this work by suggesting that we consider a new model of the privacy right, and I have offered here some key components and potential applications of such a right. A future study would do well to propose a strategy for bringing such a model to fruition in the courts for the direct benefit of battered women.

CONCLUSION

The story of the right to privacy and its impact on intimate partner violence is still being written. As I write today in 2006, the issues of "homeland security"—and the attendant focus on civil liberties—as well as growing concern about protecting individual privacy over the internet are at the forefront of our national consciousness. With concerns about privacy on the minds of citizens and scholars alike, the issue is currently the subject of regular debate and scrutiny. This level of dialogue focused on issues of privacy suggests that the old models are ripe for reevaluation, and that this may be a particularly good time for proposing and introducing new models. While no one can predict exactly how these issues will unfold, what is clear is that the development of the privacy right has historically played and will continue to play a crucial role in the judicial response to domestic violence. It is, therefore, imperative that feminist scholars, activists, and lawyers seize this moment to shape the future of the right to privacy.

NOTES

1. See, for example, *Fulgham v. State*, 46 Ala. 143 (1871), in which the batterer was a former slave.
2. *People of the State of New York v. Mario Liberta*, 64 N.Y.2d 152 (1984).

3. *Thurman v. Torrington*, 595 F. Supp. 1521 (1984).

4. *Sorichetti v. City of New York*, 65 N.Y.2d 461 (1985).

5. *DeShaney v. Winnebago County Department of Social Services*, 489 U.S. 189 (1989).

6. *Castle Rock v. Gonzales*, 125 S. Ct 2796 (2005).

7. *Bowers v. Hardwick*, 478 U.S. 186 (1986).

8. See Catharine A. MacKinnon, *Toward a Feminist Theory of the State* (Cambridge: Harvard University Press, 1989).

9. Patricia Boling, *Privacy and the Politics of Intimate Life* (Ithaca: Cornell University Press, 1996): 34.

10. Dorothy Roberts, "Punishing Drug Addicts Who Have Babies: Women of Color, Equality, and the Right of Privacy," *Harvard Law Review* 104 (1991).

11. Elizabeth Schneider, "The Violence of Privacy," in *The Public Nature of Private Violence: The Discovery of Domestic Abuse*, ed. Martha Albertson Fineman and Roxanne Mykitiuk (New York: Routledge, 1994): 36–58.

12. Patricia Boling, *Privacy and the Politics of Intimate Life* (Ithaca: Cornell University Press, 1996): 34.

13. Ibid., 34.

14. Dorothy Roberts, "Punishing Drug Addicts Who Have Babies: Women of Color, Equality, and the Right of Privacy," *Harvard Law Review* 104 (1991): 1477–78.

15. Ibid., 1479–82.

16. Elizabeth Schneider, "The Violence of Privacy," in *The Public Nature of Private Violence: The Discovery of Domestic Abuse*, ed. Martha Albertson Fineman and Roxanne Mykitiuk, 36–58 (New York: Routledge, 1994): 53.

17. 410 U.S. 113.

18. Ibid., 211–13.

19. *Olmstead et al. v. U.S.*, 277 U.S. 438.

20. See, for example, *U.S. v. Grunewald*, 233 F.2d 556 (1956); *Silverman et al. v. U.S.*, 365 U.S. 505 (1961), http://laws.findlaw.com/us/365/505.html (full text), http://www.oyez.org/cases/case?case=1960-1969/1960/1960_66 (audio); *Tehan v. U.S.*, 382 U.S. 406 (1966), http://laws.findlaw.com/us/382/406.html (full text); *Katz v. U.S.*, 389 U.S. 347 (1967), http://laws.findlaw.com/us/389/347.html (full text), http://www.oyez.org/cases/case?case=1960-1969/1967/1967_35 (audio); *Stanley v. Georgia*, 394 U.S. 557 (1969), http://laws.findlaw.com/us/394/557.html (full text), http://www.oyez.org/cases/case?case=1960-1969/1968/1968_293 (audio); and *Winston v. Lee*, 470 U.S. 753 (1985), http://laws.findlaw.com/us/470/753.html (full text), http://www.oyez.org/cases/case?case=1980-1989/1984/1984_83_1334 (audio).

21. *Olmstead*, 478.

22. Elizabeth Schneider, "The Violence of Privacy," in *The Public Nature of Private Violence: The Discovery of Domestic Abuse*, ed. Martha Albertson Fineman and Roxanne Mykitiuk (New York: Routledge, 1994): 36–58; see esp. p. 53.

23. *Fitzgerald v. Porter Memorial Hospital*, 523 F.2d 716 (1975): 719–20, qtd. in *Bowers*, 217.

24. Ibid.

25. See, e.g., The Declaration of Independence, para. 2 (U.S. 1776) and the Preamble to the U.S. Constitution.

26. Rebecca L. Brown, "Liberty, The New Equality," *New York University Law Review* 77 (2002): 1495.

27. Elizabeth Schneider, "The Violence of Privacy," in *The Public Nature of Private Violence: The Discovery of Domestic Abuse*, ed. Martha Albertson Fineman and Roxanne Mykitiuk, 36–58 (New York: Routledge, 1994): 53.

28. *Roe*, 214–15.

29. Dorothy Roberts, "Punishing Drug Addicts Who Have Babies: Women of Color, Equality, and the Right of Privacy," *Harvard Law Review* 104 (1991): 1479.

30. 665 N.E.2d 1180 (1996).

31. *Griswold v. Connecticut*, 381 U.S. 479 (1965).

32. *Eisenstadt v. Baird*, 405 U.S. 438 (1972).

33. Ibid., 453.

34. *Roe*, 152–53.

35. *People v. Liberta*, 64 N.Y.2d 152 (1984): 573.

36. Ibid., 574.

37. *Bowers*, 205–6.

38. Julie Mertus, "Turning a Liberal Feminist Lens on Post-Agreement Kosovo: The Radical Future of Liberal Feminism?" unpublished paper, 2003, p. 5.

39. *Bruno v. Codd*, 419 N.Y.S.2d 901 (1979).

40. *Scott v. Hart*, No. C-76-2395 (N.D. Cal., filed Oct. 28, 1976).

APPENDIX

This appendix provides detailed information regarding the methods of case selection that I adopted in chapters two through five. While I have provided information specific to each chapter below, there were several guiding principles that informed the project as a whole, and I will discuss those here first.

Throughout the book, I chose the cases upon which to focus my research by adopting a multi-layered approach. First, I examined via archival research the work and writing of contemporary activist organizations, in order to ascertain which cases they perceived to be the most significant (as evidenced by their participation in those cases). Because this book examines the role of activists—and the interaction between courts and activists—in shaping and responding to the problem of domestic violence, I adopted this method as a means of ensuring that I did not exclude any cases in which activists had (or attempted to have) a significant influence. This method of preliminary case identification was most important and most useful during those periods when anti-domestic violence efforts focused on litigation (i.e., since the 1980s). This method played a less important role in determining which cases I discussed from earlier periods, when activists placed less emphasis on litigation strategies. Likewise, in some instances, secondary sources were helpful in confirming or supplementing my research, by identifying cases that had received substantial attention from activists and/or legal scholars.

Second, I chose to focus my research almost exclusively on appellate-level cases. While the majority of domestic violence litigation occurs at the local and lower-court levels, this study focuses on appellate cases for two reasons. In a practical sense, individual appellate cases can be studied in greater depth because the opinions in these cases, unlike those of lower courts, are often published. In addition, these opinions, while fewer in number than the judgments rendered by trial courts, have precedential value and often present the court's perspective on the case within historical and social context. In other words, the opinions issued by appellate courts often serve several functions. In addition to resolving the case itself, appellate opinions also consider the central issue within the context of other, related cases. Furthermore, these opinions frequently provide judicial commentary or guidance on the issue more broadly, as well as on relevant legal concepts (such as the right to privacy). Because this work examines the impact of judicial attitudes on the problems of privacy and domestic violence, each of the various functions served by such appellate decisions are important to this study. As a means of obtaining these opinions, I searched the LexisNexis Academic Universe database using categories and keywords germane to each chapter (details below).

The case selection method I have adopted here has been extremely beneficial to this study. Yet, like all methodological approaches, this one has inherent limitations that should be understood. The approach I have taken has proven particularly useful for understanding the role of activists as well as courts in responding to the problem of domestic violence in this country. It has also provided important insight into the historical development of concepts of privacy, in both legal and cultural contexts. Such an approach would be of little or no use, however, in a study that sought to quantify the numbers of domestic violence cases heard at the local level in a given area, or to identify patterns of case disposition by trial courts.

In fact, the multitude of cases that do not result in published opinions are undeniably significant to the issue of domestic violence. Furthermore, judicial tactics and responses at the trial level do not always mirror—and indeed, they sometimes contradict—those exhibited at appellate levels. This study, therefore, should not be viewed as a comprehensive analysis of all judicial attitudes toward and responses to the problems of domestic violence and privacy. Instead, by adopting the case selection method I have described here, I have been able to trace broadly both the historical development of the right to privacy in the United States, and the role of privacy in the most significant domestic violence cases of the nineteenth, twentieth, and early twenty-first centuries. Ultimately, this approach has enabled me to explore the interaction of courts and activists with regard to the issues of privacy and domestic violence. I now turn to the individual chapters to review the method of case selection for each one.

CHAPTER TWO

As the problem of domestic violence (or "chastisement") was still gaining legal recognition during the nineteenth century, the number of domestic violence court cases brought during this era was fairly small, and the number of appellate-level cases even smaller. This chapter, therefore, examines all of the cases brought in state appellate courts for assault and battery of wives by husbands. As divorces began to be granted on the grounds of cruelty during this era, this chapter also examines the published opinions from those cases. Additionally, the research undertaken by Elizabeth Pleck to identify such cases matches my own findings and suggests that the cases I examine here represent a comprehensive whole.

CHAPTER THREE

During the period of the 1970s examined in this chapter, domestic violence cases proliferated within trial courts. Activity at the appellate level, however, was much slower to appear. This chapter thus focuses primarily on the interrelationships of the anti-rape, reproductive rights, and battered women's movements, culminating in a critical case study of *People* v. *Liberta*. I argue that the most significant cases to emerge from the late 1970s were in fact the *Bruno* v. *Codd* and *Scott* v. *Hart* cases, which are discussed in chapter four as precursors to the decade of civil litigation that developed during the 1980s.

CHAPTER FOUR

Many of the cases in this chapter were selected by their prominence in the literature of the National Center on Women and Family Law and the National Battered Women's Law Project, organizations that were keeping meticulous track of the litigation in this area nationwide; disseminating that information to shelters, activists, and attorneys; and writing numerous articles about the significance of this wave of cases. This extensive documentation led me to many of the cases examined in this chapter. In addition, I supplemented the lists I developed through these archival materials by searching LexisNexis for federal cases brought on grounds of "Section 1983" that also included the phrases "domestic violence," "domestic abuse," "family violence," "spousal abuse," or "battered wom!," or the word combinations "husband OR wife OR boyfriend OR girlfriend OR spouse W/3 [within three words' proximity to] violen! OR abus! OR murder! OR kill! OR batter! OR assault!" (Note that exclamation points are wildcard symbols used to retrieve words with variant endings—so that, for example, a search for violen! will retrieve documents containing violence and violent, and a search for abus! will retrieve documents containing abused, abusive, abuse, abuser, abused, etc.)

CHAPTER FIVE

Like chapter two, this chapter explores an area of law containing a relatively small number of cases. Numerous factors—including the uneasy relationship that has historically existed between homosexuals and the judicial system in this country, as well as homophobia within police departments and courtrooms—have contributed to low rates of arrest, reporting, and judicial response to cases of same-sex domestic violence. Again, the number of appellate cases is even smaller. As a result, the number of relevant cases that exist at the appellate level is so small that I am able to discuss all of them in this chapter. In order to find these cases, I turned to LexisNexis to search each state's appellate cases for those that employed the following terms: "gay OR lesbian OR homosex!" AND "relationship OR boyfriend OR girlfriend OR partner OR dating" W/3 [within three words of] "violen! OR abus! OR murder! OR kill! OR batter! OR assault! OR domestic violence OR family violence OR domestic abuse."

In this appendix I have explained the priorities and principles that informed my case selection for the book in an overarching sense, as well as the details that are specific to each chapter. By examining the methods that I used to locate the cases for my research, I hope to further explain the ways in which I developed my analysis of the interaction and influence of activists and courts on the issues of domestic violence and privacy.

BIBLIOGRAPHY

ARCHIVAL MATERIALS

National Center on Poverty Law archives. Chicago, Illinois

Bruno v. Codd, Index No. 21946/76 (Sup. Ct. N.Y.). Clearinghouse No. 19,951.
Scott v. Hart, Index No. C-76-2395-WWS (N.D. Cal.). Clearinghouse No. 19,947.

Schlesinger Library, Radcliffe Institute for Advanced Study, Harvard University

Aegis, the Magazine on Ending Violence Against Women.
Andrea Dworkin papers.
National Center on Women and Family Law records / National Battered Women's
    Law Project records.
National Organization for Women records.

National Organization for Women Legal Defense and Education Fund archives.
Yolanda Bako papers (including Papers of the National Coalition Against Domestic
　　Violence).

United States Library of Congress, Online

Buck, photographer. ["Suffragist Margaret Foley distributing the Woman's Journal
　　and Suffrage News."] 1 photograph: print; 4.5¥6.5 in. Nov.–Dec. 1913. From Li-
　　brary of Congress: *Photographs from the Records of the National Woman's Party.*
　　http://memory.loc.gov/cgi-bin/query/r?ammem/mnwp:@field(DOCID+@lit
　　(mnwp000378)) (accessed January 15, 2007).
Photographer unknown. ["Elizabeth Cady Stanton, seated, and Susan B. Anthony,
　　standing, three-quarter length portrait."] 1 photographic print. Between 1880 and
　　1902. From Library of Congress: *By Popular Demand: "Votes for Women" Suffrage
　　Pictures, 1850–1920.*
　　http://memory.loc.gov/cgi-bin/query/r?ammem/suffrg:@field(NUMBER+@band
　　(cph+3a02558)) (accessed January 15, 2007).
Photographer unknown. ["Florence F. Noyes as "Liberty" in suffrage pageant."] Pho-
　　tograph. March 1913. From Library of Congress: *By Popular Demand: "Votes for
　　Women" Suffrage Pictures, 1850–1920 [George Grantham Bain Collection].*
　　http://memory.loc.gov/cgi-bin/query/r?ammem/suffrg:@field(NUMBER+@band
　　(cph+3b17779)) (accessed January 15, 2007).
Photographer unknown. ["Head of suffrage parade, Washington, D.C."] Photograph.
　　March 3, 1913. From Library of Congress: *By Popular Demand: "Votes for Women"
　　Suffrage Pictures, 1850–1920 [George Grantham Bain Collection].*
　　http://memory.loc.gov/cgi-bin/query/r?ammem/suffrg:@field(NUMBER+@band
　　(cph+3a23348)) (accessed January 15, 2007).
Photographer unknown. ["Henry Browne Blackwell, photo mechanical print and
　　80th birthday poem by William Lloyd Garrison."] photographic print. After Sep-
　　tember 7, 1900. From Library of Congress: *Miller NAWSA Suffrage Scrapbooks,
　　1897–1911; Scrapbook 8; page 58.*
　　http://memory.loc.gov/cgi-bin/query/r?ammem/rbcmillerbib:@field(DOCID+@lit
　　(rbcmiller003744)) (accessed January 15, 2007).
Photographer unknown. ["Lucy Stone, head-and-shoulders portrait, facing right."] 1
　　photographic print. Between 1840 and 1860. From Library of Congress: *By Popular
　　Demand: "Votes for Women" Suffrage Pictures, 1850–1920.*
　　http://memory.loc.gov/cgi-bin/query/r?ammem/suffrg:@field(NUMBER+@band
　　(cph+3a52181)) (accessed January 15, 2007).
Photographer unknown. ["Official program—Woman suffrage procession, Washing-
　　ton, D.C. March 3, 1913 / Dale."] 1 photomechanical print: color. 1913. From Li-

brary of Congress: *By Popular Demand: "Votes for Women" Suffrage Pictures,* *1850–1920 [George Grantham Bain Collection].*

http://memory.loc.gov/cgi-bin/query/r?ammem/suffrg:@field(NUMBER+@band (cph+3a21392)) (accessed January 15, 2007).

Photographer unknown. ["The first picket line—College day in the picket line line."] 1 photographic print. February 1917. From Library of Congress: *By Popular De-* *mand: "Votes for Women" Suffrage Pictures, 1850–1920 [National Woman's Party* *Collection].*

http://memory.loc.gov/cgi-bin/query/r?ammem/suffrg:@field(NUMBER+@band (cph+3a32338)) (accessed January 15, 2007).

United States Supreme Court Archives, Online

Bowers v. Hardwick, 478 U.S. 186 (1986)

Case materials:

Petition for a Writ of Certiorari (July 25, 1985).

Brief of Respondents in Opposition to Petition for Writ of Certiorari (September 12, 1985).

Joint Appendix (December 17, 1985), including:

- Letter from District Attorney Lewis Slaton, (January 7, 1983).
- Order of the District Court for the Northern District of Georgia (Civil Action No. C83-273A) (filed April 18, 1985).

Brief of Petitioner in Reply to Respondent's Brief in Opposition to Petition for Writ of Certiorari (October 8, 1985).

Brief of the Catholic League for Religious and Civil Rights, Amicus Curiae, in Support of Petitioner (December 13, 1985).

Brief of Petitioner Michael J. Bowers (December 17, 1985).

Brief of David Robinson, Jr., as Amicus Curiae in Support of Petitioner (December 18, 1985).

Brief of the Rutherford Institute et al., Amicus Curiae, in Support of Petitioner (December 19, 1985).

Brief of Concerned Women of America, Amicus Curiae, in Support of Petitioner (December 19, 1985).

Brief Amicus Curiae of the Association of the Bar of the City of New York, in Support of Respondent Hardwick (January 27, 1986).

Brief Amicus Curiae of for Lesbian Rights Project et al, in Support of Respondent (January 29, 1986).

Brief for (and of) Respondent (January 31, 1986).

Brief of the American Jewish Congress, Amicus Curiae, in Support of Respondents (January 31, 1986).

Brief of National Gay Rights Advocates et al., in Support of Respondents (January 31, 1986).

Amicus Curiae Brief on Behalf of the Respondents by Lambda Legal Defense and Education Fund, Inc., et al. (January 31, 1986).

Brief of Amici Curiae the Presbyterian Church (U.S.A.), et al., (in Support of Respondents) (January 31, 1986).

Brief of the Attorney General of the State of New York, Joined by the Attorney General of the State of California, as Amici Curiae in Support of Respondents (January 31, 1986).

Brief of the National Organization for Women as Amicus Curiae in Support of Respondents (January 31, 1986).

Brief of Amici Curiae American Psychological Association and American Public Health Association in Support of Respondents (January 31, 1986).

Reply Brief of Petitioner Michael J. Bowers, Attorney General of Georgia (March 21, 1986).

Oral Argument of *Bowers* v. *Hardwick, Landmark Briefs and Arguments of the Supreme Court of the United States* vol. 164. Washington: University Publications of America: 631–57.

Lawrence v. *Texas*, 539 U.S. 558 (2003)

Case materials:

Brief for Amici Curiae American Psychological Association, American Psychiatric Association, National Association of Social Workers, and Texas Chapter of the National Association of Social Workers in Support of Petitioners (January 10, 2003).

Brief Amici Curiae of the American Civil Liberties Union and the ACLU of Texas in Support of Petitioner (January 15, 2003).

Brief of Amici Curiae Consitutional Law Professors Bruce A. Ackerman, Jack M. Balkin, Derrick A. Bell, Jr., Paul Brest, et al. in Support of Petitioners (January 15 2003).

Brief of Petitioners (January 16, 2003).

Amicus Brief of Human Rights Campaign; National Gay & Lesbian Task Force; Parents, Families & Friends of Lesbians & Gays; National Center for Lesbian Rights; Gay and Lesbian Advocates and Defenders; Gay and Lesbian Alliance Against Defamation; Pride at Work, et al. in Support of Petitioners (January 16, 2003).

Brief of Amici Curiae Republican Unity Coalition and the Honorable Alan K. Simpson in Support of Petitioners (January 16, 2003).

Brief of the Cato Institute as Amicus Curiae in Support of Petitioners (January 16, 2003).

Brief of the National Lesbian and Gay Law Association, the Asian American Legal Defense and Education Fund, Action Wisconsin, the Bay Area Lawyers for Individual Freedom, the Bay Area Transgender Lawyers' Association, et al. as Amici Curiae in Support of Petitioners (January 16, 2003).

Brief of the Alliance of Baptists, the American Friends Service Committee, the Commission on Social Action of Reform Judaism, the Most Rev. Frank T. Griswold, III, Presiding Bishop of the Episcopal Church, the Methodist Federation for Social Action, et al as Amici Curiae Supporting Petitioners (January 16, 2003).

Brief of Professors of History George Chauncey, Nancy Cott, John D'Emilio, Estelle B. Freedman, Thomas C. Holt, et al. as Amici Curiae in Support of Petitioners (January 16, 2003).

Brief of the Institute for Justice as Amicus Curiae in Support of Petitioners (January 16, 2003).

Amici Curiae Brief of the Log Cabin Republicans and Liberty Education Forum in Support of the Petitioners (January 16, 2003).

Brief of the American Bar Association as Amicus Curiae in Support of Petitioners (January 16, 2003).

Brief of the American Public Health Association, National Mental Health Association, et al. in Support of Petitioners (January 16, 2003).

Brief Amici Curiae of Mary Robinson, Amnesty International U.S.A., Human Rights Watch, Interights, the Lawyers Committee for Human Rights, and Minnesota Advocates for Human Rights in Support of Petitioners (January 16, 2003).

Brief of NOW Legal Defense and Education Fund as Amicus Curiae in Support of Petitioners (January 16, 2003).

Brief Amicus Curiae of United Families International in Support of Respondent (February 13, 2003).

Brief Amicus Curiae of the Center for the Original Intent of the Constitution in Support of Respondent (February 14, 2003).

Respondent's Brief (February 17, 2003).

Brief of Amici Curiae Texas Legislators, Representative Warren Chisum, et al., in Support of Respondent (February 18, 2003).

Brief in Support of Respondent on behalf of Amici Curiae Texas Physicians Resource Council, Christian Medical and Dental Associations and Catholica Medical Association (February 18, 2003).

Amicus Brief of the American Center for Law and Justice in Support of Respondent (February 18, 2003).

Brief of Amici Curiae Center for Arizona Policy and Pro-Family Network in Support of Respondent (February 18, 2003).

Brief Amicus Curiae of Public Advocate of the United States, Conservative Legal Defense and Education Fund, Lincoln Institute for Research and Education, Help and Caring Ministries, Inc., and Citizens United Foundation in Support of Respondent (February 18, 2003).

Brief of Amici Curiae, Pro-Family Law Center, Traditional Values Coalition, Traditional Values Education & Legal Institute and James Hartline, in Support of Respondent (February 18, 2003).

Brief of the States of Alabama, South Carolina, and Utah as Amici Curiae in Support of Respondent (February 18, 2003).

Brief of Amicus Curiae Concerned Women for America, in Support of the State of Texas, Respondent (February 18, 2003).

Brief of Texas Eagle Forum, Daughters of Liberty Republican Women, Houston, Texas and Spirit of Freedom Republican Women's Club as Amici Curiae in Support of Respondent (February 18, 2003).

Brief Amicus Curiae of the Family Research Council, Inc. and Focus on the Family in Support of the Respondent (February 18, 2003).

Brief Amici Curiae of the Center for Marriage Law in Support of Respondent (February 18, 2003).

Brief of the Center for Law and Justice International as Amicus Curiae in Support of Respondent (February 18, 2003).

Brief of Amicus Curiae Agudath Israel of America in Support of Respondent (February 19, 2003).

Petitioner's Reply Brief (March 10, 2003).

Castle Rock v. *Gonzales*, 125 S. Ct 2796 (2005)

Case materials:

Petitioner's Opening Brief (December 23, 2004).

Brief of Amici Curiae International Municipal Lawyers Association and National League of Cities, National Sheriffs' Association, and County Sheriffs of Colorado in Support of Petitioner (December 23, 2004).

Brief for the United States as Amicus Curiae Supporting Petitioner (December 23, 2004).

Brief of Amicus Curiae the Denver Police Protective Association, the Peace Officers Research Association of California Legal Defense fund, and the Colorado Association of Chief's [sic] of Police in Support of Petitioner (December 23, 2004).

Brief of International Law Scholars and Women's, Civil Rights and Human Rights Organizations as Amici Curiae in Support of Respondents (February 9, 2005).

Brief Amicus Curiae of AARP in Support of Respondent (February 10, 2005).

Brief of Amicus Curiae of the Family Violence Prevention Fund, National Center on Domestic and Sexual Violence, and others in Support of Respondent (February 10, 2005).

Brief of National Coalition Against Domestic Violence and National Center for Victims of Crime as Amici Curiae in Support of Respondent (February 10, 2005).

Brief of Peggy Kerns, Former Member of the House of Representatives of the State of Colorado, and Texas Domestic Violence Direct Service Providers, as Amici Curiae in Support of Respondent (February 10, 2005).

Brief Amicus Curiae of the American Civil Liberties Union and ACLU of Colorado, Hon. John J.Gibbons, Hon. Timothy K. Lewis, AALDEF, California Women's Law Center, National Asian Pacific American Women's Forum, National Partnership for Women and Families, Northwest Women's Law Center and Women's Law Project in Support of Respondent (February 10, 2005).

Brief Amicus Curiae of the National Association of Women Lawyers and the National Crime Victims Bar Association in Support of Respondent (February 10, 2005).

Brief of National Black Police Association, National Association of Black Law Enforcement Officers, Women in Federal Law Enforcement, National Center for Women and Policing, and Americans for Effective Law Enforcement, Inc., as Amici Curiae Supporting Respondent (February 10, 2005).

Respondent's Brief on the Merits (February 10, 2005).

Petitioner's Reply Brief (March 15, 2005).

Oral Argument of *Castle Rock v. Gonzales*, Alderson Reporting Company, available at U.S. Supreme Court Online, (March 21, 2005).

http://www.supremecourtus.gov/oral_arguments/argument_transcripts/04-278.pdf

Interviews

George Brenning, November 3, 2002

Marjory Fields, January 22, 2002

Pauline Gee, May 24, 2002

Barbara Hart, May 1, 2002

Elizabeth Holtzman, December 21, 2001

Kathleen Sullivan, November 19, 2002

Barbara Underwood, December 20, 2001

Sarah Weddington, November 26, 2002

Kathleen Wilde, October 30, 2002

Joan Zorza, December 14, 2001

Cases and Laws

Entick v. Carrington, 19 Howell's State Trials 1029 (1765)

Bradley v. State, 1 Miss. (1 Walker) 158 (1824)

Poor v. Poor, 8 N.H. 307 (1836)

State v. Buckley, 2 Del. 552 (1838)

People v. Mercein, 3 Hill (N.Y.) 399 (1842)

Richards v. Richards, 1 Grant (P.A.) 389 (1857)

Joyner v. Joyner, 59 N.C. 322 (1862)

State v. Black, 60 N.C. (Win.) 268 (1864)

Commonwealth v. Wood, 97 Mass. 225 (1867)

State v. Rhodes, 61 N.C. (Phil. Law) 453 (1868)

Commonwealth v. McAfee, 108 Mass. 458 (1871)

Fulgham v. State, 46 Ala. 143 (1871)

Knight v. Knight, 31 Iowa 451 (1871)

State v. Oliver, 70 N.C. 60 (1874)

Shackett v. Shackett, 49 Vt. 195 (1876)

Boyd v. U.S., 116 U.S. 616 (1886)

Harris v. State, 14 So. 266 (Miss. 1894)

Meyer v. Nebraska, 262 U.S. 390 (1923)

Pierce v. Society of Sisters, 268 U.S. 510 (1925)

Olmstead et al. v. U.S., 277 U.S. 438 (1928)

State of Connecticut v. Roger B. Nelson et al., 11 A.2d 856 (1940)

Skinner v. Oklahoma, 316 U.S. 535 (1942)

Tileston v. Ullman, 318 U.S. 44 (1943)

Prince v. Massachusetts, 321 U.S. 158 (1944)

U.S. v. Provoo, 215 F.2d 531 (1954)

Benway v. Watertown, 1 A.D.2d 465 (1956)

U.S. v. Flores-Rodriguez, 237 F.2d 405 (1956)

U.S. v. Grunewald, 233 F.2d 556 (1956)

People v. Beasley, 328 P.2d 834 (1958)

Poe v. Ullman, 367 U.S. 497 (1961)

Silverman et al. v. U.S., 365 U.S. 505 (1961)

Morgan v. County of Yuba, 230 Cal.App.2d 938 (1964)

Griswold v. Connecticut, 381 U.S. 479 (1965)

Jones v. Herkimer, 51 Misc.2d 130 (1966)

Tehan v. U.S., 382 U.S. 406 (1966)

Boutilier v. Immigration and Naturalization Service, 387 U.S. 118 (1967)

Huey v. Barloga, 277 F.Supp. 864 (1967)

Katz v. U.S., 389 U.S. 347 (1967)

People v. Spencer, 458 P.2d 43 (1969)

Stanley v. Georgia, 394 U.S. 557 (1969)

Anonymous v. Anonymous, 67 Misc. 2d 982 (1971)

Baker v. Nelson, 191 N.W.2d 185 (1971)

Canosa v. City of Mt. Vernon, 327 N.Y.S.2d 843 (1971)

Reed v. Reed, 404 U.S. 71 (1971)

Board of Regents v. Roth, 408 U.S. 564 (1972)

Byrd v. Brishke, 466 F.2d. 6 (1972)

Eisenstadt v. Baird, 405 U.S. 438 (1972)

Doe v. Bolton, 410 U.S. 179 (1973)

Jones v. Hallahan, 501 S.W.2d 588 (1973)

Paris Adult Theatre I v. Slaton, 413 U.S. 49 (1973)

Perez v. State, 491 S.W.2d 672 (1973)

Roe v. *Wade*, 410 U.S. 113 (1973)

Murray v. *Vandevander*, 522 P.2d 302 (1974)

Doe v. *Commonwealth's Attorney for Richmond*, 403 F.Supp. 1199 (1975)

Fitzgerald v. *Porter Memorial Hospital*, 523 F.2d 716 (1975)

Ponter v. *Ponter*, 135 N.J. Super. 50 (1975)

State v. *Schweppe*, 237 N.W.2d 609 (1975)

Bellotti v. *Baird*, 428 U.S. 132 (1976)

People v. *Washington*, 58 Cal. App. 3d 620 (1976)

Planned Parenthood of Central Missouri v. *Danforth*, 428 U.S. 52 (1976)

Scott v. *Hart*, No. C-76-2395 (N.D. Cal., filed Oct. 28, 1976)

Zibbon v. *Town of Cheektowaga*, 387 N.Y.S.2d 428 (1976)

Beal v. *Doe*, 432 U.S. 438 (1977)

Carey v. *Population Services International*, 431 U.S. 678 (1977)

Maher v. *Roe*, 432 U.S. 464 (1977)

Monell v. *Department of Social Services*, 436 U.S. 658 (1978)

Bruno v. *Codd*, 419 N.Y.S.2d 901 (1979)

Bruno v. *Codd* Consent Judgment (1978) (reprinted in Woods 1978: 32–33)

Crawford v. *State*, 404 A.2d 244 (1979)

Thomas v. *City of Los Angeles*, CA No. 00572/79 (Cal. Sup. Ct., filed Aug. 16, 1979, settled Nov. 4, 1985)

White v. *Rochford*, 592 F.2d 381 (1979)

Harris v. *McRae*, 448 U.S. 297 (1980)

People v. *Onofre*, 51 N.Y. 2d 485 (1980)

Zagarow v. *Zagarow*, 105 Misc. 2d 1054 (1980)

In Interest of Jones, 429 A.2d 671 (1981)

Doe v. *Belleville*, No. 81-5256 (S.D. Ill., filed Sept. 15, 1981; settled Sept. 9, 1983)

Adams v. *Howerton*, 673 F.2d 1036 (1982)

Harlow v. *Fitzgerald*, 457 U.S. 800 (1982)

City of Akron v. *Akron Center for Reproductive Health, Inc., et al.*, 462 U.S. 416 (1983)

Jackson v. *City of Joliet*, 715 F.2d 1200 (1983)

Nearing v. *Weaver*, 295 Ore. 702 (1983)

New York v. *Uplinger*, 464 U.S. 812 (1983)

Wiley v. *Florida*, 427 So.2d 283 (1983)

Wright v. *Ozark*, 715 F.2d 1513 (1983)

People of the State of New York v. *Mario Liberta*, 64 N.Y.2d 152 (1984)

People v. *Woodhull*, 481 N.Y.S.2d 749 (1984)

Thurman v. *Torrington*, 595 F.Supp. 1521 (1984)

Dudosh v. *Allentown*, 629 F. Supp. 849 (1985)

Lowers v. *City of Streator*, 627 F.Supp. 244 (1985)

Tennessee v. *Herron*, 1985 Tenn. Crim. App. LEXIS 3087 (1985)

Sorichetti v. *City of New York*, 65 N.Y.2d 461 (1985)

Winston v. *Lee*, 470 U.S. 753 (1985)

Bartalone v. *County of Berrien*, 643 F. Supp. 574 (1986)

Bowers v. *Hardwick*, 478 U.S. 186 (1986)

Hardwick v. Bowers, 760 F.2d 1202 (1985) (Eleventh Circuit opinion)

Bowers v. Hardwick, 474 U.S. 943 (1985) (U.S. Supreme Court granting certiorari)

Hardwick v. Bowers, 804 F.2d 622 (1986) (Circuit Court opinion vacated and remanded subsequent to U.S. Supreme Court opinion)

Escamilla v. City of Santa Ana, 796 F.2d 266 (1986)

Williams v. State, 494 So.2d 819 (1986)

Anderson v. Creighton, 483 U.S. 635 (1987)

Collins v. Kings County, 742 P.2d 185 (1987)

Sherrell v. City of Longview, 683 F. Supp. 1108 (1987)

Shunn v. State, 742 P.2d 775 (1987)

Tarantino v. Baker, 825 F.2d 772, 774 (1987)

Turner v. City of North Charleston, 675 F.Supp. 314 (1987)

Balistreri v. Pacifica Police Department, 855 F.2d 1421 (1988); amended as *Balistreri v. Pacifica Police Department*, 901 F.2d 696 (1990)

Bowen v. Kendrick, 487 U.S. 589 (1988)

Hynson v. City of Chester, 864 F.2d 1026 (1988)

Turner v. Dammon, 848 F.2d 440, 443 (1988)

Watson v. Kansas City, 857 F.2d 690 (1988)

Allegheny v. ACLU, 492 U.S. 573 (1989)

DeShaney v. Winnebago County Department of Social Services, 489 U.S. 189 (1989)

McKee v. City of Rockwall, 877 F.2d. 409 (1989)

Stanford v. Kentucky, 492 U.S. 361 (1989)

State of North Carolina v. Norman, 378 S.E. 2D 8 (1989)

Webster v. Reproductive Health Services, 492 U.S. 490 (1989)

Brown v. City of Elba, 754 F.Supp. 1551 (1990)

Coffman v. Wilson, 739 F. Supp. 257 (1990)

Freeman v. Ferguson, 911 F.2d. 52 (1990)

Raucci v. Rotterdam, 902 F.2d 1050 (1990)

Gilpin v. State, 1991 Tex. App. LEXIS 1396 (1991)

Hurlman v. Rice, 927 F.2d 74 (1991)

Ohio v. Hadinger, 573 N.E.2d 1191 (1991)

People v. Newbern, 579 N.E.2d 583 (1991)

Siddle v. City of Cambridge, 761 F.Supp. 503 (1991)

Duong v. County of Arapahoe, 837 P.2d. 226 (1992)

Lutheran Day Care v. Snohomish County, 829 P.2d 746 (1992)

Roy v. City of Everett, 738 P.2d 1090 (1992)

Bailey v. Texas, 1993 Tex. App. LEXIS 1253 (1993)

Bryant v. Burnett, 624 A.2d 584 (1993)

Rotondo v. State, 860 S.W.2d 575 (1993)

Sinthasomphone v. Milwaukee, 838 F.Supp. 1320 (1993)

Allen v. State, 871 P.2d 79 (1994)

Cusseaux v. Pickett, 652 A.2d 789 (1994)

Ricketts v. City of Columbia, 36 F.3d. 775 (1994)

Defense of Marriage Act, 104 P.L. 199 (1996)

People v. Humphrey, 921 P.2d 1 (Cal. 1996)
State v. Linner, 665 N.E.2d 1180 (1996)
Ward v. Ward, 742 So.2d 250 (1996)
Ireland v. Davis, 957 S.W.2d 310 (1997)
Rucks v. Florida, 692 So.2d 976 (1997)
Baehr v. Miike, 994 P.2d 566 (1999)
Cosco v. Uphoff, 195 F. 3d. 1221 (1999)
Weigand v. Houghton, 730 So.2d 581 (1999)
Ex parte H.H.; (In re: D.H. v. H.H.), 2002 Ala. LEXIS 44 (2002)
In re: J.M., Supreme Court of Georgia, 2003 Ga. LEXIS 2, January 13 (2003)
Lawrence v. Texas, 539 U.S. 558 (2003)
Lawrence v. Texas, 41 S.W.3d 349 (2001)
Peterman v. Meeker, 855 So. 2d 690 (2003)
Annette F. v. Sharon S., 119 Cal. App. 4th 1146 (2004)
Castle Rock v. Gonzales, 125 S. Ct 2796 (2005)
Jessica Gonzales v. City of Castle Rock, Civil Action No. 00-D-1285 (2001)
Jessica Gonzales v. City of Castle Rock, 307 F.3d 1258 (2002)
Jessica Gonzales v. City of Castle Rock, 366 F.3d 1093 (2004)
In re Lowe, 130 Cal. App. 4th 1405 (2005)

Primary Sources

Cobbe, Frances Power. "Legal Relief for Assaulted Wives." *The Woman's Journal* (July 6, 1878a): 212.
———. "Wife-Torture in England." *Woman's Journal* (June 1, 1878b): 174–77.
———. "Declaration of Rights and Sentiments." Seneca Falls, 1848.
Goodell, Lavinia. "Ownership of Wives." *Woman's Journal* (October 28, 1876): 348–49.
Leslie, Cora. "A Chapter on Young Men." *The Lily*. April 1, 1849: n. pg.
Munger, Rhoda. "A Woman's Wrongs in Arkansas." *Woman's Journal* (August 31, 1878): 280.
Stanton, Elizabeth Cady. "Governor Geary and Hester Vaughan." *Revolution* (December 10, 1868a): 353–55.
———. "The Solitude of Self." *Woman's Journal* (January 23, 1892): n. pg.
———. "St. Paul on Duties of Wives." *Revolution* (August 6, 1868b): 73.
Swisshelm, "Mrs." "Plain Talk." *The Lily* (June 1, 1849): n. pg.
Unknown author. "The Case of Hester Vaughan." *Revolution* (December 10, 1868): 357–58.
———. "Centennial Crimes Against Women." *Woman's Journal* (June 17, 1876): 199.
———. "Christian England Gives Two Pounds for Whipping Your Wife." *Revolution* (August 6, 1868): 71.

———. "Crimes Against Women." *Woman's Journal* (January 15, 1876): n.pg.

———. "Crimes Against Women." *Woman's Journal* (August 31, 1878): 280.

———. "Crimes of a Single Day." *Woman's Journal* (January 29, 1876): 34.

———. "Feminine Suffrage." *The Lily* (December 1, 1851): 90–91.

———. "Infanticide." *Revolution* (August 6, 1868): 74.

———. "Married Women and Law." *Woman's Journal* (July 13, 1878): 222.

———. "The Monster Intemperance." *The Lily* (May 1, 1849): 39.

———. "The Rathbun Tragedy." *The Lily* (September 1, 1849): n. pg.

———. "The Subjection of Wives." *Woman's Journal* (September 2, 1876): 288.

———. Untitled article. *The Lily* (April 1, 1849): n. pg.

———. "Wife-Killing From Affection." *Woman's Journal* (April 20, 1878): 126.

———. "A Wife-Whipper Whipped by Women." *Revolution* (August 6, 1868): 74.

———. "Woman's Rights." *The Lily* (October 1, 1849): n. pg.

Books, Articles, and Films

Ahrens, Lois. "Battered Women's Refuges: Feminist Cooperatives vs. Social Service Institutions." *Radical America* 14, no. 3 (1980): 41–47.

Aliaskari, Mahsa. "U.S. Asylum Law Applied to Battered Women Fleeing Islamic Countries." *American University Journal of Gender, Social Policy and the Law* 8 (2000): 231.

Allen, Charlene and Beth Leventhal. "History, Culture, and Identity: What Makes GLBT Battering Different." In *Same-Sex Domestic Violence: Strategies for Change*, ed. Leventhal, Beth and Sandra E. Lundy, 73–82. Thousand Oaks, CA: Sage, 1999.

Amar, Akhil Reed and Daniel Widawsky. "Child Abuse as Slavery: A Thirteenth Amendment Response to *DeShaney*." *Harvard Law Review* 105 (1992): 1359.

Ames, Lynda J. "The Dilemmas of Policy Success: Evaluating Domestic Violence Programs." *American Sociological Association* Paper, 2000.

Ammons, Linda L. "Discretionary Justice: A Legal and Policy Analysis of a Governor's Use of the Clemency Power in the Cases of Incarcerated Battered Women." *Journal of Law and Policy* 3 (1994): 2.

Anderson, Greg. "*Sorichetti v. City of New York* Tells the Police that Liability Looms for Failure to Respond to Domestic Violence Situations." *University of Miami Law Review* 40 (1985): 333.

Baker, Carrie N. "Sex, Power, and Politics: The Origins of Sexual Harassment Policy in the United States." Ph.D. diss., Emory University, 2001.

Barden, J.C. "Wife Beaters: Few of them Even Appear Before a Court of Law." *New York Times*. October 21, 1974. n. pg.

Basch, Norma. *In the Eyes of the Law: Women, Marriage, and Property in Nineteenth-Century New York*. Ithaca: Cornell University Press, 1982.

Becker, Christine Noelle. "Clemency for Killers? Pardoning Battered Women Who Strike Back." *Loyola of Los Angeles Law Review* 29 (1995): 297.

Bevacqua, Maria. *Rape on the Public Agenda: Feminism and the Politics of Sexual Assault*. Boston: Northeastern University Press, 2000.

Bishop, Gary M. "Section 1983 and Domestic Violence: A Solution to the Problem of Police Officers' Inaction." *Boston College Law Review* 30 (1989): 1357–90.

Blackstone, William. *Commentaries on the Laws of England*. Oxford: Clarendon Press, 1765.

Boling, Patricia. *Privacy and the Politics of Intimate Life*. Ithaca: Cornell University Press, 1996.

Bordin, Ruth. *Woman and Temperance: The Quest for Power and Liberty, 1873–1900*. Philadelphia: Temple University Press, 1981.

Borgmann, Caitlin E. "Battered Women's Substantive Due Process Claims: Can Orders of Protection Deflect *DeShaney?*" *New York University Law Review* 65 (1990): 1280.

Brand, P.A. and A.H. Kidd. "Frequency of Physical Aggression in Heterosexual and Female Homosexual Dyads." *Psychological Reports* 59 (1986): 1307–1313.

Brotherson, Sean E. and Jeffrey B. Teichert. "Value of the Law in Shaping Social Perspectives on Marriage." *Journal of Law & Family Studies* 3 (2001): 29.

Brown, Rebecca L. "Liberty, the New Equality," *New York University Law Review* 77 (2002): 1495.

Browne, Susanne M. "Due Process and Equal Protection Challenges to the Inadequate Response of the Police in Domestic Violence Situations." *Southern California Law Review* 68 (1995): 1295.

Buechler, Steven. *Women's Movements in the United States*. New Brunswick: Rutgers University Press, 1990.

Bush, Diane Mitsch. "Women's Movements and State Policy Reform Aimed at Domestic Violence Against Women: A Comparison of the Consequences of Movement Mobilization in the U.S. and India." *Gender and Society* 6, no. 4 (1992): 587–608.

Butler, Judith. *Gender Trouble: Feminism and the Subversion of Identity*. London: Routledge, 1990/1999.

Cahn, Naomi R. "Civil Images of Battered Women: The Impact of Domestic Violence on Child Custody Decisions." *Vanderbilt Law Review* 44 (1991): 1041.

Coker, Donna. "Shifting Power for Battered Women: Law, Material Resources, and Poor Women of Color." *U.C. Davis Law Review* 33 (2000): 1009.

Cole, Patricia and Sarah M. Buel. "Safety and Financial Security for Battered Women: Necessary Steps for Transitioning from Welfare to Work." *Georgetown Journal on Poverty Law and Policy* 7 (2000): 307.

Collins, Patricia Hill. *Black Feminist Thought: Knowledge, Consciousness, and the Politics of Empowerment*. London: Routledge, 1990.

Crane, Beth, et al. "Lesbians and Bisexual Women Working Cooperatively to End Domestic Violence." In *Same-Sex Domestic Violence: Strategies for Change*, edited by Beth Leventhal and Sandra E. Lundy, 125–34. Thousand Oaks, CA: Sage, 1999.

A *Cry for Help: The Tracey Thurman Story.* Dir. Robert Markowitz. Perf. Nancy McKeon, Bruce Weitz. Lifetime Original Movies, 1989.

Cuthbert, Carrie and Kim Slote. "Bridging the Gap Between Battered Women's Advocates in the U.S. and Abroad." *Texas Journal of Women and the Law* 6 (1997): 287.

Daniels, Christine and Michael V. Kennedy, eds. *Over the Threshold: Intimate Violence in Early America.* New York: Routledge, 1999.

Daniels, Cynthia, ed. *Feminists Negotiate the State: The Politics of Domestic Violence.* Lanham, MD: University Press of America, 1997.

Dannenbaum, Jed. "The Origins of Temperance Activism and Militancy Among American Women." *Journal of Social History* 15 v.2 (1981): 235–52.

Davis, Angela Y. *Women, Race and Class.* New York: Vintage, 1983.

Davis, Nanette. "Shelters for Battered Women: Social Policy Response to Interpersonal Violence." *Social Science Journal* 25, no. 4 (1988): 401–419.

DiStefano, Christine. *Configurations of Masculinity: A Feminist Perspective on Modern Political Theory.* Ithaca: Cornell University Press, 1991.

DuBois, Ellen Carol. *Feminism and Suffrage: The Emergence of an Independent Women's Movement in America, 1848–1869.* Ithaca: Cornell University Press, 1978.

Eaton, Mary. "Abuse by Any Other Name: Feminism, Difference, and Intralesbian Violence." In *The Public Nature of Private Violence: The Discovery of Domestic Abuse,* edited by Martha Albertson Fineman and Roxanne Mykitiuk, 195–223. New York: Routledge, 1994.

Egelko, Bob. "Sonoma County abuse suit settled; $1 million wife abuse settlement Family says woman's pleas were ignored." *The San Francisco Chronicle* June 19, 2002, pg. A13.

Elliott, Pam. "Shattering Illusions: Same-Sex Domestic Violence." In *Violence in Gay and Lesbian Domestic Partnerships,* edited by Claire M. Renzetti and Charles Harvey Miley, 1–8. New York: Haworth Press, 1996.

Elshtain, Jean Bethke. *Public Man, Private Woman: Women in Social and Political Thought.* Princeton: Princeton University Press, 1981.

Ely, John Hart. "The Wages of Crying Wolf: A Comment on *Roe v. Wade.*" *Yale Law Journal* 82 (1973): 920.

Enos, V. Pualani. "Prosecuting Battered Mothers: State Laws' Failure to Protect Battered Women and Abused Children." *Harvard Women's Law Journal* 19 (1996): 229.

Eskridge Jr., William N. *Gaylaw: Challenging the Apartheid of the Closet.* Cambridge, MA: Harvard University Press, 1999.

Ewing, Charles Patrick. *Battered Women Who Kill: Psychological Self-Defense as Legal Justification.* Lexington, MA: Lexington Books, 1987.

Ferraro, Kathleen. "Negotiating Trouble in a Battered Women's Shelter." *Urban Life* 12, no. 3 (1983): 287–306.

Ferguson, Jim. "Law Enforcement Liability in the Wake of *Castle Rock v. Gonzales.*" *The Source, Newsletter of the Stalking Resource Center* 6 (Winter 2006): 1, 8–9.

Fineman, Martha Albertson. *The Autonomy Myth: A Theory of Dependency.* New York: New Press, 2005.

Fineman, Martha Albertson and Roxanne Mykitiuk, eds. *The Public Nature of Private Violence: The Discovery of Domestic Abuse.* New York: Routledge, 1994.

Fray-Witzer, Evan. "Twice Abused: Same-Sex Domestic Violence and the Law." In *Same-Sex Domestic Violence: Strategies for Change,* edited by Beth Leventhal and Sandra E. Lundy, 19–41. Thousand Oaks, CA: Sage, 1999.

Garrow, David J. *Liberty and Sexuality: The Right to Privacy and the Making of Roe v. Wade.* New York: MacMillan, 1994.

Gee, Pauline. "Ensuring Police Protection for Battered Women: The *Scott v. Hart* Suit." *Signs: Journal of Women in Culture and Society* 8 (1983): 554–67.

Ginsburg, Ruth Bader. "Some Thoughts on Autonomy and Equality in Relation to Roe v. Wade." *North Carolina Law Review* 63 (1985): 375.

Goldstein, Anne. "History, Homosexuality, and Political Values: Searching for the Hidden Determinants of *Bowers v. Hardwick.*" *Yale Law Journal* 97 (1988): 1073.

Gordon, Linda. *Heroes of Their Own Lives: The Politics and History of Family Violence.* New York: Viking, 1988.

Grant, Jennifer. "An Argument for Separate Services." In *Same-Sex Domestic Violence: Strategies for Change,* edited by Beth Leventhal and Sandra E. Lundy, 183–91. Thousand Oaks, CA: Sage, 1999.

Green, Lisa R. "Homeless and Battered: Women Abandoned by a Feminist Institution." *UCLA Women's Law Journal* 1 (1991): 169.

Greenhouse, Linda. "Supreme Court Roundup; Justices to Reconsider Ruling Against Sex Between Gays." *New York Times* December 3, 2002, Section A, pg. 26.

Grossberg, Michael. *Governing the Hearth: Law and Family in Nineteenth-Century America.* Chapel Hill: University of North Carolina Press, 1985.

Halley, Janet E. "Reasoning About Sodomy: Act and Identity in and After *Bowers v. Hardwick.*" *Virginia Law Review* 79 (1993): 1721.

Hamberger, L. Kevin. "Intervention in Gay Male Intimate Violence Requires Coordinated Efforts on Multiple Levels." In *Violence in Gay and Lesbian Domestic Partnerships,* edited by Claire M. Renzetti and Charles Harvey Miley, 83–92. New York: Haworth Press, 1996.

Harper, Laura S. "Battered Women Suing Police for Failure to Intervene: Viable Legal Avenues After *DeShaney v. Winnebago County Department of Social Services.*" *Cornell Law Review* 75 (1990): 1393–1425.

Hart, Barbara. "Preface." In *Naming the Violence: Speaking Out About Lesbian Battering,* edited by Kerry Lobel, 9–16. Seattle: Seal Press, 1986.

Hasday, Jill Elaine. "Contest and Consent: A Legal History of Marital Rape." *California Law Review* 88 (2000): 1373.

Hathaway, Carolyne R. "Gender Based Discrimination in Police Reluctance to Respond to Domestic Assault Complaints. *Thurman v. City of Torrington.*" *Georgetown Law Journal* 75 (1986): 667.

Hilden, Julie. "Must the Government Protect Its Citizens if It Learns They Are in Danger? The Supreme Court Considers How Far Responsibility Reaches." Findlaw.com, Mar. 29, 2005: http://writ.news.findlaw.com/hilden/20050329.html.

Hobbes, Thomas. "De Cive," Chapter 8, Section 8.1. In *Selections*. Computer version of selected works of Thomas Hobbes, transcribed principally from the Molesworth ed. of 1843. http://chaucer.library.emory.edu/htprop/beck.html.

Hoff, Joan. *Law, Gender, and Injustice: A Legal History of U.S. Women*. New York: New York University Press, 1991.

Hollis, Martin. *Models of Man: Philosophical Thoughts on Social Action*. Cambridge, England: Cambridge University Press, 1977.

Irons, Peter. *The Courage of Their Convictions*. New York: Free Press, 1988.

Jacobs, Michelle S. "Requiring Battered Women Die: Murder Liability for Mothers Under Failure to Protect Statutes." *Journal of Criminal Law and Criminology* 88 (1998): 579.

Johnson, Dirk. "Abused Women Get Leverage in Connecticut." *New York Times*. June 15, 1986: Section 4; Page 8.

Johnson, John M. "Program Enterprise and Official Cooptation in the Battered Women's Shelter Movement." *American Behavioral Scientist* 24, no. 6 (1981): 827–42.

Johnson, Robb. "Groups for Gay and Bisexual Male Survivors of Domestic Violence." In *Same-Sex Domestic Violence: Strategies for Change*, edited by Beth Leventhal and Sandra E. Lundy, 111–23. Thousand Oaks, CA: Sage, 1999.

Jones, James T. R. "Battered Spouses' Section 1983 Damage Actions Against the Unresponsive Police After *DeShaney*." *West Virginia Law Review* 93 (1991): 251–358.

Jones, Ruth. "Guardianship for Coercively Controlled Battered Women: Breaking the Control of the Abuser." *Georgetown Law Journal* 88 (2000): 605.

Keiser, Laurie. "The Black Madonna: Notions of True Womanhood from Jacobs to Hurston." *South Atlantic Review* 60 (Jan. 1995): 97–109.

Kent, James. *Commentaries on American Law*. New York: O. Halstead, 1827.

Kraditor, Aileen S. *The Ideas of the Woman Suffrage Movement, 1890–1920*. New York: Columbia University Press, 1965.

Krause, Joan H. "Of Merciful Justice and Justified Mercy: Commuting the Sentences of Battered Women Who Kill." *Florida Law Review* 46 (1994): 699.

Kurtz, Howard. "Meese Clears Disputed Grant for Aid to Battered Women; Group is 'Pro-Family,' Conservative Critics Told." *Washington Post*. (August 10, 1985): p. A2.

———. "Meese Delayed Grant When Conservatives Balked; Decision on Coalition Against Domestic Violence Indicates Split in Ranks." *Washington Post*. (August 9, 1985): p. A8.

Kwan, Peter. "Intersections of Race, Ethnicity, Class, Gender and Sexual Orientation: Jeffrey Dahmer and the Cosynthesis of Categories." *Hastings Law Journal* 48 (1997): 1257.

Leventhal, Beth and Sandra E. Lundy, eds. *Same-Sex Domestic Violence: Strategies for Change*. Thousand Oaks, CA: Sage, 1999.

Lobel, Kerry, ed. *Naming the Violence: Speaking Out About Lesbian Battering*. Seattle: Seal Feminist Press, 1986.

Locke, John. *Two Treatises of Government*. Edited by Peter Laslett. Cambridge, England: Cambridge University Press, 1960.

Loke, Tien-Li. "Trapped in Domestic Violence: The Impact of United States Immigration Laws on Battered Immigrant Women." *Boston University Public Interest Law Journal* 6 (1997): 589.

Lum, Joan. "Battered Asian Women." *Rice* (1988): 50–52.

MacKinnon, Catharine A. "Reflections on Sex Equality Under Law." *Yale Law Journal* 100 (1991): 1281.

———. *Toward a Feminist Theory of the State.* Cambridge: Harvard University Press, 1989.

Martin, Del. *Battered Wives.* San Francisco: Glide Publications, 1976.

Martin, Douglas. "The Rise and Fall of the Class Action Lawsuit." *New York Times.* Jan. 8, 1988: p. B7.

Martin, Emily J. and Caroline Bettinger-Lopez. "*Castle Rock* v. *Gonzales* and the Future of Police Protection for Victims of Domestic Violence." *Domestic Violence Report* 11 (October/November 2005): 1, 11–15.

Matthews, Nancy A. *Confronting Rape: The Feminist Anti-Rape Movement and the State.* London: Routledge, 1994.

McFarlane, Lauren L. "Domestic Violence Victims v. Municipalities: Who Pays When the Police Will Not Respond?" *Case Western Reserve Law Review* 41 (1991): 929.

Melner, Amy R. "Rights of Abused Mothers vs. Best Interest of Abused Children: Courts' Termination of Battered Women's Parental Rights Due to Failure to Protect Their Children From Abuse." *Southern California Review of Law and Women's Studies* 7 (1998): 299.

Mertus, Julie. "Turning a Liberal Feminist Lens on Post-Agreement Kosovo: The Radical Future of Liberal Feminism?" unpublished paper, 2003.

Mill, John Stuart. *On Liberty.* Edited by Edward Alexander. Peterborough, Ontario: Broadview Press, 1999.

Morgan, Patricia. "From Battered Wife to Program Client: The State's Shaping of Social Problems." *Kapitalistate* 9 (1981): 17–39.

Murray, Susan B. "The Unhappy Marriage of Theory and Practice: An Analysis of a Battered Women's Shelter." *National Women's Studies Association Journal* 1, no. 1 (1988): 75–92.

Nix, Crystal. "For Police, Domestic Violence is no Longer a Low Priority." *New York Times.* December 31, 1986: Section B; Page 1.

"N.Y. Police Will Begin Arresting Wife Beaters." *Washington Post.* June 28, 1978. Final Edition, p. A10.

Okin, Susan Moller. *Women in Western Political Thought*, revised edition. Princeton: Princeton University Press, 1992.

Omolade, Barbara. *The Rising Song of African-American Women.* New York: Routledge, 1994.

Peled, Einat. "The Battered Women's Movement Response to Children of Battered Women: A Critical Analysis." *Violence Against Women* 3, no. 4 (1997): 424–46.

Pence, E. "Integrating Feminist Theory and Practice: The Challenge of the Battered Women's Movement." In *Feminist Perspectives on Wife Abuse*, edited by Kersti Yllo and Michele Bograd, 282–98. Newbury Park, CA: Sage Publications, 1988.

Plant, Morgan. "Abortion is a battered women's issue." *AEGIS* 33 (1982): 32–35.

Pleck, Elizabeth Hafkin. "Criminal Approaches to Family Violence, 1640–1980." In *Family Violence*, edited by Lloyd Ohlin and Michael Tonry, 16–39. Chicago: University of Chicago, 1989.

——. *Domestic Tyranny: The Making of Social Policy Against Family Violence from Colonial Times to the Present.* New York: Oxford University Press, 1987.

——. "Feminist Responses to 'Crimes Against Women,' 1868–1896." *Signs* 8 (1983): 451–65.

——. "Wife Beating in Nineteenth-Century America." *Victimology* 4, no. 1 (1979): 60–74.

Poorman, Paula B. "Forging Community Links to Address Abuse in Lesbian Relationships." In *Intimate Betrayal: Domestic Violence in Lesbian Relationships*, edited by Ellyn Kaschak, 7–24. New York: Haworth Press, 2001.

Posch, Pamela. "The Negative Effects of Expert Testimony on the Battered Women's Syndrome." *American University Journal of Gender, Social Policy and Law* 6 (1998): 485.

Reagan, Leslie J. *When Abortion Was a Crime: Women, Medicine, and Law in the United States, 1867–1973.* Berkeley: University of California Press, 1997.

Reinelt, Claire. "Fostering Empowerment, Building Community: The Challenge for State-Funded Feminist Organizations." *Human Relations* 47, no. 6 (1994): 685–705.

——. "Moving Onto the Terrain of the State: The Battered Women's Movement and the Politics of Engagement." In *Feminist Organizations*, edited by Myra Marx Feree and Patricia Yancey Martin, 84–104. Philadelphia: Temple University Press, 1995.

Renzetti, Claire M. *Violent Betrayal: Partner Abuse in Lesbian Relationships.* Newbury Park, CA: Sage, 1992.

Richie, Beth. "Battered Black Women: A Challenge for the Black Community." In *Words of Fire*, edited by Beverly Guy-Sheftall, 398–404. New York: New Press, 1995. Reprinted from *Black Scholar* 16 (1985): 40–44.

Rivera, Rhonda R. "Our Straight-Laced Judges: The Legal Position of Homosexual Persons in the United States." *Hastings Law Journal* 30 (1979): 799–955.

Roberts, Dorothy. "Punishing Drug Addicts Who Have Babies: Women of Color, Equality, and the Right of Privacy." *Harvard Law Review* 104 (1991): 1419.

Robson, Ruthann. "Lavender Bruises: Intra-Lesbian Violence, Law and Lesbian Legal Theory." *Golden Gate University Law Review* 20 (1990): 567–91.

Rodriguez, Noelie Maria. "Transcending Bureaucracy: Feminist Politics at a Shelter for Battered Women." *Gender and Society* 2, no. 2 (1988): 214–17.

Rousseau, Jean-Jacques. *The Social Contract and the First and Second Discourses.* Ed. Susan Dunn. New Haven: Yale University Press, 2002.

Ruiz, Vicki L. and Ellen Carol DuBois. *Unequal Sisters: A Multi-Cultural Reader in U.S. Women's History.* New York: Routledge, 1990.

Schechter, Susan. *Women and Male Violence: The Visions and Struggles of the Battered Women's Movement.* Boston: South End Press, 1982.

Schneider, Elizabeth M. *Battered Women and Feminist Lawmaking.* New Haven: Yale University Press, 2000.

——. "The Violence of Privacy." In *The Public Nature of Private Violence: The Discovery of Domestic Abuse,* edited by Martha Albertson Fineman and Roxanne Mykitiuk, 36–58. New York: Routledge, 1994.

Seith, Patricia A. "Escaping Domestic Violence: Asylum as a Means of Protection for Battered Women." *Columbia Law Review* 97 (1997): 1804.

Seligman, Joel and Lindsey Hunter. "Rule 23: Class Actions at the Crossroads." *Arizona Law Review* 39 (1997): 407.

Siegel, Reva B. "The Rule of Love: Wife Beating as Prerogative and Privacy." *Yale Law Journal* 105 (1996): 2117–2207.

Sigler, Robert T. 1989. *Domestic Violence in Context.* Lexington, MA: Lexington Books.

Skinazi, Heather R. "Not Just a 'Conjured Afterthought:' Using Duress as a Defense for Battered Women Who 'Fail to Protect.'" *California Law Review* 85 (1997): 993.

Special to *The New York Times.* "Court of Appeals Tells City to Pay $2 Million to Girl Father Stabbed." *New York Times.* July 10, 1985: Section B; p. 4.

Staff report. "Millions Awarded Beaten Wife Who Sued Connecticut Police." *Washington Post.* June 26, 1985: First Section; p. A7.

Stanton, Elizabeth Cady, Susan B. Anthony, and Matilda Joslyn Gage, eds. *History of Woman Suffrage vol. 1: 1848–1868.* Salem, NH: Ayer Company, 1881.

Sullivan, Gail. "Cooptation of Alternative Sources: The Battered Women's Movement as a Case Study." *Catalyst* 4, no. 2 (1982): 39–56.

Thomas, Kendall. "Beyond the Privacy Principle." *Columbia Law Review* 92 (1992): 1431.

Tice, Karen W. "A Case Study of Battered Women's Shelters in Appalachia." *Affilia* 5, no. 3 (1990): 83–100.

Tierney, Kathleen. "The Battered Women Movement and the Creation of the Wife Beating Problem." *Social Problems* 29, no. 3 (1982): 207–20.

Tonsing, Heather. "Battered Woman Syndrome as a Tort Cause of Action." *Cleveland State University Journal of Law and Health* 12 (1997): 407.

Unknown author. "Gonzales Ruling a 'Serious Blow' to Victims of Violence Who Need Police Protection." *Speaking Up* [online publication of the Family Violence Prevention Fund] vol. 11, issue 9 (June 27, 2005): top story.

U.S. Commission on Civil Rights. *Battered Women: Issues of Public Policy.* Washington, D.C.: January 30–31, 1978.

U.S. Department of Justice. Office of Justice Programs. *Violence by Intimates.* Bureau of Justice Statistics Factbook (NCJ-167237). Washington, D.C.: Bureau of Justice Statistics, 1998.

VanBurkleo, Sandra F. *"Belonging to the World": Women's Rights and American Constitutional Culture.* New York: Oxford University Press, 2001.

Walker, Lenore E. "Why Battered Women Kill and How Society Responds." *Harvard Law Review* 103 (1990): 1384.

Weddington, Sarah. *A Question of Choice.* New York: Putnam, 1992.

Welter, Barbara. "The Cult of True Womanhood." *American Quarterly* 18 (1966): 151.

Wermuth, Laurie. "Domestic Violence Reforms: Policing the Private?" *Berkeley Journal of Sociology* 27 (1982): 27–49.

Wharton, Carol S. "Establishing Shelters for Battered Women: Local Manifestations of a Social Movement." *Qualitative Sociology* 10, no. 2 (1987): 146–63.

White, Evelyn C. *Chain, Chain, Change: For Black Women Dealing with Physical and Emotional Abuse.* Seattle: Seal Feminist Press, 1985.

Woods, Laurie. "Litigation on Behalf of Battered Women." *Women's Rights Law Reporter* 5 (1978): 7–3.

——. "Litigation on Behalf of Battered Women" (update). *Women's Rights Law Reporter* 7 (1981): 39–45.

Zambrano, M. M. *Mejor Sola que Mal Acompanada: Para la Mujer Golpeada/For the Latina in an Abusive Relationship.* Seattle: Seal Feminist Press, 1985.

Zorza, Joan. "The UCCJEA: What is it and How Does it Affect Battered Women in Child-Custody Disputes?" *Fordham Urban Law Journal* 27 (2000): 909.

——. "Things We Still Can Do After the *Castle Rock* v. *Gonzales* Decision, *Domestic Violence Report* 11 (October/November 2005): 1–2, 10.

LaVergne, TN USA
31 December 2009
168409LV00005B/4/P